THE JESUS HEIST

THE
JESUS
HEIST

RECOVERING THE GOSPEL
FROM THE CHURCH

C. ANDREW DOYLE

 Church Publishing
NEW YORK

Unless otherwise noted, all quotations from the Bible are taken from Bruce M. Metzger and Roland E. Murphy, eds. *The New Oxford Annotated Bible with Apocrypha: New Revised Standard Version* (New York: Oxford University Press, 1994).

Church Publishing
19 East 34th Street
New York, NY 10016
www.churchpublishing.org

Cover design by Marc Whitaker, MTWdesign
Typeset by PerfecType, Nashville, Tennessee

Library of Congress Cataloging-in-Publication Data
Names: Doyle, C. Andrew, author.
Title: The Jesus heist : recovering the Gospel from the church / C. Andrew Doyle.
Description: New York : Church Publishing, 2017. | Includes bibliographical references.
Identifiers: LCCN 2017012631 (print) | LCCN 2017027195 (ebook) | ISBN 9780819233523 (ebook) | ISBN 9780819233516 (pbk.)
Subjects: LCSH: Bible. Gospels--Criticism, interpretation, etc. | Church renewal. | Church growth.
Classification: LCC BS2555.52 (ebook) | LCC BS2555.52 .D69 2017 (print) | DDC 226/.06--dc23
LC record available at https://lccn.loc.gov/2017012631

Printed in Canada

Dedicated to the people of the Diocese of Texas, who long to be faithful missionaries of the gospel of God in Christ Jesus. They make me want to be a better bishop of the Church of God, and for that challenge I am most grateful.

I do not mind at all if the loud-mouthed, or flatterers, or the mock-modest, or fault-finders, gossips, title-tattlers, talebearers, or any sort of grumbler, never see this book. I have never meant to write for them. So they can keep out of it.

—Author of the *Cloud of Unknowing*[1]

CONTENTS

FOREWORD

This book is a wake-up call! It's not another call to work harder, in our own little corner of the church, to work harder at holding the building up, harder at increasing attendance, harder at defining and advertising our little niche in the religious market. It's a call to wake up and remember Jesus, wake up and hear him, wake up and follow him, wherever he goes even when he goes out of our church doors and well out of our comfort zone. It's a call to be with Jesus when he is in the strange places and with the odd people with whom we see him in the gospel. And what are those places? Who are those people? When we blow the dust off our Gospels and read them afresh, as Andy Doyle does in this book, we find that the places Jesus goes are not the churches but the streets, not the comfortable lounges but the wide open spaces and the wilderness, and when he *is* in the religious buildings—as for example when he goes to the temple—he's usually making trouble. And the most significant place of all, if we are to follow Jesus? The place no one wants to go: the dumping ground, the rubbish tip, Golgotha. The place where he was crucified and the place from which, and for which he unleashed the radical all-transforming love and forgiveness that is still alive and loose in the world, even if some of the followers of Jesus have tried to keep it confined in a church-shaped box. And the people, who are those people Jesus meets? Not, on the whole the religious, the pious, or the righteous, but the lost, the bewildered, the damaged and the damaging, the wounded and the wounding. Meeting Jesus sometimes changes their lives, but he seems happy to meet them where they are and before their lives are changed, even though such meetings scandalize the powers that be.

How is it that the church, which is after all the society of friends and followers of Jesus, has been content for so long to sit in a holy huddle bickering with each other about who remembers Jesus best, whilst Jesus himself is long gone, out there, living and loving in the world he died to save? Andy Doyle suggests that it is because we have gradually turned our attention from Jesus himself to the institutions and traditions to which we belong and we only read his gospel through the lens of our churchy preoccupations.

So this book is a call to wake up and listen again to our lord and master, to Jesus himself, not just to our highly selective and sanitized version of what we think he said. As Andy Doyle says in this book, we must "set aside our ideas of church and its institution, opening our minds to the imagination of the gathered community that followed Jesus."

But this is easier said than done. As it happens, before I met Andy, I had myself been trying over the course of a year or so to free myself from other preoccupations and sit again at Jesus's feet and somehow hear afresh what he was saying, and I was doing so by composing a series of sonnets each focusing on a saying of Jesus, listening to it, wrestling with it, responding to it as honestly as I could. These sonnets were a work in progress when Andy invited me to come and read poetry with a diverse and highly interesting group of people gathered at his house. I read them a poem on the saying, "he who has ears to hear let then hear," a poem which Andy quotes in this book, so it may help to tell you something about how it was written. I was wrestling with the very problem Andy tackles in this book: how to hear Jesus afresh, really hear him and follow him, not just hear the edited version I have been reading through my cultural lens. When I started the poem, I thought the problem was that the Scriptures had become too familiar, that they were covered with a film of familiarity and the dust of years and that it would just be a case of peeling back the film and blowing away the dust, so I wrote:

> How hard to hear the things I think I know,
> To peel aside the thin familiar film
> That wraps and seals your secret just below:
> An undiscovered good, a hidden realm,

But as I wrote the poem, I suddenly realized that the film and the wrappings weren't really on the Scripture at all—they were on me! It wasn't a case of my unwrapping the Scriptures—it was a question as to whether I would dare to let the Scriptures unwrap me! So the poem went on to see that the kingdom Jesus was describing was:

> A hidden realm
> A kingdom of reversal, where the poor

Are rich in blessing and the tragic rich
Still struggle, trapped in trappings at the door
They never opened, Life just out of reach . . .

Then came the turn in the sonnet where I had to turn to Jesus himself and say Help! Unbandage me! How foolish I was to think I had to bring your teachings back to life: it is your teachings that have to bring me back to life!

Open the door for me and take me there.
Love, take my hand and lead me like the blind,
Unbandage me, unwrap me from my fear,
Open my eyes, my heart, my soul, my mind.
I struggle with these grave clothes, this dark earth,
But you are calling "Lazarus come forth!"*

Little did I know when I read this poem that Bishop Doyle was in the same place and making the same prayer, and indeed that there were Christians all over the world, in every denomination and church, feeling this urgent call: Wake up! Begin again!

When Jesus raised Lazarus, he gave the beautiful commandment "Unbind him, and let him go" (John 11:44). In many ways the institutional church has become like Lazarus, trapped in trappings, wrapped up in its own concerns, dead on its feet. But Jesus didn't leave Lazarus that way and he is not going to leave his church that way either. This book, I believe, is part of that call to the church to rise up, come forth, and be unbound and set free again to follow Jesus.

It can't have been very comfortable for Lazarus, even after three days of wrapped up stasis, suddenly to be called to stand and be unbound, and so it's not going to be comfortable for the church to come out after centuries in the familiar dark tomb of its monuments and religious wrappings. You won't find this book a comfortable read. It will nettle you and sting you and pull at you in painful ways (it always hurts when a bandage comes off!) but stay with it, because this book will also unbind you, breathe some life back into you, and invite you to the freedom and adventure of following Christ beyond your church door.

Malcolm Guite, musician, theologian, and poet

---

*This poem is now published in my collection of sonnets on the sayings of Jesus, *Parable and Paradox* (London: Canterbury Press, 2016) 28.

PREFACE

Gracious Father, we pray for thy holy Catholic Church. Fill it with all truth, in all truth with all peace. Where it is corrupt, purify it; where it is in error, direct it; where in any thing it is amiss, reform it. Where it is right, strengthen it; where it is in want, provide for it; where it is divided, reunite it; for the sake of Jesus Christ thy Son our Savior. Amen.
—William Laud, a tailor's son, scholar,
and archbishop of Canterbury[1]

The institutional church has stolen the gospel by reading her indispensability into the Scriptures and into the hearts and minds of her people. Our task in this book is to understand this hermeneutical act and to offer as an alternative the ecclesia of Jesus. We will reread portions of the Scripture with a new hermeneutic in mind and, I hope, provide a provocative story that will free the gospel from the institutional church for the sake of mission. First, we will need to understand the lens we are using. Then, we will ponder the idea of the ecclesia of Jesus and seek to create a new lens. We will, along the way, reread portions of Scripture with this new lens in mind.

The ecclesia, the society of humans bound by Christ, is the outcome of God in Christ Jesus giving himself over to humanity in love. One does not join the holy fellowship of God by belief alone, acceptance of a dogma, or membership and participation in an institution. The church is not a means to salvation. It is instead our invitation to participate in this life of God within a community of narrative.

The problem with viewing the church as a means to salvation is that the only means to salvation is through God in Christ Jesus and his work upon the cross. Even baptism, while an outward and visible sign of the inward working of grace, cannot defensively be articulated as a means to salvation. As soon as you articulate baptism this way, the church becomes the stage where our

salvation is achieved, rather than Calvary. If viewing the church as a means
of salvation is a common theological error, so too is it to say that the ecclesia
of the New Testament is the contemporary church. Instead we know, as the
theologian Emil Brunner wrote, that the contemporary church is a product
"of a long and complicated history, through a process of development, transformation and retrogression, out of the New Testament ecclesia."[2]

We in the church are prone to two theological errors: (1) reading the
church and sundry tasks as a sure means to salvation, which deemphasizes the
cross and tomb in favor of the altar and pew, or (2) equating the contemporary church, with its multiple malignancies and institutional baggage, with
the church of Jesus.

Jesus speaks of one ecclesia, but there are today many. Which form of
this church idea is *the* form? No instances of earthly church have enjoyed
pure communion between God and humanity, or between one member
and another. And much of earthly church is pure bureaucratic institution.
Therefore, no contemporary ecclesia can be the ecclesia Jesus speaks about.

Martin Luther understood this and tried not to use the word "church"
because of the misconception that it was either fulfilling the communion
perfectly or that it was a means to salvation. We should credit Luther's teachings with helping us understand that the New Testament ecclesia is not an
"it"—a thing or an institution—but rather a personal relationship with God
and with others. The New Testament is speaking of a communion with God
through Jesus Christ with others.

The ecclesia of the New Testament always and everywhere refers to this
oneness with Christ and others by faith and love. This fellowship is not bound
by membership or participation in an institution because God in Christ Jesus
came for the whole world.

Brunner, in *The Misunderstanding of the Church,* writes that "religion is
always attempting to point towards God but it is always something bound by
our human nature in the world and so is always a mere reflection of the ecclesia."[3] It is always and in every age, therefore, the work of the leadership of the
church to question how best to receive this idea of ecclesia as the society of the
friends of Jesus and how best to reform the institution of church so that it ever
more closely reflects the true fellowship with Christ and with all humanity.[4]

CHAPTER ONE

THE RABBIT-HOLE

The idea of churchmanship was to be wholly unattractive. I was not in the least anticlerical, but I was deeply antiecclesiastical. . . .

But though I liked clergymen as I liked bears, I had as little wish to be in the Church as in the zoo.

It was, to begin with, a kind of collective; a wearisome "get-together" affair. I couldn't yet see how a concern of that sort should have anything to do with one's spiritual life. To me, religion ought to have been a matter of good men praying alone and meeting by twos and threes to talk of spiritual matters.

And then the fussy, time-wasting botheration of it all! The bells, the crowds, the umbrellas, the notices, the bustle, the perpetual arranging and organizing. Hymns were (and are) extremely disagreeable to me. Of all musical instruments I liked (and like) the organ least. I have, too, a sort of spiritual gaucherie which makes me unapt to participate in any rite.

—C. S. Lewis, theologian and author[1]

A re you willing to imagine a different church than the one that is even now passing away? Imagine a church renewed, alive, filled with meaning, relevant to the experience of life lived in this new millennia. If you believe in a church of the future that is more in line with Jesus's mission, if you believe in a church at work in the world in fifty years—and thriving in service to others by giving itself away to and for the world—then this book is meant for you. We must begin, though, with our gut. We know that something isn't quite right. We can sense that there is more to church than the institution is offering us. We aren't sure what this "more" is because we are so enmeshed in a bureaucratic way of being church that has metastasized to encompass everything. This is true in hierarchical, catholic, congregational, denominational, and nondenominational church organizations alike.

Richard Rohr, a Franciscan friar and Roman Catholic priest, wrote, "We worshiped Jesus instead of following him on his same path. We made Jesus into a mere religion instead of a journey toward union with God and everything else. This shift made us into a religion of 'belonging and believing' instead of a religion of transformation."[2] I have found in many conversations that when we ponder the reality posed in the Gospels alongside the church organization, we are all a bit befuddled. We don't really know what to do, or how to begin to unravel the gospel from the organization itself. Meanwhile, the very nature of this predicament affects all of our mission work in the most profound ways.

My generation was shaped by a dystopian movie called *The Matrix*. It is about a man who wakes up to find that his life isn't real but a symptom of forces that have enslaved him for their own purposes. Sentient machines are using the life force of human beings—their heat and electrical impulses—as an energy source. Reality as perceived by humans is called "the Matrix" and the hero of the movie, Neo, is mentored by a rebel leader, Morpheus, to understand the truth and eventually lead a rebellion against the machines and their primary weapon, Mr. Smith, a sentient computer program that sees Neo and other enlightened people as bugs in the system destined for elimination.

There is a fantastic scene where Neo is told the truth by Morpheus and has to choose to live within this dystopic reality or continue to live within the Matrix and its false world. This scene gives Morpheus occasion to hold forth on the nature of the Matrix. He begins by comparing Neo's adventure thus far to Lewis Caroll's *Alice's Adventures in Wonderland*. Like the Cheshire Cat, Morpheus explains that we are taught to accept the world as it is presented. He questions Neo as to his knowledge about the Matrix. He then goes on to explain that we know the Matrix is present because every once in a while we experience a feeling that our life and everything around us is, well, not quite right. He explains that it is a gnawing truth like a "splinter in your mind." Morpheus then reveals to Neo that the Matrix is everywhere, and that it is a super-structured computer program that artificially creates a world inside our minds. Meanwhile, the computers live off of our bio-electric energy.

Morpheus says, "It is the wool that is pulled over our eyes to blind you from the truth. That you are a slave." Slaves to the machine that is literally consuming us. Morpheus tells him that all humanity is born into this bondage, this way of experiencing and seeing the world. Moreover, the only way to be freed from the prison is to take a pill. Morpheus then gives Neo a choice: he can take either the red pill or the blue pill. If Neo takes the blue pill, he will wake up as if nothing has changed and all of this was just a dream. However, if he takes the red pill, he will exit the Matrix and will find out exactly how far the rabbit hole goes. Morpheus is offering Neo a vision of the truth, a truth he knows is real but only sees dimly through the overlay of the Matrix.[3]

The point here is that *reality* as Neo experiences it is not real. It isn't that the Matrix is a mere illusion of reality: it is an experience that has no underlying connection to what it represents.

What the film's writers and directors, Lilly and Lana Wachowski, aka the Wachowski Brothers, analogize in this scene and throughout the movie is the philosophy of Frenchman Jean Baudrillard, specifically his seminal work *Simulacres et Simulation*.[4] In this text, Baudrillard examines the alienating entropy of symbolic society in its perpetual reproduction. The title of the book comes from the notion that "simulacra" are copies of things, representations, and as they pile up, one atop another, each copy becomes more degenerate from the original. In essence, simulacra are endless imitations of an original that degrade with each iteration.[5]

Critical of postmodern, technographic society, Baudrillard argues that humans are symbol-making creatures. We have over time imbued our original reality with a host of symbols, signs, and metaphors. Today our world is awash in these symbols and because of the endless reproduction made possible by our digital world, they have lost their meaning. These symbols are no longer in continuity with the actual reality that spawned them. They cannot represent or mediate reality. Instead the limitations inherent in their reproduction prevents these symbols from making sense of our experiences.[6]

Mircea Eliade, a religious phenomenologist, argues that the world that came before the Information Age was awash with coherent signs and rich with symbolic meaning.[7] By contrast, today we have more and more information and less and less meaning. Baudrillard expands on this, arguing that this state of affairs has come about because we are mired in an anemic, media-constructed symbolic copy of reality that dictates what we believe, think, do, and buy. The very marrow of our culture in the West, and quickly being exported globally, is endlessly branded but lacking in meaning. These meaningless, endlessly reproduced symbols are what Baudrillard calls "simulacra." In *Simulacres et Simulation,* Baudrillard narrates the four stages of simulation that result in this symbolic degradation.

Baudrillard's first stage is sacramental order. Here the sign is intimately connected to its originator. It is a reflection of a "profound reality."[8] Baudrillard writes: "Such would be the successive phases of the image: it is the reflection of a profound reality; it masks and denatures a profound reality; it masks the absence of a profound reality; it has no relation to any reality whatsoever: it is its own."[9] While the original copy, the original symbol, is connected well to its initiator, those that come after are not.

The second stage is a perversion of this first reality and has to hide its secondary origins. It hints at the existence of the originator but obscures the connection.

The third stage masks completely any relationship the symbol might ever have had with the first mover, the reality that originated it. In this stage, the truth of the symbol is now completely encapsulated in a hermetically sealed container, a vessel, an organization, or a system. It completely lacks any reference to the original and only references itself.

Finally, the system simply simulates and replicates itself. The symbol is now utterly self-referential and bereft of meaning. It is the *simulacrum*.[10] Baudrillard is clear: "Today abstraction is no longer that of the map, the double, the mirror, or the concept. Simulation is no longer that of a territory, a referential being or substance. It is the generation by models of a real without origin or reality: A hyperreal."[11]

The institutional church is implicated in Baudrillard's historical process of simulation. He casts the premodern era, with a certain relationship to a definite creator, as an artificial placeholder—the symbol once removed if you will. Disconnected from the primeval relationship with the original, the premodern era replicates from the archaic a system that claims irreproducibility.[12] During this period, the church itself leaves far behind the church of the first disciples and the first apostles, accepting instead a symbolic religion connected to the state and power. From fishermen's clothes to the vestments of emperors, symbols are invested with meaning that reshapes the original ecclesia of Jesus and his followers.

Baudrillard describes the second era of Western history as modernity. Modernity is intimately connected to the Industrial Revolution. During this era, symbols and signs are mass-produced. They become commodities and are easily purchasable and owned. This overproduction takes the symbol one more step away from reality. While it may look like the popular version of the original, its meaning and authority are now in the hands of the owner. The power in this mass production resides in the fact that the copy looks and feels just as real as the prototype. The authority now lies in the hands of the owner.

In terms of the Western Church, from the period of the Reformation to the 1970s church growth movement, we see the same mass production of community, sign, and symbol. We see the proliferation of style and type: the diversification and exhaustive experimentation of everything from building, type of church organization, and liturgy. Bitter arguments over language and liturgy are the high watermark of this period of church history. There is a complete erosion of the link between copies of church and its original, now over a thousand years in the distant past. In fact, the church of this time period looks less and less like even the second- and third-generation concepts of itself. The church idea now only references itself.

As we reach the new millennium, the end of modernity, and late capitalism, the brands—the "simulacrum" as Baudrillard calls them—collapse the connection between reality and representation.[13] I believe that the institutional church has reached this stage. It isn't that there is something wrong with the people of the West so much as humans who are sense-making creatures know when the symbols are no longer connected. The symbol's original purpose is lost. The interested observer will look at the postmodern church and see precious little that reminds her of its original progenitor.

Recently, a friend took his three-year-old child to church. The little girl looked at the wall. There was a picture of me in my Episcopal bishop's vestments. I held my wooden crozier, or shepherd's crook. I was wearing a mitre and a chasuble, much like high priests of the first century or kings and emperors of the third and fourth century. She asked her father, "Is that the King or the Shepherd?" He shared this with me in a text. I said, "That is a good question." And I told him the story of how one time a little boy went home after my visitation to his church and told his father that he had met the king of church that day. My friend said that he tried to explain that the man in the picture was the bishop. My friend wrote, "She simply repeated the question more loudly as though we didn't understand what she was asking." I then wrote back, "Exactly! Tell her the church likes to dress their shepherd servants up in princess clothes so they are less threatening to the establishment."

This little girl was wrestling with a process of simulation that took place within a very short period of time and exemplifies Baudrillard's process. While there was great meaning in a tradition of following Jesus passed down from shepherd-servant to shepherd-servant, it did not take long for the shepherd-servant to look and act like the king or queen of church. The symbol is removed from its originator to a degree that it must begin to build a closed system to support and justify itself.

The media (internet, television, music, film, print) are all carriers of simulacra. One author called it the "mass-ification" of society itself.[14] This influx of symbols has blurred the lines between those which have resonance and meaning left to help us navigate the complexity of our lived experience and those simulacra defunct of meaning but marketed to us for the purpose of pure profit. Baudrillard would say that, in the final evaluation, all value is lost, that even the commercial value is lost in the process of endless simulation.[15] The vacuous, valueless economic reality that confronts us today must be grappled with by any church seeking to reconnect with its originating singularity.

The danger of such a valueless economic reality is evident in the story of art through Western history. Art was a primary symbol bearer deeply rooted in the original symbolic worldview. It eventually became representational and then finally reached the watershed moment after the World Wars when art started to exist solely for art's sake. In the modern era, all symbolic meaning is jettisoned so that the symbol of art could be self-referential and complete. At the end of modernity, art's value has shifted yet again from symbolic self-sufficiency to an economic model, where art is valued in reference to markets and currency. And now that the market dictates the value of art, all symbol, meaning, and original connection to reality is lost in a multiplication and media driven expansion of value.

The institutional church finds itself within a similar economic bankruptcy. More and more bereft from its originating singularity—Jesus—the church has self-referenced itself out of any meaning or value except in the hearts and minds of a select few. The multiplication of religions and spiritual pilgrimages undertaken by one-time and would-be Christians because of their desperate search for meaning exemplifies the insolvency of the institutional church at its worst.

Charles Taylor, in his book *The Sources of Self*, rightly says that the only way that this impoverishment can be undone is by "connecting ourselves rightly to the significance of things."[16] This is a process that is never ending for the church. We as church institution will have to do this over and over again. Thomas Tierney argues, in his work on the nature of self and death, that Baudrillard relies upon Max Weber's undertaking on disenchantment and is struggling to generate a system of reconnection beyond the meaninglessness of our present circumstances.[17]

This is what Morpheus seeks to do for Neo. Morpheus wants Neo to unplug (quite literally) from the sentient machines' construct of false reality. Baudrillard helps us sort through the simulacra that bind us so that we can seek out the real and the meaningful. I am inviting the church to awaken from her institutional torpor to see that we are living within and promulgating a series of impoverished simulacra—self-referencing symbols that prop up an economic system sapped of meaning. We are imprisoned in a kind of Matrix, and we inadvertently serve a different master than was originally intended. We know something is not quite right, but we are unable to put our finger on what it is. It is not difficult to see the symptoms within our own organizations. And I am wondering if you are willing to see how deep the rabbit-hole goes? Or will you be content with what you have been fed?

Like a glitch in the system, I first noticed something was wrong with how I viewed the ministry of the institutional church as I traveled and spoke to people following the publication of my books, *CHURCH* and *Generous Community*. I was struck by an overwhelming sense that there was an unspoken truth about our work of ministry. The institutional church of our ministry (the building, structures, and inward-focused goals) was not the church Jesus envisioned. Whether they be Episcopal, Lutheran, Methodist, or any manner of denomination or nondenominational organization, countless good and faithful clergy and laity talked to me about how their church was not the community of the reign of God that Jesus spoke about. Privately and publicly people shared their frustration that the actual work they were doing was nothing like the work they were called to undertake. They were disconnected and much of their daily grind seemed meaningless when compared to

the profound truth they believed was present in the gospel. The transformation of lives, community, and world failed in comparison to vast amounts of
time and energy expended each day and week on the survival of bureaucratic
structures on which churches have come to rely. A bureaucracy, mind you,
that is far more complex and ornery than any nonprofit service organization
out there.

A new covenant has been unwittingly created, a covenant and system that
incorporates whatever it chooses to interpret. It is not a covenant with God,
but rather with the parishioner and money. The ordained are vassals to a new
lord. Clergy and pastors dare not tell their parishioners what they really think
because of their economic relationship with them. If the preacher were to
preach without paying heed to economic viability, she might make someone
mad. That disgruntled person would then abandon her community in favor
of another.

Over these last eight years as bishop, I have watched the clergy of my diocese tie themselves in knots trying to be faithful to the gospel and not anger
their supporters. In this way the modern Western preacher is far more like a
politician who runs for office each week than they are like Jesus. People long
to hear the words of Jesus preached. They are also aware that in church there
is a kind of matrix overlaying their experience of the gospel, though they are
not sure what it is. Priest and parishioner are puzzled by this, and while they
are genuinely stuck, don't quite know what to do with the flicker of truth that
catches their eye from just beneath the surface.

While the gospel of God in Christ Jesus is meant for the doubter, the
unbeliever, the sinful, sin-sick, and broken soul, the institutional church is
not particularly meant for the nonbeliever, the none, the seeker, or the person with questions. The institutional church exists primarily for those who
belong. Despite quotes like, "The Church is the only organization that does
not exist for itself, but for those who live outside of it" being thrown around,
the vast majority of our time and energy is spent on preparing for and show-
ing up for a few hours on Sunday morning. Our attention is given to those
who show up on Sunday morning and exist inside the organization.[18]

This relentless focus on supporting the system as we have received it
is evinced by the hard truth that all our attention to invitation and evangelism has the ultimate goal of increasing Sunday morning attendance.
Everything seems so very focused on increasing the economic strength of the

organization. I have actually had people tell me, "So if we do this, will it mean more people in the pews? If not, explain to me again why we should do this? Tell me what good is working with our neighbor for the betterment of our community if they don't come to our church?" Such questions reveal that we serve an economic system, not the gospel. We will do anything to perpetuate our institutional Matrix, our field of pet simulacra. In a book entitled *The Art of Neighboring*, I was reminded that the "ulterior" motive of much of what we do is the hidden agenda of "butts in pews."[19] This "bait and switch paradigm is engrained into our thinking," write authors Jay Pathak and Dave Runyon.[20] Our goal has never purely been to gather people to Jesus, but simply to keep the church machine running. This is Christian community at its worst.

The idea that all this questionable labor is done in the name of healthy churches infected every conversation I had over the last two years. People could not remove themselves from the bottomless needs of the institutional church when they did their Bible reading. Everything they read was impacted and influenced by an urgent belief that the logical endpoint of all our mission work and the work of Jesus was the institutional church: the swelled local congregation, the expansive building, and an endless longevity for these things. It began to dawn on me that we had made a huge shift in our reading of Scripture. It turns out that such a shift has been subtly at work over many millennia, though it may have been solidified during the last one hundred years of a particular kind of congregational life. I found that people within the church could not separate out their congregation from the Scripture's vision of community. It was like we had blinders on.

A sermon on the Good Samaritan is turned into a churchgoer's moral play about doing good for others; the Widow's Mite is turned into a sermon about stewardship and the church budget; and the Pearl of Great Price is less about the kingdom. The Call of the Disciples becomes about invitations for people to come to church while Lazarus at the gate becomes about the poor outside the church door. There is continually in our preaching and teaching an ever-so-subtle hermeneutic that says that the Gospels are really talking about our church and our congregation. So it is that over the years, the weight of institution has ever so slightly reoriented our focus upon domesticating a gospel that is actually quite critical of centralized worship and religion.

If the church took a massive inventory, measured its time spent, the money spent on service, outreach, and community engagement, and then compared it to worship, and measured how much time we spend getting ready for and undertaking a liturgy, the number of people involved in doing that work (tends to be about 10 percent of the community each week), and where it spends its money (salary breakout, electricity, mortgage, maintenance, supplies), we would find that it is manifestly focused internally on the perpetuation of the institution. Institutional preservation is not the only purpose of worship; worship of God is not the only purpose of the gospel. But if you look at where our hearts are as an organized church, you would have a difficult time based upon our balance sheets understanding where our mission lies. By the pure numbers, the church's mission lies on Sunday morning.

I do not believe congregational churches spending most of their time and resources on worship during a few hours once a week was Jesus's intent. If Jesus was to come back today, I don't think the institutional church and its leaders would much like to hear what he had to say; and we would probably defend ourselves and our work, revealing the sinfulness of it all. Now, do I believe that the church as congregation and buildings needs to be broken down and given away in some kind of mass reform? No. I do not. I reject such an idea. I believe the strength and power of the church with its assets focused on the mission of Jesus could be a very sizable part of the reign of God. The work of mission must hold in hand the tension between the work of Jesus in this world and the invitation to be with Jesus in the world to come. A church separate from the world is no good to anybody—least of all the mission of God. A church separate from the work of preparing people for the life to come is also no good. We must have both the church institution and its mission. But this is out of balance today. The service of the church to its own institutional ends far outweighs its service to others.

It might seem as though, as an Episcopal bishop, I am simply painting the whole church with a series of concerns specific to my own limited context. I am concerned about the Episcopal Church in particular, that is true. But the fact is that church attendance is decreasing across all denominational and nondenominational churches in the West. As I point out in my book *CHURCH,* our inherited congregational models have only really existed for the last sixty plus years or so. The vast majority of what the West accepts as normative church does not look much like the active, lively society of friends who follow Jesus and are sent out and leave behind a second generation of church just as missional.

We cannot lie to ourselves any longer. We have to wake up. We have to take the red pill. We must see that what we have inherited is not what is meant to be. We must unplug. We must admit that we have been stealing Jesus from the world and dressing him up as a Sunday churchgoer of the good guy establishment. We have cleaned him up and tamed his language—lest he offend. We have watered down his teachings and his warnings so as to escape his critical view of our institution. We have dismantled his concern for the world and anger at unjust structures in order to woo power and free us to enjoy and profit from our globalized consumer society. All that we have left is a spiritual Jesus relegated to a privatized faith that has no voice in the world and no relevance to the situations in which we find ourselves. Jesus did not silence himself. The world did not neuter his power. The institutional church did this for the sake of its own self-perpetuation—for the sake of maintaining the Matrix.

Worshiping God in Christ Jesus, breaking bread together weekly, reading the Scriptures, praying together, serving the poor, sharing what we have with those who have less, and continuing to do what the first followers did is not sinful. The clergy, pastors, and people of God's churches have done powerful and profound work and continue to do so every day. I bear witness to it daily as a bishop. People's lives are different and better because people who love God sat with them at their parent's bedside as they died. Because people who love Jesus prayed with them in that moment when they needed a power from beyond to help them get through the next few hours or days of their lives. In cancer, in poverty, in crisis, in birth, marriage, and love, in war and peace, and in all manner of life, the people who love God in Christ Jesus have been the faithful hands and feet of our Lord to those in need.

Yet at the same time, we the people who follow Jesus remain imprisoned by the structures of church we have thought were our sanctuary. We have pledged our loyalty to buildings and structures instead of Jesus. And we have been peddling an idea that many of us today believe, a false truth, a matrix, that what the churches and our people do on Sunday morning for an hour fulfills our covenant with God. That is the sinful deception at work.

I mean to be provocative here and to unplug from the foundations of the institutional church.

So join me and take the plunge. You are brave to have purchased this book and an even braver soul if you choose to keep reading it. Let there be no mistake—this is a book that aims to open your eyes to a reality that has been kept hidden from you. I believe it has been unintitionally hidden from you, but it has been hidden nonetheless. We are all part of the great deception. I invite you to join a movement that seeks to transform and change the institutions we have inherited. We shall journey together, if you choose to turn the page, take the red pill, and read the Scriptures again for the first time without the perpetuation of the institutional church as our primary looking glass.

CHAPTER TWO

ONE GREAT FELLOWSHIP

Not for yourself, O church, do you exist, any more than Christ existed for himself. His glory was that he lay aside his glory, and the glory of the church is when she lays aside her respectability and her dignity, and counts it to be her glory to gather the outcast, and her highest honor to seek amid the foulest mire the priceless jewels for which Jesus shed his blood. To rescue souls from hell and leave to God, to hope, to heaven, this is her heavenly occupation. O that the church would always feel this.
—Charles Spurgeon, British Baptist preacher[1]

The church does not exist for itself. The church exists for the mission and work of God. The church only has meaning when its relationship to Christ is inseparable, and it has humbly given away its need for self-preservation. The church is most itself when it is completely dependent upon God and, like God in Christ Jesus, gives itself away to the world. I do believe that God intends the church to flourish in its myriad forms and manifestations—to flourish, that is, as Christ's body in the world. But the flourishing of the church is not the chief or ultimate goal of God or the gospel. God is unconcerned with the survival of the church and its institution.

Our inability to see this clearly is in part due to our choice of focus. We no longer see clearly our mandate because of a multitude of other competing work we have made our ministry. When the church focuses on morality[2] and behavior for the sake of salvation and happiness, it has gone astray. When the church supports itself and its mission through a reliance on trite syllogisms it is lost. William Stringfellow wrote in his book *An Ethic For Christians and Other Aliens in a Strange Land*:

> I am called in the Word of God—as is *everyone* else—to the voca-
> tion of being human, nothing more and nothing less. . . . To be a
> Christian means to be called to be an exemplary human being. And,
> to be a Christian *categorically* does not mean being religious. Indeed,
> all religious versions of the gospel are profanities. . . . In the face of
> death, live humanly. In the middle of chaos, celebrate the Word.
> Amidst babel, I repeat, speak the truth. Confront the noise and ver-
> biage and falsehood of death with the truth and potency and efficacy
> of the Word of God. Know the Word, teach the Word, nurture the
> Word, preach the Word, define the Word, incarnate the Word, do
> the Word, live the Word. And more than that, in the Word of God,
> expose death and all death's works and wiles, rebuke lies, cast out
> demons, exorcise, cleanse the possessed, raise those who are dead in
> mind and conscience.[3]

For Stringfellow the church was simply the fellowship of people about this holy work. There was no being a Christian alone. Stringfellow wrote: "There is no unilateral, private, insulated, lonely, or eccentric Christian Life. There is only the Christian as the member of the whole body."[4] The church is to be such a society of friends of Jesus. It is not a membership-only moral society of individuals who gather symbolically to hope and pray for the extension of the institutional church, or to arrive at their own self-satisfaction.

My friend David Zahl, a theologian, often says, "Christianity is not about good people getting better. It is about real people coping with their failure to be good."[5] Morality and ethics are flawed prescriptive discourses obsessed with behavior. They rely upon human evaluations of human activities and they only recognize sure and certain results. These systems frame right or wrong, good or bad in terms that benefit the powers and authorities of this world. These powers and authorities created systems of morality and ethics, so that we might be compelled to obey them.[6]

Morality and ethics are fundamentally syllogistic discourses: if you do these good behaviors, then these good effects will accrue. No matter how you go about talking of morality and ethics, you always end up with a behavior first, and a promised end second. This is exactly what Zahl is picking at. In contrast, the gospel declares that salvation is achieved by the mercy and grace of God in Jesus Christ. Those who wish to respond to this gift are invited to do so.

Christianity is not a propositional ethic. Anyone who teaches you that access to the grace of Jesus Christ depends on good behavior is no Christian preacher. Furthermore, if you heard this in church, then your church, however reverent, historical, stately, and Bible-believing it may claim to be, is not a fellowship of the friends of Jesus.

I know what you are saying, "But bishop, isn't the church supposed to tell us how to live? Isn't that the point? If we go to church, aren't we good people?" This is neither the message, nor how grace works. Here is the root of our problem: Because we get everything all backwards, we completely misread the Bible and are confused about why we go to church in the first place. And, quite honestly, the leadership of the institutional church is afraid that if laypeople knew the truth, they wouldn't come anymore. These leaders are wrong, of course. If we were friends of the Jesus movement rather than the moral society of do-gooders (who aren't), we would be a much healthier, more appealing family of broken people making our way in the world.

In his book *Mere Christianity*, C. S. Lewis describes how following Jesus gets confused with propositional ethics. When the church offers a faith that is not at all about who Jesus is or where he goes or what he does, it is no faith at all. When the church simply focuses its members' attention on making a good response to Jesus within the footprint of the church, a living faith is not in play. If an invitation to respond to Jesus does not plunge a church member deeper into the teaching of Jesus, and into the places he goes and the things he does, then it is no invitation to follow Jesus at all. All such churches are simulacra. Their members' faith consists of assenting to some long-dead thinker's implicit theory about the good life. Lewis writes, "If what you call your 'faith' in Christ does not involve taking the slightest notice of what He says, then it is not Faith at all—not faith or trust in Him, but only intellectual acceptance of some theory about Him."[7]

It is always hard to tease out where God's grace ends and where our work begins, when we are truly making a response to the grace, mercy, and forgiveness offered to us by Jesus Christ. It is difficult because the Bible tells us that we should make our response with fear and trembling, as though our own salvation depends upon it. Paul writes in the letter to the Christian community emerging in Philippi (2:3–5, 12–13), "Do nothing from selfish ambition or conceit, but in humility regard others as better than yourselves. Let each of you look not to your own interests, but to the interests of others. Let the same mind be in you that was in Christ Jesus. . . . Work out your own salvation with fear and trembling; for it is God who is at work in you."[8] It is so easy to focus on the work and get ourselves completely backwards. We want to believe that our goodness will provoke the love of God, the ultimate good parent. The problem is that neither God nor parents work this way. Lewis writes:

> I think all Christians would agree with me if I said that though Christianity seems at the first to be all about morality, all about duties and rules and guilt and virtue, yet it leads you on, out of all that, into something beyond. One has a glimpse of a country where they do not talk of those things, except perhaps as a joke. Every one there is filled full with what we should call goodness as a mirror is filled with light. But they do not call it goodness. They do not call it anything. They are not thinking of it. They are too busy looking at the source from which it comes. But this is near the stage where the road passes over the rim of our world. No one's eyes can see very far beyond that: lots of people's eyes can see further than mine.[9]

The church is simply a group of broken people following Jesus. It is a collection of discouraged, wounded people. The church is the gathering of the society of friends of Jesus. It is so much more than membership, rules, and roles. It is more than average Sunday attendance, budgets, and building maintenance. The church is a spiritual creature of God's making.

This spiritual creature, in the Gospels, is called the *ecclesia*. This ecclesia is simply people in relationship to Jesus and one another. There is a spirit of love between them. This spirit of love is called *koinonia* in the Gospels.[10] *Ecclesia* and *koinonia* are fancy ancient Greek words used throughout the Gospels, but they describe something important—the fellowship of those who follow Jesus and who are loved by him and who love each other. For the remainder of this book I intend to use "ecclesia" to describe this spiritual creature created by God and existing in this world. When I use the word "church" for the remainder of this book, I intend to mean that church which is the religious institution, regardless of jurisdiction or affiliation. What I am getting at here is that this religious institution we call church has become a simulacrum that rarely mirrors the ecclesia. Like William Stringfellow, I do not intend here to imply that all churches are hopelessly corrupted by the world in which they are rooted. Yet I recognize that any time we begin to talk about the church victorious or as any piece of the kingdom of God on earth, we, in Stringfellow's words, "diminish the spontaneity and momentary character of the reality" of the ecclesia.[11]

Emil Brunner writes that the ecclesia at its best is a group of people "bound" together by the mutuality of God's Good News. That ecclesia is relational through a mystical union with Christ through the Holy Spirit. It is not a "thing" or an "it." It is not captive to the structure, organization, or institution of the church. Instead, it is always and everywhere a living body of Christ. [12] American Christianity today is all too eager to proclaim truth and untruth. This church religion of our day is perfectly willing to be the moral voice of our society in the West. But nothing could be further from the priorities of the ecclesia. The truth that is found in the ecclesia is simply the love of God in Christ Jesus. It is the love of God manifest in the person of Jesus. It is the love of God manifest in the fellowship of those who are loved and are willing to love. This is not an "abstract or neutral truth or truths."[13]

This truth, this love of God, is not some systematic theology of the church. It is not propositional. This is the very love experienced by the first followers of Jesus, and experienced by those whom they loved, and the continual love that has been present in the midst of the fellowship of friends of Jesus for over two thousand years. This love is exemplified by Christ Jesus, who gives himself over to and for the world. And it is a love exemplified by the first followers, who gave themselves over to and for the world. It is always and everywhere only going to be the love manifested through the ecclesia, that spiritual and incarnate creature, that gives itself up completely to and for the world. This love will never be a truth held theologically by a church for the sake of morality.

Martin Luther, the great reformer, would not use the word "church" to describe this fellowship of the friends of Jesus. He called church an "obscure ambiguous" term.[14] Like Brunner, he believed that the ecclesia was not an "it," a "thing," an "institution." Instead, he believed it was "a unity of persons, a people, a communion."[15] Emil Brunner points out that though he understood that this was an idea rooted in both the Old and New Testament, his followers would soon, in the post-Reformation era, return to their own version of church.

It is all too easy for the ecclesia to become church. As soon as humans attempt to organize around dogma and doctrine, the ecclesia is out the window.[16] We are immediately about creating systems of morality and religion for the ordering of society. Brunner questions:

> Who can establish criteria to judge whether or not the Holy Ghost is really active in a human heart to which God is only just beginning to reveal Himself? Who would wish to propose criteria of membership which in certain circumstances would exclude precisely those whom God in secret has begun to draw unto Himself? The boundaries of the Church face to face with the world must therefore remain invisible to the eyes of men; a full dogmatic confession can deceive just as much as the entire absence of any such a thing.[17]

The church is always and everywhere forced into making judgments and policies and creating systems that do exactly this. I believe the church is still a good vehicle for the work of the gospel. Our work must be that the church's mission, purpose, and forms of gathering resemble more the ecclesia rather than the institution of our own devising.

The great challenge will be to move forward and create a defensible account of the "unalienating copy," the church that is NOT ultimately a simulacrum. Baudrillard's work suffers from a nihilism rooted in the universality of his diagnosis. That universality is that everything that we make can only be a worse, more meaningless copy of what preceded it. This is the weakness we inherit and must avoid in our discourse. Certainly the church as a human construction erodes from sin. At the same time the church is not left without the Holy Spirit. We understand then that the ecclesia is distinct, and intermittently present during Christian history, before itself succumbing to the entropy of symbolic reproduction.[18]

For this reason, in every season the church must be reformed. Such reformations force the church to look at itself in the mirror and confess that it is not fully the ecclesia. We know this has been done throughout history. The reforms have always come when the church has become ineffective because of its complete enmeshment within the culture. To believe that the church can ever truly become the ecclesia in our lifetime may indeed be a fool's errand. But it is the work of being a Christian. It is our work to constantly reject religion for complete dependence upon God and upon his grace. We seek to be the people of God, the fellowship of the friends of Jesus. We seek to be one with Christ and one with one another. This ecclesia is first and foremost relational. It is the first sign and symbol of the kingdom before a proliferation of simulacra crowd it out.

At the dramatic climax of *The Matrix*, at that moment when Neo is truly waking up to his potential, seeing the world again for the first time, Morpheus explains to him, "There is a difference between knowing and walking the path."[19] We have much work still to do before we go a bit further. We must take our first steps deeper into the rabbit hole.

CHAPTER THREE

THE TEMPLE-ROOTED CHURCH

I tell you, something greater than the temple is here.

—Jesus (Matt. 12:6)

Jesus's bold assertion remains true: there is something here that is greater than our temple faith, our church faith. In order to see the ecclesia more clearly, we must strip away our inherited narrative about the church and its purpose. This struggle to see beyond religious institution is not a uniquely Christian conundrum. Humanity has a long legacy of struggling between order and chaos, of being caught between religion and relationship. The Christian experience of this universal struggle is given depth by a survey of the Scripture.[1]

As an Episcopalian I remember the prayer on Scripture that Thomas Cranmer wrote for the first Book of Common Prayer. We recite it during the fall. We pray: "Blessed Lord, who caused all holy Scriptures to be written for our learning: Grant us so to hear them, read, mark, learn, and inwardly digest them, that we may embrace and ever hold fast the blessed hope of everlasting life, which you have given us in our Savior Jesus Christ; who lives and reigns with you and the Holy Spirit, one God, for ever and ever. Amen."[2] Yet, reading the Bible does not guarantee that we plumb its depths, breaking the text down and digesting it with the aid of deep scholarship to unlock meaning.

Our failure to be rigorous readers makes the face of Jesus harder to see in the
Scripture. Instead of Jesus, we unwittingly behold our own reflection staring
back at us through a dim-looking glass caked with ages of dirt (1 Cor. 13:12).
In our immaturity, we stubbornly read Scripture relying on nothing but our
own individual wisdom, a wisdom that avoids challenge and interruption,
that is boastful, arrogant, and insisting on its own way.

For the vast majority of seminary-educated clergy, survey courses of the
Old and New Testament have not produced a mature reading of Scripture,
enriched by scholarship. A cursory review of preaching (my own included)
will show how the needs of the institutional church are unconsciously
woven into our readings of Scripture. The history of Christianity and
even the history of our sacred texts are taught so that we accept as simple
providence the progression from Moses, Mount Sinai, and the covenant
at Shekem to the first and second great temples on Mount Zion to their
destruction and the natural emergence of the institutional church from the
fledgling synagogue system.

This unquestioned certainty of revelational progress is a secret recapitula-
tion of modernity, which saw everything naturally leading to the industrial
and now technological revolutions. According to this narrative, humanity
has naturally arrived at this moment of culture—a human fulfillment meant
to be. A careful reading of the Scripture will help us ponder exactly how the
narrative of modernity has shaped us.

The problem is that every Sunday across the vast Western expanse of
Christianity we perpetuate a church-oriented gospel. What is worse, we have
passed this along around the globe through mission. What was once the colonizing lens of Jerusalem—Mount Zion, and its intertwining of politics and
religious practice—has metastasized across the West and has been exported
as a church-oriented focus today. There is an overemphasis of Mount Zion
and Jerusalem in our exegesis. Scholars are even discovering an overemphasis
on Zion and the temple within biblical archeology, revealing that institutional concerns have driven scriptural interpretation for some time.[3] The Old
Testament Sinai tradition has been redacted by the servants of Mount Zion,
and the servants of the institutional church have perpetrated the same redaction in the scriptural deposit left behind by the apostles.[4]

To say this in another way, the Sinai vs. Zion dichotomy, as we shall see,
directly maps onto the idea of ecclesia vs. institutional church.

The temple imprisons and subdues religious impulses that are messy and organic in order to provide structure and routine. Prophetic traditions rise up to correct this perpetual tendency to substitute a structured, routine status quo for a dynamic relationship with God. The ancient battle for supremacy between the prophets and the temple is often settled in favor of the temple, because more people invest in power, authority, and longevity than in an authentic relationship with God. This ancient battle is particularly evident in the Zionist strand of Old Testament Judaism. The Scriptures themselves reveal that the church's current crisis has very ancient roots. To understand these roots, a short excursus on the Sinai prophetic tradition and the temple religion of the Old Testament is necessary.

Our excursus begins with the prophet Jeremiah, who vigorously opposed the centralized religious authority symbolized by the temple in Jerusalem. In the year Josiah, the king of Judah, died (around 609 BCE), Jeremiah and his school of prophets were writing. He continued to write until after the destruction of Solomon's temple. He had a prophetic ministry that spanned the reigns of Josiah, Jehoahaz, Jehoiakim, Jehoiachin, and Zedekiah, and is responsible for a good bit of the history we have from that time.

Jeremiah was not happy with the way Israelite religion was beholden to forces other than God. In Jeremiah 26, during the reign of Jehoiakim, Jeremiah stood before the Lord's house at Topeth, in the valley of Ben-hinnom, more than likely a local shrine to God. There he prophesied that the people needed to turn from their worship of other gods in order to be spared by God's coming judgment. But, he continued, if the people did not relent in their idolatry, then God would bring the whole city of Jerusalem down around the shrine. Well, as you can imagine, this did not go over very well. The people and the priests and prophets who maintained the shrine at Topeth turned on Jeremiah:

> "You shall die! Why have you prophesied in the name of the Lord, saying, 'This house shall be like Shiloh, and this city shall be desolate, without inhabitant?' And all the people gathered around Jeremiah in the house of the Lord. When the officials of Judah heard these things, they came up from the king's house to the house of the Lord and took their seat in the entry of the New Gate of the house of the Lord. Then the priests and the prophets said to the officials and to all the people, 'This man deserves the sentence of death because he

has prophesied against this city, as you have heard with your own ears.'" (Jer. 26:8–11)

Topeth stood on the border between the wilderness and the entrance to Jerusalem. A short walk from the Temple Mount, at the time of Jeremiah Topeth was remembered for human sacrifice and the worship of local gods like Baal. Jeremiah came from the wilderness of Judah to the very gate of the great city of Jerusalem, stood at a historically compromised shrine that physically separated God's chosen people and their high religious tradition of Zion from all the rest of Israel, declared the city's idolatrous wickedness, and promised that this wickedness would spell the doom of Jerusalem. With great power, Jeremiah prophesied God's judgment on the institutional theology of Mt. Zion.

Our excursus begins with Jeremiah because he was steeped in the tradition of Moses, Mount Sinai, and the covenant made between God and Abraham's descendants at Shekhem. Jeremiah was very concerned with the living out of relationship between God and God's people, and his writing exemplifies a tradition of criticism that we might call the Sinai prophets. All of whom write of their suspicion of the temple religion at Jerusalem and specifically on Mount Zion.

Think of it this way. The patriarch Abraham is promised a great generation. His descendants migrate to Egypt, eventually becoming slaves to the Egyptians. God raises them out of Egypt through the ministry of Moses. Then God makes a new covenant with them from Mount Sinai and at Shekhem. The people wander in the desert for forty years because of their unfaithfulness, then inherit the Promised Land. Here they transfer their faith, founded at Sinai and Shekhem, to a religious faith centralized on Mount Zion in Jerusalem. Eventually the kings of Israel unite the kingdom of north and south and build the great temple on the Temple Mount—today the dome of the rock. All scholars of the Old Testament and the religion of Israel imagine this as a "historical succession."[5]

Jon Levenson, a scholar of the Hebrew Bible, argues that the tradition of Sinai was never fully consumed by the temple on Mount Zion in Jerusalem. The Sinai tradition stood outside the centralization and politicization of religion in Israel and was very critical of it. Likewise, the proponents of the religious institution emerging on Mount Zion were critical of the Sinai tradition. Both of these groups recognized each other as kin, as fellow representatives of the people freed from Egypt. But this kinship did not stop them from arguing about which form of relationship with God was the best. It isn't so much that one was right and the other wrong, or that they thought of themselves as wholly different traditions. On the contrary, they would have understood themselves as inheritors of the tradition of the people freed from Egypt. This did not keep them from having very strong opinions about which tradition was a better way of being in relationship with God.

Part of what makes this sorting out of the traditions so difficult is the process by which their stories were collected. The books, you see, were not written in the order in which they are found in the Bible today. They were collected over time from traditions and narratives rooted deeply in the cultic mind of the Hebrews and then the people who came to live in Israel. A good portion of the books were collected and put together by the kings. Remember the kings are the ones interested in centralizing all the faith at the Temple Mount and Jerusalem—the center of political power.[6] We don't need to go into all the scholarship here (I have included a brief paragraph in the endnotes). But it is important to understand that the redaction that took place was important and sought to explain both the rise and fall of the people of Israel almost two hundred years after the original authors wrote.[7]

Why is this little detour important? Because the redaction—the editing and gathering of the texts—was done in relationship to and around the building and eventual destruction of the temple and its rebuilding. There was a movement from a faith of the people to a faith oriented around the central powers of the theocratic state. The temple became essential to the redactors of the Hebrew Bible and it overshadows and obscures much of the original language about relationship between God and his people, the tradition powerfully advocated by the prophets of Sinai. This temple faith was rooted in a belief that if the people were faithful, if they observed all of the law and honored the prophets, the reign of God would be enacted in Jerusalem.

The people and the king were vassals of the most high God. The messianic hope of Israel was rooted in fulfillment of the law, and embedded in the theocratic culture of Jerusalem and Mount Zion. The Messiah was to bring about the perfect Davidic kingdom.[8] The state and religion were entwined. This is a key departure from the prophetic voice of Sinai, which did entertain concerns of state. To the Zion supporter in Israel, the prophetic voice over and against a king appointed by God was a "political absurdity."[9] This is not unlike what will happen in the third and fourth centuries after Christ as the church becomes the central governing power of the West and reenacts similar redaction.

This Mount Zion temple theology reduced the stature of the Sinai covenant, and even altered its forms.[10] "The two covenants thus stand in diametric opposition. One had to give way, and since the Davidic could marshal political support, it was the Sinaitic which waned in Judah," Levenson (following E. W. Nicholson's theory) argues that the Davidic covenant traditions eventually took precedence over the older Sinaitic tradition and developed it in such a manner as to alter its normative form and reduce it to its secondary position. Scholars believe that there were shrines in both the north and south of Judah that predated the temple and continued to coexist during the time of the temple and long after. Levenson writes, "The fact is that there existed a plurality of shrines in the South [as well as the North] throughout the Davidic monarchy. The Deuteronomy program of centralization [redaction] (Deuteronomy 12) was late and it failed. There is no basis for the assumption that alienation from the royal theology celebrated upon Mount Zion was particularly northern."[11] Certainly, at the time of Jesus a disbursed religious system existed in the networks of local synagogues.

When the people freed from Egypt arrived in the Land of Canaan, they deposited their tent shrine (which they had carried with them since their time with God on Mount Sinai) at Shiloh (1 Sam. 1:9, 3:3). It was the greatest shrine of Israel for three hundred years until the reign of David and the centralization of faith in Jerusalem. We are told that the land was divided up among the tribes in chapter 13 of the book of Joshua. Archeologists and biblical scholars believe there are at least seventeen recognizable sites where the tradition of the Sinai covenant continued.[12] This means that there were likely more than seventeen, for these are the ones that survive in the Scripture and through the archeological evidence. Furthermore, we know that archeology is revealing that at the city walls and gates of some communities there were shrines as well.[13] Just as the land was divided among the tribes, so the covenant was to be kept in each place and these shrines were the bearers of the ongoing Sinai tradition.[14]

The variance between the traditions of Sinai and Zion is hotly debated in part because most Old Testament scholars are inclined to argue too expansively for a victory of one tradition over the other. Many scholars believe the

shrines and Sinai tradition were destroyed by David and the religion centralized in Jerusalem. Further, they argue that these shrines were all destroyed by
the religious reforms of Hezekiah. I am inclined to come down on the side
of those who argue for a more diversified kingdom, where the local shrines
continued to exert power. Weaker and fewer by the time we reach the two
hundred years before Jesus, these shrines still played an important role in the
local life of Israel.

These shrines were emphatically not minitemples; the institution of centralized faith and kingship were denounced by the Sinai tradition as "treach-
ery against God." As an example, we might consider the exchange between
the judge Gideon and the people of Israel in Judges 8:22–23:[15] "Then the
Israelites said to Gideon, 'Rule over us, you and your son and your grandson
also; for you have delivered us out of the hand of Midian.' Gideon said to
them, 'I will not rule over you, and my son will not rule over you; the LORD
will rule over you.'" Gideon took up a collection and built a shrine and the
people worshiped there. The Sinai worship tradition saw the demand for a
human king as a rejection of the divine king—Yahweh.[16] At the same time,
however, the Sinai tradition and its prophets did not slavishly endorse everything that went on at local shrines. We know, for instance, that prophets like
Amos and Hosea forcefully disavowed local shrines where gods other than
Yahweh featured among the objects of worship.[17]

The proponents of the Sinai tradition viewed the centralization of state
and religious power in Jerusalem as a kind of detestable suzerainty. Suzerainty
is a political relationship by which the local people of a nation may have
autonomy while remaining a part of the occupying power and subservient to
it. The Sinai perspective was that Mount Zion propped up a different king
in the place of God, and organized a dubious, novel set of disciplines around
the Mosaic faith received in the desert. It is clear that this institution-creep
was perpetual.

While the vast majority of the Old Testament reveals the priorities of the
institution-phobic Sinai tradition, later editors attempted to answer Sinai crit-
ics with their redactions. The edited text allows for the suzerainty of a Davidic
monarchy under the power of god. But even so, Deuteronomy 17–18 make
it clear that the Mosaic covenant, the Sinai prophetic tradition, and the rule
of God will continue. The redactors hold that the king will be accountable to
God, to Sinai, and to Sinai's prophets.[18]

The prophets Elijah and Elisha were about exactly this accountability work. Steeped in the Sinai tradition, both of these illustrious prophets maintained a passionate focus on the relationship between the people and their God. In 1 Kings 21 Elisha powerfully reminds the king and the centralized religion that they are answerable to a higher power. Like an episode of *Scandal* or *House of Cards*, King Ahab has killed a man for love of his wife and vineyard. So God sends Elisha the Tishbite to remind Ahab that God and his justice will prevail:

> Then the word of the LORD came to Elijah the Tishbite, saying: Go down to meet King Ahab of Israel, who rules in Samaria; he is now in the vineyard of Naboth, where he has gone to take possession. You shall say to him, "Thus says the LORD: Have you killed, and also taken possession?" You shall say to him, "Thus says the LORD: In the place where dogs licked up the blood of Naboth, dogs will also lick up your blood." Ahab said to Elijah, "Have you found me, O my enemy?" He answered, "I have found you. Because you have sold yourself to do what is evil in the sight of the LORD, I will bring disaster on you; I will consume you, and will cut off from Ahab every male, bond or free, in Israel." (1 Kings 21:17–21)[19]

The prophet Hosea also works in the shadow of Sinai. His singular calling is to reform and renew the local shrines that dotted the Israelite landscape. Hosea warns, in 12:11: "In Gilead there is iniquity, they shall surely come to nothing. In Gilgal they sacrifice bulls, so their altars shall be like stone heaps on the furrows of the field."[20]

Perhaps it is the prophet Micah who outlines the Sinai covenant in the clearest terms. In Micah, chapter 6, the prophet calls the people to plead their case to God: "For I brought you up from the land of Egypt, and redeemed you from the house of slavery; and I sent before you Moses, Aaron, and Miriam. O my people, remember now what King Balak of Moab devised, what Balaam son of Beor answered him, and what happened from Shittim to Gilgal, that you may know the saving acts of the LORD" (Mic. 6:4–5). Micah declares that God has acted in history for God's people. In light of this fact, God suggests what the proper response to his action is *not*: "With what shall I come before the LORD, and bow myself before God on high? Shall I come before him with burnt-offerings, with calves a year old? Will the LORD be pleased with thousands of rams, with ten thousands of rivers of oil? Shall I give my firstborn for my transgression, the fruit of my body for the sin of my soul?" (Mic. 6:6–7).

Micah has crafted a direct attack on the temple tradition, a bold critique of Zion and its unfaithfulness. The proper response to God's salvific action is summed up succinctly in the famous passage from Micah 6:8: "He has told you, O mortal, what is good; and what does the LORD require of you but to do justice, and to love kindness, and to walk humbly with your God?"[21]

The sixth chapter of the book of Micah outlines the foundation of the Sinai tradition. God is the God of the holy mountain of Sinai. The desert is the place where that God dwells. God does not dwell in the cities of men, in temples, or even in shrines. God is not interested in offerings but in faithfulness. This God—whether upset at kings, angry because of his people's idolatry, or concerned with the tension between religion and faith—is a God who is in relationship with his people.

Jon Levenson writes, "The mountain of God is a beacon to the slaves of Egypt, a symbol of a new kind of master and radically different relationship of people to state. Sinai is not the final goal of the Exodus, but lying between Egypt and Canaan, it does represent YHWH's unchallengeable mastery over both."[22] It is in the desert that the people learned dependence upon God but also how to respond faithfully to God. The God of the Sinai covenant is a God who is angered with the temple religion or the religious authorities who collude to reorient the faith toward the state. When this happens, the God of the Sinai prophets sees nothing more than Egypt remade. Centralized religion, especially when it is connected to the power and authority of this world, will inevitably recreate a system of slavery. God is the Lord and the King—there shall be no others in his place.

In this way then, Israel was not a state, a theocracy, or a religious kingdom. No, Israel was forever a people in relationship with God. The people were to renew their relationship every day and every night. This is the power of the Shema. It is one of the oldest prayers in Judaism. "Hear, O Israel: the LORD our God, the LORD is one" (Hebrew: שְׁמַע יִשְׂרָאֵל ה' אֱלֹהֵינוּ ה' אֶחָד), found in Deuteronomy 6:4. God is God and will forever be about the work of freedom. God has acted by raising the people out of Egypt. This abounding Sinai grace precedes and trumps Israel's response as the faithful witness.

While the Sinai tradition could never be completely rooted out of the Old Testament and the Tanahk by the Deuteronimists, this essential biblical voice was, unfortunately, displaced in the Christian tradition by the second generation of Jesus followers. The New Testament and the emerging church of the late first century relocates the ministry of Jesus in the temple. Removing traces of Moses and the Sinai prophets, the Gospel and Epistle authors recast Jesus as the Messiah of the temple faith. Moreover, the second and third generation of followers accepted him as such. This squarely placed Jesus, and consequently the writers themselves, as inheritors of the temple religion.

No matter how much we have tried over two thousand years, the church has not been able to reform itself out of an obsession with its own specialness, the assumption that what we do as an institution qualifies as faithfulness and courts God's pleasure. The church has historically read the Old Testament as a story about the dispensation of the law, and the keeping of the law as an appropriate response to God's freeing act in Egypt, leaving the Sinai covenant impotent as a guide to a faithful relationship with God. Even worse is the pure temple debate where the church declares itself the sole arbiter of law and morality, the only place where we can go so that God will be pleased with us. The tragedy of the church's perpetual trajectory is that Sinai is the true predecessor to a faith of grace and the human response to God's grace—not the temple religion.

I believe that Jesus himself, of Bethlehem, of Nazareth, is aligned not with the temple but with the Sinai prophetic tradition. Jesus takes up the work of Micah, Elisha, Elijah, and Hosea. He is critical, not of the shrines or synagogues, but of the Temple Mount of Zion and the religious authorities of his day. Jesus and the first friends of Jesus imagined and created a different kind of community. They were a community in relationship with God, who loved in response to God's grace, mercy, and forgiveness. They did not mean to found a new temple. Jesus and the Jesus movement did not give birth to the church to replace the shrine, synagogue, or temple. No, Jesus and his followers intended something quite different. Jesus intended something quite different from the temple and the church. Jesus calls us back to Mount Sinai and our covenant response to God alone rather than into renewed bondage to human systems of power and authority.

Jesus is the inheritor of a Sinai tradition where the central relationship with God is that of love. Sinai is where the people who share this loving relationship with God attempt to live. It is the Sinai prophetic tradition that reminds us of how easily we forget God and God's love. Moreover, such forgetfulness opens the door to a dark substitution, where other kings are made to rule in God's place. The temple, the state, our own needs, the church, take the center space instead of Yahweh. The Sinai tradition of ancient Israel can be summed up by this very basic truth: the believers of this God, gathered together in their local context, will always be the best determinants of how a response to God's love shall be lived out. Only in these local communities can Leviticus become a response to God's acts. As Old Testament scholar Roy Heller wrote recently to me, "Leviticus is primarily about telling the reader about how things are, and the image of reality is that which is present in Genesis 1: a beautiful, orderly, balanced, almost poetic vision of reality . . . and how to keep it from going into the ditch!"[23]

It is my contention that we must reclaim Jesus as a prophet of Sinai or else miss out on the revelation of preceding grace and our response. Without a Sinai Jesus, we are left with a church that is only about a morality for this world.

By contrast, the Sinai tradition holds something more for us. While the high temple religion sought to create a divided order between the "Holy/Clean/Unclean," attempting to "reestablish a simple schema of outsider/insider," a Sinai Jesus returns the faith to the people, an expansive people that includes the whole world, every tribe and every nation.[24] Jesus explodes the Sinai tradition even further by welcoming all people to witness the action of God. God does not desire for us to suffer slavery to the state, systems of religion, the powers and principalities of this world, and of the next. God will trample down even death in God's desire to set God's people free. God raised Jesus from the dead after first raising the people of Israel out of Egypt.[25]

On Mount Sinai, in the midst of the desert, after being freed from Egypt, Moses bowed his head toward the earth, and worshiped. Moses then said, "If now I have found favor in your sight, O Lord, I pray, let the Lord go with us. Although this is a stiff-necked people, pardon our iniquity and our sin, and take us for your inheritance." God replied, "I hereby make a covenant. Before all your people I will perform marvels, such as have not been performed in all the earth or in any nation; and all the people among whom you live shall see the work of the Lord; for it is an awesome thing that I will do with you" (Exod. 34:8–10).

The temple religion and its redaction attempted to reverse this formula in which God's actions always came before the covenant. It made the fulfillment of the law essential to the arrival of God and a true messianic kingdom.

The temple proponents argued that God's grace comes only in response to faithfulness by God's people.[26] By the time of Jesus, the Sinai tradition had diminished, becoming a minor player in the discourse of the Israelite faith. The centrality of the temple at the time of Jesus and its religion was archetypal for the second generation of followers of Jesus, who took the church left behind by the first friends of Jesus, and made a Church out of it.

CHAPTER FOUR

BABYLON TEARS

I do not conclude that no Christians can be found on churchly prem-
ises, including those which most blatantly are Babylonian shrines. I am
saying that if you look for the Jerusalem reality of Church among the
established ecclesiastical and churchly bodies, what you will find is chaos.
—William Stringfellow, lay theologian[1]

William Stringfellow was part of the confessing movement of American
Christians following in the steps of great theologians and Christian
saints like Dietrich Bonhoeffer and Karl Barth. In fact, when Barth came
to the United States, the only person that he wished to meet was William
Stringfellow. Now certainly Stringfellow believed that not all Christian
communities were lost and not all churches were devoid of practicing faithful people. But, like a long line of modern and postmodern Sinai prophets,
he believed that any organization concerned with itself could not be the
ecclesia of God. Any organization that needed to perpetuate its own power
could not be the ecclesia. We get ahead of ourselves, though. We must
continue to look back before we can clearly see our present circumstance.

The lens of institution took time to infect our reading of Scripture. We see
how it slowly made its way from Sinai to the temple in Jerusalem. From there
it would travel into the Christian faith. We now move our gaze onward to
the New Testament and the events that transpired after the ministry of Jesus,
his death, and resurrection. The well-regarded Roman Catholic bible scholar,

Raymond E. Brown, and his book *The Churches the Apostles Left Behind* will be our companion and guide as we explore the emergence of the early church.

Brown points out that within a relatively short amount of time the generation that followed Jesus quickly dissipated and that a second generation of followers emerged before we even reached the end of the first century CE.[2] Brown argues that the first century of Christian history can be grouped into thirds: the first third of the first century was occupied with the work of Jesus himself and his first followers. The second third of the century saw these budding Christian communities expand under the leadership of Jesus's first followers. Then by the time we reach the end of the first century, a second generation of leaders is in place.

Brown reminds us that the vast majority of our Scripture comes from the last third of the first century and this second generation of church leaders. Each of the communities represented in the New Testament express a story about their own triumph, and the particulars of these narratives have concretized into textual norms for the church. In the vernacular of Jean Baudrillard, the Scripture does not reflect the originating singularity of the ecclesia—the work of Jesus in community. Instead, the Scriptures reflect the concerns of the second generation of Christians. Once removed from the originating singularity, this second copy of the church conceals its generational remove from Christ himself. It hints at the existence of the originator but it obscures the connection.[3]

In this section I intend to follow Brown by examining several separate witnesses to the church in its second generation. The first is the work of Paul and the letters that reflect the pastoral concerns of the church. Brown places a majority of his argument on Paul's own advice to his followers found in Titus 1:5,7, "I left you behind in Crete for this reason, that you should put in order what remained to be done, and should appoint elders in every town, as I directed you," and "a bishop, as God's steward, must be blameless." Paul's answer to structure was hierarchy wherein the heads of the community, these "presbyter-bishops" would help unify the community as well as provide sound teaching.[4] Now these bishops are nothing like me or like most bishops over the last 1,800 years. Paul's concern here is a unified teaching of the gospel, his gospel. Remember, he is most fearful of those who would woo away his community members, either toward the ancient faith of their forbears or toward faith that didn't resemble the internal faith of the community.

Paul is constantly worried about false teachers. Paul himself was called a false teacher. Furthermore, Titus and Timothy should gather around them more than simply presbyters. They should have people who are pastors—teachers—but Paul makes no mention of missionaries.[5] Make no mistake, while Paul was a preacher to the people, he desired hierarchy and structure. Not unlike the temple, here we see that Paul may have some elements of a Sinai grace, but he has imported orderly structure and teaching. While most scholars do not believe Paul wrote Colossians and Ephesians, they clearly fall within the Pauline school and reflect, like other portions of Paul, a desire for structure and hierarchy.[6]

Typical of the second generation of Baudrillard's symbols, we see that Paul is intent on crafting his own catechism. What is interesting, of course, is that such a catechism must be inferred from his teaching letters. He never actually tells Titus or Timothy the parameters of his formation program. There is a holiness within this hierarchy. The other pastoral epistles echo Paul's concern about power, greed, money, and arrogance.[7] Here is the spotless bride of Paul (Eph. 5:27) holding on to what is good (1 Thess. 5:12–28), to what has been attained (Phil. 3:14–4:1), to Paul's words (Rom. 12:9–21).

The weakness here is that Paul has replicated a temple/church idea—even though it is part of a message of grace for all people. It is hard, Brown writes, "reforming a spotless bride. What emerges then is an idea that the center of the life of the community is the church itself."[8] This is not true, of course. The center is wherever and whenever people gather to hear the Word, to offer prayers, and to break bread together. The holiness does not belong to the church but to the people. Paul marginalizes the people by overemphasizing the notion that God's plan is concentrated on the development of church. Like Paul's followers, we are likely to be overly focused on the church as the center, and we are likely to see everything within the dominion of the spotless bride as good and everything without bad. This bifurcated world we have inherited from Paul is simply not real.[9]

To overcome the Pauline version of the church, this inheritor of the temple religion, we must embrace a more democratic ecclesiology: truly where two or three are gathered in his name there is the ecclesia. We must jettison the notion that the church is the people gathered for liturgy, doing the work of liturgy, in the church. The work of being the ecclesia is out in the world with the people of the world.

The next group of Scripture that Brown reviews is the work of Luke and Acts. For the author of these texts, Brown writes, the church is the logical inheritor of the tradition.[10] The line leads from the temple, to Jesus, to followers, to mission, to church. In Luke/Acts the Messiah has ushered in the new age and that new age will be the kingdom—even though we don't know when that will be.[11] This kingdom will be ushered in through the work of the disciples as they proclaim the Good News of the gospel to the ends of the earth. The Spirit will bring people into the community and will empower people for the work of the gospel. The Spirit will be the unifying agent of the kingdom of church.[12] Luke imagines a church that is faithful, and in touch with the Spirit, growing and thriving all the while.

The weakness of Luke's triumphant vision is that we all know perfectly faithful, good people who are part of shrinking churches. We know that the whole movement of growth and expansion of Christian community took place in a variety of contradictory forms and not as an orderly procession of imparted teachings and the bequeathing of the Holy Spirit to the next generation. Brown reflects on his own tradition and remarks on the need for reform—how greed and corruption can lead to abuse. He notes how chaos reigns in a system that is not truly free enough to have reform and diversify itself.[13]

What we see and know is that the church is at its worst when it attempts to control and order particular forms, rites, and structures without the allowance for growth and experimentation. I love the Gospel of Luke and the stories of Acts. They are a powerful witness to one community's experience of Christ in the world. However, Luke/Acts is also responsible for giving today's Christians the notion that if their church is faithful to the apostolic mission, it will automatically thrive and grow.

The heritage of Peter is expressed in the two epistles that bear his name, 1 Peter and 2 Peter. These epistles view the church, the rightful people of God, as inheritors of the late temple theology of insiders/outsiders that Roy Heller articulated above. One of the great strengths of the tradition of Peter is that the people who are members of the church matter very much. The church is "worthwhile" and benefits its members. The church is the place where people love you as imitators of God. This emphasis on charitable kinship in the churches formed by the Petrine tradition made these communities especially distinct. These churches formed a tight-knit family that has enabled "the unique people of God . . . to survive over 3,000 years of world history."[14] It is what will allow Christian community to continue.

But Peter's teachings, enshrined in 1 and 2 Peter, also promote a dark insider/outsider dynamic. The people inside have a "sovereign assurance" that they are God's people. Membership is highly prized and very important. There is no holiness for outsiders in this tradition. This insider/outsider dynamic can make the church myopic and singularly focused on itself. There is no mission, and very little service, to the outside community. Truly in this model of church, already present at the end of the first century, the purpose is the survival of the unique people of God gathered together.

Brown then turns his attention to the work of John and the other authors who wrote in what is often called the Johannine school. He describes them as people "personally attached to Jesus."[15] The community is a community bound by the Holy Spirit—what is called the paraclete. For John, the Holy Spirit is an advocate. This advocate builds up the holy community of God's people. This gospel assumes a new community, a new creation. This community is not the continuation of the old. Therefore, there is a great divide, a radical dualism about the world and the people in it. The people within the community can bear witness to God, but the outsiders will only do so by seeing the truth proclaimed by the insiders. There is no room in this gospel for revelation from outside of the community.

John's spiritual priority of community means that he ignores the structural, hierarchical concerns of other early writers, and he completely neglects the sacraments of Eucharist or baptism, which feature prominently in Matthew, Mark, and Luke. This does not mean that Johannine Christians did not practice baptism or share a common meal. It is simply to say that they had very few guidelines for these things. Everything is oriented around the revelation brought by the Spirit.[16] This ritual fluidity demonstrates the strength of the Johannine community and also preserves an echo of the ecclesia. The Johannine community wanted to continue the egalitarianism of Jesus.[17] It is very difficult in a church with liturgy and sacraments to maintain a sense that we are all doing equal work.[18] When a church spends most of its time, energy, and money on Sunday morning Eucharist, then it is natural for there to be a growing separateness and holiness for those who are set apart to do this ministry. John sees ministry as many hands at work. The love of Jesus binds them together and propels them forward.

Unfortunately, the second generation of leaders writing epistles in the Johannine community enhance the dark outsider/insider dynamic at play in the Gospel of John. Brown argues that the Johannine church suffers from "one sidedness."[19] The charismatic norms of the Johannine community marginalize doubters and critical thinkers. Eventually a number of schisms emptied the Johannine churches. Their exclusive focus on the divinity of Jesus and their expulsion from the Jewish synagogues pushed the community to the fringe of the Jesus movement,[20] and it very quickly turned in on itself. This led inevitably to "excommunication."[21] This turn toward extreme polemic created schism and chaos, because anyone who is criticizing anyone else can defend their claim based upon the Holy Spirit.[22] Not unlike what we have seen across the West, and will see globally in time, John's charismatic church grows and then divides until it vanishes amidst internal division.

The Johannine community left its darkness in the DNA of the church, a darkness that presumes righteousness, that pretends a populist view of the structure, and possesses a florid polemics that leave people out.

Matthew is next on Brown's list. Matthew embraces the temple religion and applies it to the community of followers of Jesus. Jesus is called rabbi, teacher, and master.[23] The Jewish religious practices of the day find a home in Matthew's Gospel. In Matthew, it is easy for grace to be lost as the Gospel attempts to describe how we are to live. The members of Matthew's community were rule followers, first and foremost. While holding forth on how best to follow the law and imitate Jesus's own following of the law, the author mixes in a good bit of pastoral care.[24] This enables some flexibility, and the community appears to be relieved from some of the polemical conflict of the Johannine community. We might think of the Pauline message highlighting "the good news of God done by Jesus Christ."[25] Or Mark's views of himself as a herald of the kingdom who outlines the deeds that this kingdom required. Brown asserts that Matthew molds these two major trends into one and tempers them with fresh teachings of Jesus.[26]

In other words, Matthew's Gospel builds an impenetrable wall of works around keeping the covenant. It looks like Sinai and smells like Sinai. But Matthew's Gospel then weaves into the text the fact that it is the church, helping to parse out Jesus's teachings, that will be the final arbiter of truth. Here the church becomes "a self-sufficient entity, ruling (in the name of Christ, to be sure) by its own authority, its own teaching, and its own commandments."

Brown continues, "Matthew accepts institution, law, and authority, but wants a unique society where the voice of Jesus has not been stifled and remains normative."[27] I fear that the institutional church has, like a camel, gotten its nose under the tent. In Matthew's reading, the church remains the primary arbiter of faith and following of Jesus.

While I have been critical of these traditions and their influence on ensuing generations, the point that Raymond Brown is making in *The Churches the Apostles Left Behind* is that these habits of being would lead to church success. Despite their weakness for our conversation, these structural realities brought about a great explosion in followers of Jesus. A second generation of Christians would grow and build a great church organization.

Think just for a moment about what has taken place over the past two thousand years. We have gone from small house churches to groups of Jesus followers transforming and creating clubs, guilds, and associations. There were colleague groups and burial societies.[28] These were organized a bit differently than the house communities and the larger city clusters. There was in fact still another type of community that was being generated during the same period of time. Many of the first followers of Jesus were Jews and so they founded communities within synagogues. These groups would soon be identified as Christians and kicked out of the synagogues, but the nature and liturgy of synagogue worship remained important to them. In time and throughout the Mediterranean region, unused or abandoned synagogues would be reinhabited or taken over by Christians. So some of the first buildings we might call churches began their lives as synagogues. The ones we know of from Paul's letters and archeological digs are Duro Europos, Stobi, and Delos.[29] Schools were still another kind of Christian community. Rural communities and those situated in the desert developed a more communal expression of early Christianity. Sects, special groups, and movements of God fearers had been part of Middle Eastern life for centuries before the time of Jesus.

By the time we reach the middle of the second century, there are a lot of different kinds of communities. There are many more bits and pieces of narratives about Jesus, letters from early followers to their communities, and collections of Jesus sayings floating around. Internal strife and division about what was considered Scripture quickly became an issue, as the many churches and their leaders were trying to sort out God, Jesus, and the Holy Spirit. By the end of the second century, the majority of the New Testament was put together and agreed upon. This sorting is attested to by Athanasius, Jerome, and Augustine among many others. When we reach the great gathering of church leaders at Carthage in 397, we have a closed canon. The Eastern churches would wait almost another one hundred years to decide on the final books.[30]

Here the church enters into the third stage of Baudrillard's system. It closes the canon, and begins to unify liturgies. Rules about membership, training, and formation begin to take shape. Rooted in the testimony of the second-generation biblical narratives and their own experience of church, the institution begins to grow and support itself. What is happening in the third century is the creation of an abstraction that no longer mirrors the society of friends of Jesus but instead relies upon the power, authority, and economy of a centralized church. Growth of the church continues, but a new suzerainty is taking shape; a new political relationship is emerging. The church and its leadership are building an autonomous government (based on the local Roman practice) by which the organized kingdom might be governed in this world. Not unlike the centralization from Sinai to Zion, we see even stronger governance by the church structure that differs greatly from the ecclesia imagined by Jesus. The church rules in place of God, and iterates a different set of disciplines around their inherited faith than that which was received from Jesus. This is easy enough to see when one considers the church responded to the sack of Rome by stepping in to govern, raise armies, and organize the state anew. This is reflected in a series of new symbols.

Think about the symbols of Jesus's life and ministry. Simple bread, a wooden cup, a basin of water, sitting in the field, in a home, at a handmade table, teaching out in the open. The church had to change, though this change was highly controversial. At the end of the fifth century, in a homily on the Gospel of Matthew, St. John Chrysostom warned against adorning the Church building at the expense of caring for the suffering people. He argued for the ecclesia to remember its work was to do the work as Jesus did the work, be in relationship with people Jesus was in relationship with, eat with and feed the poor and hungry. He wrote:

> Do you want to honor Christ's body? Then do not scorn him in his nakedness, nor honor him here in the church with silken garments while neglecting him outside where he is cold and naked. For he who said: *This is my body*, and made it so by his words, also said: *You saw me hungry and did not feed me, and inasmuch as you did not do it for*

one of these, the least of my brothers, you did not do it for me. [Matt. 25:34ff) What we do here in the church requires a pure heart, not special garments; what we do outside requires great dedication. . . .

Give [Christ] the honor prescribed in his law by giving your riches to the poor. For God does not want golden vessels but golden hearts. . . . Of what use is it to weigh down Christ's table with golden cups, when he himself is dying of hunger? First, fill him when he is hungry; then use the means you have left to adorn his table. Will you have a golden cup made but not give a cup of water? What is the use of providing the table with cloths woven of gold thread, and not providing Christ himself with the clothes he needs? What profit is there in that?

Tell me: If you were to see him lacking the necessary food but were to leave him in that state and merely surround his table with gold would he be grateful to you or rather would he not be angry? What if you were to see him clad in worn-out rags and stiff from the cold, and were to forget about clothing him and instead were to set up golden columns for him, saying that you were doing it in his honor? Would he not think he was being mocked and greatly insulted?

Apply this also to Christ when he comes along the roads as a pilgrim, looking for shelter. You do not take him in as your guest, but you decorate floor and walls and the capitals of the pillars. You provide silver chains for the lamps, but you cannot bear even to look at him as he lies chained in prison.

Once again, I am not forbidding you to supply these adornments; I am urging you to provide these other things as well, and indeed to provide them first. No one has ever been accused for not providing ornaments, but for those who neglect their neighbor a hell awaits with an inextinguishable fire and torment in the company of the demons. Do not, therefore, adorn the church and ignore your afflicted brother, for he is the most precious temple of all.[31]

Chrysostom associates for his readers the suffering brother and sister as the true and highest locus of God's church. It is in the relationship and service to and with the poor, marginalized, and those in need that we are to find true Christian community.

By the eighth century, the ordinary has become the special. The ordinary household materials gathered and used for the breaking of common bread in whatever place the faithful gathered are now transformed. The pottery cup and plate taken from the cupboard now are gold and silver formed for the special purpose of the Lord's Supper. Along with the special vessels comes the standardization of the service itself.[32] Buildings are now specifically being built for worship.

By 1517, buildings and liturgy are no longer about the people but about the action. People no longer are participants in the way they were in the early days. The liturgy is no longer for the hearing or the responding. People are distant and what is happening is mysterious and not very earthly. While we can imagine that in some early communities there were hosts, we know for sure that many were simply householders. By the sixteenth century, we have a high priesthood that is in charge of the holy item.[33] The holy world is wholly separate from the real world, and the heavenly banquet table is carefully and ritually prepared by the professional.

Now we have arrived at the Reformation. The great divide is also the great moment of reinvention of the church. The great movements of the Reformation were about the Bible, liturgy, and language. There was a rediscovery of a living theology. All of this was broadcast in the language of the people. Homes and churches were filled with a new vibrancy of faith. People gathered to read Scripture. People gathered to talk about God. People gathered to break bread together. The importance of this turning over of the church to people cannot be understated. The reform would eventually spread and Christianity would continue to grow. But it grew within the vessel that had become the norm—a church building. The church was the building where the people go for the sacraments (Roman) or to hear the living Word preached (reformed). What happens during the succeeding three hundred years is a bumpy road but mostly unchanged until the invention of free time, as a result of the Industrial Revolution.

While some will want to focus next on the monastic reformations, or the discoveries of ancient manuscripts, or liturgical revivals, I want to focus on the creation of free time. The Victorians are responsible for this invention. No matter what we look at, the creation of public parks, the decrease of the work week, the increase in what people called pastime, the invention of baseball as the best way to spend that pastime, or the growing understanding of something called "childhood," all emerged during the nineteenth century.[34]

During the Industrial Revolution, Victorians were the first to begin to think differently about time that was not spent working.

Think about it for just a moment. Prior to the Victorian age, most people worked all the time. It was survival that set the hours of the day. From sunup to sundown, people worked every day of the week. They might break to make their way to the local shrine for the holy feast day of their town. But with the Industrial Revolution, there is time. And one of the things people did with their free time was go to church. The church began to grow in attendance. The minister and preaching were some of the best entertainment on offer. So people habitually return from their homes and pubs and societies to gather at church. Institutional church once more supplants the great populist reformation. All the modern denominations took shape during this time, building up their structures, buying property, and constructing buildings. Ironically, this vast and aging infrastructure is now a great millstone around the neck of a waning church institution.

The expansion of cities, growth in population in the American West, and the unchallenged sacred time of Wednesday nights and Sunday mornings saw the great expansion—explosion—in church attendance. This was a triumphant moment in church history not unlike the very high Middle Ages. We had a great capacity and the church expanded. By the end of this boom in the 1950s, the diocese I serve had planted five congregations a year for a decade. It almost doubled membership for the previous century. The Diocese of Texas was not alone in this expansion. Resources of the empire-rich Western church began to build monolithic bureaucracies and hierarchies. In our own tradition, our presiding bishop appeared on the cover of *Time* magazine! Money rich, we sent out missionaries, and our church itself began to expand into new countries, completing the global vision of the nineteenth-century mission movements.

We also turned inward. New scholarship allowed for a reinvention of liturgy in our tradition—though this was true for all the mainline denominations. By the twentieth century, the liturgical movement had returned the central action of the Eucharist to weekly worship. The liturgical renewal movement also brought with it a new liturgical fundamentalism; we became overly focused on the words we say, the words the priest says, and the words of the Bible. Fundamentalism sneaked in and Christians began to argue over inerrancy. Politics crept in and we began to argue about culture issues. Words and their meaning became important and we argued over the gender of God, sexuality, the gender of ministers, divorced people. We argued and we argued. Along with the rest of the Western culture, we divided ourselves into camps at war with one another. We began to break apart our churches, as if playing out C. S. Lewis's *The Screwtape Letters* in which a senior devil instructs the disciple to keep the Christians fighting amongst themselves so that the mission will never happen. Saint Paul's epistles have similar warnings about division. Yet, as we became disputing arbiters of truth, the great dismantling of Western Christianity began. We were not worried about anything outside of the church structure, because the great church society was all there was. Sure, there were prophets along the way, many of whom I am depending upon for this book. The confessing movement of William Stringfellow and Karl Barth or Dietrich Bonhoeffer were some. Women like Dorothy Day refused to be coopted by the institution. There have been many . . . but the institution is a powerful and seductive mistress.

This great dismantling was accompanied by a shift in technology. By the 1960s, all institutions felt the effects of a rapidly evolving smart culture. The world began to evolve in new and amazing ways. Technology changed people. TV and media began to take over the living room. Sacred weeknights were given to sports and after-school activities. Sacred Sundays were taken up by more sports and family activities. Did I mention there was more TV to watch? The 9-to-5 job evolved into a floating workweek. The gap between the haves and the have-nots, along with our desire to shop every day of the week, means that many, if not most, of the people in our country work shifts with schedules that fluctuate. New media and communications mean you can get all the spiritual information you need in the privacy of your own home. The expansion of wealth and travel means you can go on your own pilgrimage. The growth of a maker culture means you can design your own religion, and many do. The end of a great cataclysmic shift has dissolved the church's place at the center of the entertainment, communication, spirituality, family, and neighborhood life. So the church shrank, and financial burdens grew, and the culture gleefully put the nails in the coffin of the once great edifice of Western Christendom. The institutional church is crumbling in on itself.

We are left with structural elements that now are generations away from the original experience of Christ's teaching, death, and resurrection. The

church in which we live and move and have our being is one that has amplified the dark impulses of the churches the Apostles left behind. It has built an
institution upon an institution upon an institution over two thousand years
such that it no longer bears any resemblance to the organization imagined
during the subapostolic era. We rail against nonbelievers and we fear them.
We are intolerant of doubt. We are bearers of a great tradition, though most
pew-sitters could not explain at all how this came to be. We see that holiness
resides with those who perform the work of church for us, and we hate it. We
have a spotless bride who cannot be wrong, though we are sure something is
missing. We keep hoping, the fewer and fewer who sit in the pew, that if we
are just faithful enough we will be blessed. There is no longer any room for
doubt or criticism, and there is always talk of heresy. We are sure that what
we think will lead to the demise of the church. We have built up walls and a
structure that is impenetrable to reform and we wonder if there is still a Holy
Ghost in the machine. We are the people who gather on Sunday. We are no
longer the ecclesia. We practice a privatized religion for a select few.

Robert Farrar Capon, theologian and Episcopal priest, wrote, "What role
have I left for religion? None. And I have left none because the Gospel of
our Lord and Savior Jesus Christ leaves none. Christianity is not a religion;
it is the announcement of the end of religion. Everything religion tried (and
failed) to do has been perfectly done, once and for all, by Jesus in his death
and resurrection. For Christians, therefore, the entire religion shop has been
closed, boarded up, and forgotten." "Religion," Capon writes, "despite the
correctness of its insistence that something needs to be done about our relationship with God—remains unqualified bad news."[35]

The ecclesia is not religion. The church has for too long confused what it
does with the ecclesia. It is easy to do. However, this confusion has actually
been a stumbling block for us, especially as a new age of mission emerges
from the ashes of postmodernity. The institutional church has infected how
we teach the Scripture. It is a millstone around our necks when it comes to
giving ourselves to the world in mission and service. It confines us to our
buildings and city blocks. It demands that we are attentive to the needs of
Sunday worship, and internally focused church activities, while those who are
present spend the vast majority of our shared resources on ourselves. Church,
as a religion, has literally stolen Jesus from the people and put words in his
mouth as a matter of theological license.

Capon continues, "The church is not in the religion business. It never has been and it never will be, in spite of all the ecclesiastical turkeys through two thousand years who have acted as if religion was their stock in trade. The church, instead, is in the Gospel-proclaiming business. It is not here to bring the world the bad news that God will think kindly about us only after we have gone through certain creedal, liturgical, and ethical wickets; it is here to bring the world the Good News that 'while we were yet sinners, Christ died for the ungodly.' It is here, in short, for no religious purpose at all, only to announce the Gospel of free grace."[36]

In his 2005 commencement address at Kenyon College, David Foster Wallace, one of the great literary geniuses of our time, began with what he called the "deployment of a didactic parablish like story." He began with, "There are these two young fish swimming along, and they happen to meet an older fish swimming the other way, who nods at them and says, 'Morning, boys, how's the water?' And the two young fish swim on for a bit, and then eventually one of them looks over at the other and goes, 'What . . . is water?'" Then he said, "The immediate point of the fish story is that the most obvious, ubiquitous, important realities are often the ones that are the hardest to see and talk about."[37]

We are in a deep pool of water and that deep water is not the Holy Spirit's wind we are meant to breath. We have been drinking from a fountain, and we, as Jesus-loving, church-going people, must address why we have gotten so off track. When we realize that we are figuratively in Babylon, we must weep and then we must set our hearts and minds on what God is intending (Psalm 137). When Christians realize they have been drinking in something different than the gospel, we must return to Scripture and hold it up to the church, challenging one another to see how we must change to be faithful to the mission God intends. We repent and turn toward the Lord.

CHAPTER FIVE

THE LONG TALE

The church needs perpetually to recover its grip on the Gospel, the Good News of grace and forgiveness, and to protest in every age against theological models that blow the Gospel out of the water.
—Robert Farrar Capon, priest and theologian[1]

Christianity is story-centered. We tell the story of Jesus and tell people how Jesus is part of God's story. We make a habit of listening to other people describe their experiences of the divine and helping them to see how God is at work in their lives. We tell ourselves in these stories that stewardship and sharing what we have is important. We tell ourselves that resisting evil is important, as is repentance for the wrongs we do, the wrongs people do on our behalf, and the things left undone which we should have done. We have a gospel story that tells us we are never too far from God's saving grace. We have over the years repeated these stories of transformation and redemption, of new life and freedom from those things that bind us.

At the same time, mixed with this message of grace, we have over the years woven into the story we tell ourselves a different story, one of the church's self-protection and self-preservation. And in each successive season of church history, while the church has become more about sustaining its systems and structures than about the gospel, people have risen up to remind us that the Christian gospel is not a story of institutional preservation but a story about a generous community of divine love that is founded on giving ourselves away for the sake of the world.

I hope that I have shown that we come by our self-perpetuating obsession honestly. We preserve the institutional church because we need guid-
ance, systems, rules, and regulations. In the last two chapters we have spent
a good amount of time talking about the trajectory of this myopic vision of
church and the inevitable bad behaviors that emerge when we try to use it
as a tool for understanding the Scripture and our work as followers of Jesus.
I have talked about how Jesus invites us to be a gathering of friends. I have
talked about the Sinai tradition's focus on relationships and how that was
supplanted by a system of morality. I have talked about how that impulse of
institutional self-preservation shaped the communities that were left behind
by the first followers of Jesus and how the second and third generation began
a system of church building that led to a Western Christianity burdened by an
institutional structure hung around its neck like a millstone, preventing those
who seek Jesus from finding a living God in the church. These outsiders see
an organization that does some good things but all in all isn't quite what Jesus
had in mind. In fact, as I spoke to a number of church leaders, laity and clergy
alike, they all agreed with this perception. "Yes. Of course." They would say.
"No, this is not what Jesus had in mind."

Unfortunately, the problem is not as easily solved as it is to articulate.
Because underneath our twisted institutional priorities there is a worldview.
We all live, it turns out, in a secular age. The secular lens we use to understand
our religious life accounts for our inability to make change. Here, beneath the
institutional church, is the final lens that must be removed, if we are to move
forward into becoming the society of friends that Jesus intends. The secular worldview can be summarized succinctly: the immanent frame. Charles
Taylor argues that we all, the believer and unbeliever alike, have a set idea
about the world. We no longer live in a first-century world. We are not part
of a cosmos but part of a universe. We live within a secular society and we
live in a secularized church that no longer looks anything like the ecclesia of
God—that society of friends of Jesus that existed so long ago. Everything
is collapsed now into our own minds, where we arbitrate our own truth,
where we as individuals have the authority to declare what is right and what
is wrong. Individual reason rules. In his book *A Secular Age,* Taylor calls this
worldview a "mass phenomenon." Nobody is untouched.[2]

The culture is caught in an immanent frame. The mechanical world jettisoned a "hierarchy of being" and there was an "atrophy of a sense of God."[3]

The transcendent world was rejected in favor of a natural world without mystery. Reality could be explained in reference to itself. There was no need for the individual life to be dependent upon or in relationship with God. Instead, the "buffered human being" was self-sufficient.[4] Even society was able to reveal its own "blueprint" for how things are to "hang together" for the "mutual benefit" of the whole.[5] In the end there would be no need for God or religion. The church was, all in all, unprepared to speak a living Word into this culture shift. In fact, the church willingly adapted to it and settled into a diaspora relationship with the culture.

Harvey Cox wrote in his musing on the secular city: "The failure of modern theology is that it continues to supply plausible answers to questions that fewer and fewer people are asking."[6] Not unlike the twentieth century, we continue to answer questions and problems from a period that no longer exists. We imbibed deeply in a secular society. In so doing, we grew not only a powerful church machine, but a church machine that separated itself in large part from the governance of God and replaced it with its own reason and self-sufficiency. Most everyone in the Western postmodern society, Taylor and Cox would argue and I would agree, is deeply focused on the harmony of opposing views of humanism. We are no longer in Sinai, or even on the shores of the Galilean sea. Instead we have given up the whole thing to a wholly immanent understanding of human flourishing. This has led to an obsession with morality.

We live with, we preach, we offer a kind of "providential deism." Deism is the idea that God wound up the world like you might wind up an old pocket watch, and has stepped away to let it run. Providential deism is important to the church because it gives it a reason for being. God's absence has meant the church needed to act to undo the false dualism presented in the secular and sacred world.

This dualism is not a Christian idea. It is a modern idea. For Christians there is only God, the transcendent God, and all things are in relationship to this God. There are no opposing forces that can overcome this God. However, the modern church has gone awry in its response to this modern obsession with dualism. Taylor describes the church's response:

> God remains the Creator, and hence our benefactor, to whom we owe gratitude beyond all measure. We are grateful for his Providence, which has designed our good; but this Providence remains exclusively

general: particular providences, and miracles, are out. They would, indeed, defeat the kind of good which God has planned for us. And he has prepared for us an afterlife, with rewards and punishments. This, too, is for the good, because it is what motivates us to fulfill his beneficent plan.[7]

Taylor writes that in this worldview, "God's purpose for us really is simply that we flourish, and if we flourish by judicious use of industry and instrumental reason, then what possible use could we have for a Saint Francis, who in a great élan of love calls on his followers to dedicate themselves to a life of poverty?"[8]

The notion that humanity is meant for something more than our individual flourishing is difficult to square with all the preaching from the modern church with our incessant focus on the perpetual happiness of our members.

Going one step further than Taylor, I believe that there is an additional aspect of the modern church's witness: a subconscious equivalence between human flourishing and church flourishing. According to the modern church, these two flourishings taken together equal the kingdom of God. Even our outreach has become tainted by "toxic charity": churches create perpetual systems of dependence by giving money to the poor so they can flourish as well. Do not underestimate the power of an organization that builds its flourishing by promising flourishing to those who participate in it. Things are bad and we are addicted to this practice of mutual favor. It will take a great deal, and a great many conspirators to reform what has become so addictive. We have been taking the Matrix blue pill for so long that taking the red pill will be very hard to swallow.

True change will require us to remove what we might call WYSIATI Jesus—the What You See Is All There Is Jesus. Nasim Taleb is an economist and philosopher. In his book *The Black Swan,* he writes, "History is opaque. You see what comes out, not the script that produces events. . . . The generator of historical events is different from the events themselves, much as the minds of the gods cannot be read just by witnessing their deeds."[9] He also explains the reality that we have difficulty not categorizing everything. We make everything fit a lens, a worldview, or a predetermined set of expectations about what can or should be. This worldview acts as a "Procrustean bed" (Procrustes was a mythological figure who cut people down to size to fit in an iron bed), eradicating any possibility of history teaching us something unexpected. Taleb writes:

> Because our minds need to reduce information, we are more likely to try to squeeze a phenomenon into the Procrustean bed of a crisp and known category (amputating the unknown), rather than suspend categorization, and make it tangible. Thanks to our detections of false patterns, along with real ones, what is random will appear less random and more certain—our overactive brains are more likely to impose the wrong, simplistic narrative than no narrative at all.[10]

Daniel Kahneman, author and Nobel Prize winner in economics, agrees with Taleb. Kahneman writes, "The confidence that individuals have in their beliefs depends mostly on the quality of the story they can tell about what they see, even if they see little."[11] This is a principle he calls WYSIATI.[12] Kahneman says that the systematic part of our brains is lazy and so we typically jump to conclusions based upon intuitive impressions rather than difficult thinking.[13]

All this began to make me think a bit differently about the church history that I inherited and WYSIATI Jesus and WYSIATI Church. I probably should say it made me rethink my intuition about the church history I learned. Church history is taught in a linear fashion, and because you can only see what you are taught (and WYSIATI), it is no wonder that we have developed an oversimplified understanding of our church, its origins, and its perfect trajectory to this moment in time. The defense of new prayer books and liturgical movements have amplified the notion of a linear church history. Such a history goes something like this: we have always been heading in this direction so we have naturally arrived here doing exactly what was always predictable.

Of course, according to Taleb and Kahneman's suspicions about observation and history, this is crazy thinking. It is actually called a hindsight bias. Again Kahneman writes, "The mind that makes up narratives about the past is a sense-making organ. . . . A general limitation of the human mind is its imperfect ability to reconstruct past states of knowledge, or beliefs that have changed."[14] If we are going to ponder who Jesus is and what following him might look like as a society of friends, we have to come to terms with the fact that the past probably was not much like what our intuitive biases tell us it was like.

When we apply this insight to our thinking, it is easy to see that the church suffers from exactly this kind of tunnel vision. This myopia prevails whether you worship in a denominational church or a nondenominational church, with a hierarchical polity or a more congregational one. The church, that beloved mystery in which I serve as bishop, has been selling us a bill of goods. And we keep on buying it. We wonder why fewer and fewer unchurched people don't like what we have to sell.

Jesus has a little teaching that seems applicable to this question. In Matthew 7:3–5 Jesus says, "Why do you see the speck in your neighbor's eye, but do not notice the log in your own eye? Or how can you say to your neighbor, 'Let me take the speck out of your eye,' while the log is in your own eye? You hypocrite, first take the log out of your own eye, and then you will see clearly to take the speck out of your neighbor's eye." We must get beyond the WYSIATI gospel, reclaim Jesus from the institution that has housebroken him, and reorient the church toward the ecclesia of God's imagining. We must try anew to become the society of friends of Jesus. We must imagine a God intent on being in relationship with us outside the parameters of fidelity to some particular church community. In point of fact, we must reject any church that demands such fidelity as a precondition for making friends with Jesus.

Jesus saw that it is all too easy to make religious life into a transaction. Like the temple worshippers at the foot of Mt. Zion, it is all too easy to believe that the Messiah will only come if we are faithful to some institutional formulary or another. We get obsessed with the good and those who "have it." Robert Farrar Capon quips:

> You may go on saying in church that the Lamb of God takes away the sins of the world, you are actually holding that he has taken away only the sins of the church. And from there, you are in danger of waltzing yourself into the position that the world at large is damned unless it joins the church, and that even the children of Christians will go to hell if they are not baptized—and so on and on, right into the theological house of horrors that all too many people actually think is the household of faith.[15]

What do we have to reject? Matthew helps us with that question. We mustn't sit in the places of honor (Matt. 23:6). We mustn't heap heavy burdens on people, reinforcing their belief that God will not love them unless they perform well. Leaders must spend more time helping others, shoulder to shoulder, than telling people to go and do while we sit and wait. Where religion is strong we must seek to help people find grace (Matt. 23:4). We must worry less about what people think of us and likewise stop judging people. Titles of honor should be rejected (Matt. 23:7). We must not lock people out of the kingdom of heaven on account of unworthiness and dissolute living. We are not responsible for determining who is in and who is out. We should keep our mouths shut unless we are using them to welcome people into God's loving embrace (Matt. 23:13). We cannot make people promise an oath to any religion or any church (Matt. 23:16–22). Our covenant is not with church but with God. We must clean the inside of our institution. We should be about responding to God's grace. This is where true amendment of life takes place (Matt. 23:25). Jesus calls to us: "Jerusalem, Jerusalem, the city that kills the prophets and stones those who are sent to it! How often have I desired to gather your children together as a hen gathers her brood under her wings" (Matt. 23;37).

Capon writes in his book *Between Noon and Three: Romance, Law, and the Outrage of Grace*: "The Epistle to the Romans has sat around in the church since the first century like a bomb ticking away the death of religion; and every time it's been picked up, the ear-splitting freedom in it has gone off with a roar. . . . The only sad thing is that the church as an institution has spent most of its time playing bomb squad and trying to defuse it. For your comfort, though, it can't be done."[16] Think of the poet Edwin Muir who describes what the church has done to the living Word of God:

> The Word made flesh here is made word again
> A word made word in flourish and arrogant crook.
> See there King Calvin with his iron pen,
> And God three angry letters in a book,
> And there the logical hook
> On which the Mystery is impaled and bent
> Into an ideological argument.[17]

Muir would eventually leave the church and find God serving others. He was a doubter, seeker, humanist. He believed every one rehearsed the story of humanity. He worked with the poor and sought to be present in the lives of others. He is a critic of the church, but he also is a reminder that the institutional church is not fooling many people any longer.

In order to proceed, we must imagine anew what the Scripture is telling us. We must open our minds to the Jesus of God and the ecclesia dreamt by God. To do so, to find this shape, we must admit that we are simply too close to the material. We have read our beloved institution into it for way too long. We have seen the Scriptures from the vantage point of self-perpetuation, and we have even passed this habit along to our children over the ages. Our problem isn't ignorance or a failure of desire for something deeper and more real than what we experience. We have simply experienced what is deep and real in one way for so long that it is hard to break free from that perspective. We might think that what is truly needed is that our hearts be battered by this God, as in the poem by John Donne. We might pray that our walls be broken down so we can see outside for the first time. It will take a most persistent God and a humble eye to resee again Jesus and the society of friends who love and follow him.[18]

Malcolm Guite joined a few people at my home in 2016. We talked about the idea that the most difficult thing is our familiarity with ourselves. It made me think about the familiarity we have with the church's Jesus and the church's ways. He touches on this in his poem "He who has ears let them hear":

> How hard to hear the things I think I know,
> To peel aside the thin familiar film
> That wraps and seals your secret just below:
> An undiscovered good, a hidden realm,
> A kingdom of reversal, where the poor
> Are rich in blessing and the tragic rich
> Still struggle, trapped in trappings at the door
> They never opened, Life just out of reach . . .
> Open the door for me and take me there.
> Love, take my hand and lead me like the blind,
> Unbandage me, unwrap me from my fear,
> Open my eyes, my heart, my soul, my mind.
> I struggle with these grave clothes, this dark earth,
> But you are calling "Lazarus come forth!"[19]

We must unbind ourselves from our institutional grave clothes, be rid of the copy of the copy of a church where Jesus holds salvation out like a carrot we can grab if we are on good behavior.

The whole point of everything I have written before this moment was first to reveal our institutional bias and rehearse where it came from, so that we know when we are using it. You can't be rid of something you don't know about. From here on out, I'm hoping we can engage the Scripture in a new way. We have had a hermeneutic, a perspective, that assumes the institutional church. We aim for a hermeneutic that reveals Jesus and the society of friends who followed him. We desire a hermeneutic that helps us to see the ecclesia dreamt by God.

We need to first, I think, suspend belief in the church organization and read Scripture with eyes wide open.[20] Every time we read the Gospels and Scripture as a whole we must resist the temptation to justify our church existence. We must, like a person throwing a clay pot, or painting a picture, enter into the art itself, the art making itself.[21] When we turn to read, we must use an artist's eye. As Theseus says in Shakespeare's *A Midsummer Night's Dream*:

> The poet's eye, in fine frenzy rolling,
> Doth glance from heaven to earth, from earth to heaven;
> And as imagination bodies forth
> The forms of things unknown, the poet's pen
> Turns them to shapes and gives to airy nothing
> A local habitation and a name.[22]

Our artistic perspective on the Scriptures mimics what God does in the incarnation in a very real way. We are reading a word and allowing it to be embodied in our imagination. Jesus invites us to imagine this kingdom of God he keeps talking about. He doesn't give us directions or a road map. He invites us to imagine if it is like this or this or this. He offers us parables, not a map about how to get there.[23] We must do the same for the society of friends of Jesus. Jesus kept inviting them to imagine who they are together, where they might go, and what they might do. He gave us imagination about what the ecclesia is. We must return again to listen and see what he is offering. These holy imaginings give us the capacity not only to look back but also to look forward.

As we open ourselves up to this imagination, we find that we can clearly see the ecclesia of the past and future. Augustine of Hippo, a great church theologian of the fourth century, wrote in his book *The Confessions* that when it comes to the construct of time, there is no past and there is no real future.

There is only the present. In the present is the memory of the past, so that is what he calls a "present past." In the present is also the idea of the future, so that is the present future.[24] As we set aside our ideas of church and its institution, opening our minds to the imagination of the gathered community that followed Jesus and the future ingathering of community, we arrive at the present moment Augustine wrote about. When we suspend our belief that the institutional church is all that was ever meant to be and open ourselves up to the possibility of God's imagination, our gaze settles on artifacts of our present future too. What we do with this wisdom will determine our participation in God's dreamt future of mission. When we engage in the artistic, imaginative suspension of institutional priority, we use the Scripture as it is intended to be used in community. Rather than making the Scriptures a theological base for syllogistic moral behavior, the words are opened up such that we see a living, moving, inspiring, creative God. A God who draws near to us and invites us to draw near in return.

I am reminded of Martin Luther's introduction to his translation of Scripture:

> Therefore let your own thoughts and feelings go, and think of the Scriptures as the loftiest and noblest of holy things, as the richest of mines, which can never be worked out, so that you may find the wisdom of God that He lays before you in such foolish and simple guise, in order that He may quench all pride. Here you will find the swaddling-clothes and the mangers in which Christ lies, and to which the angel points the shepherds. Simple and little are the swaddling-clothes, but dear is the treasure, Christ, that lies in them.[25]

Malcolm Guite says that if we do not return to the Scripture in this way, then the Scriptures cease to be swaddling clothes in which we find the living Word of God, but become dirty rags, the "shit rags," instead of the incarnation.[26]

J. I. Packer, an evangelical pastor and teacher, writes: "We approach Scripture with minds already formed by the mass of accepted opinions and viewpoints with which we have come into contact, in both the Church and the world. . . . It is easy to be unaware that it has happened; it is hard even to begin to realize how profoundly tradition in this sense has moulded us."[27] Guite encourages us to set ourselves before the scriptural text and suspend what we already know in order to find the living God.

So if we unlock our imagination in the face of the Scriptures, what might we look for? There are three things. The first two are related to Jesus's own teaching and amplified in the teaching of St. Augustine of Hippo many years later.[28] Augustine argued that a responsible reader of texts always finds the core teaching of what she is reading, and then reads the whole text through that lens. I have been making the argument to this point that one of the key lenses we use is the church. When we do this, we steal Christ and the gospel away. I also think, by the way, that if we read morality as the primary lens, if we read sexuality as the primary lens, if we read wealth and greed as the primary lens, or if we read with some sense of self-preservation as the primary lens, then we steal the gospel of Jesus away from our people. Augustine says: find that primary lens. Here is the Jesus story that helps us with this.

During one of his many conflicts with the religious leaders of his day, Jesus was set upon by a lawyer trying to trap him into saying something prosecutable (Mark 12:28–34). The lawyer comes to Jesus and asks him, "Which commandment is the first of all?" Jesus then said to him, "The first is, 'Hear, O Israel: the Lord our God, the Lord is one; you shall love the Lord your God with all your heart, and with all your soul, and with all your mind, and with all your strength.' The second is this, 'You shall love your neighbor as yourself.' There is no other commandment greater than these.'"

The lawyer was asking Jesus for a hermeneutic, a central teaching, to use in interpreting Scripture. Jesus's response embodies the Sinai prophetic tradition we examined earlier. God loves us, God delivers us, and so what are we to do in return? Deuteronomy 6:4–9 says:

> Hear, O Israel: The LORD is our God, the LORD alone. You shall love the LORD your God with all your heart, and with all your soul, and with all your might. Keep these words that I am commanding you today in your heart. Recite them to your children and talk about them when you are at home and when you are away, when you lie down and when you rise. Bind them as a sign on your hand, fix them as an emblem on your forehead, and write them on the doorposts of your house and on your gates.

If we read a passage so that I love God less or I love others less, I am not fit to respond to God's mercy and grace in my life. Malcolm Guite said:

If I interpret any passage of the Bible in a way that diminishes my ability or anybody else's ability to love God, or in any way trammels or disables my passion for loving my neighbor, or if I have an interpretation that prevents the love of God or the love of neighbor, then I have got the wrong interpretation. I don't care how literal it is, I don't care how obvious you think the text is, if you have read it in a way that diminishes those two things that Jesus says are the meaning of the Bible, then you have got it wrong. . . . so if you read a psalm about warfare and you know, Lord, smash my enemies and you think that is your next door neighbor, then you have it wrong, maybe the enemies are in here, maybe the frontline runs directly through your heart, you have to reinterpret that.[29]

The third lens we might adopt is to actually see where Jesus goes. The ecclesia is supposed to be the body of Jesus Christ. Paul tells us this (1 Cor. 12).[30] We are supposed to respond to grace by following God's example (Eph. 5). The work of the ecclesia, the society of friends of Jesus, is solely to help us become "little Christs" as C. S. Lewis says.[31] So it is incumbent upon us to see where the actual body of Christ goes. It is incumbent upon us to notice who Jesus sits with, talks with, and touches. We should be curious about what he says to the people that he is with. We should take note of what Jesus says to the poor, the religious leaders, the women, the sick, the broken, and possessed. If the church is to make imitators of Christ, then we might organize the priorities of the ecclesia accordingly.[32] In doing this, we begin to imagine how Jesus lived out the two great commandments from Deuteronomy in his life and ministry.

I hope that a critical reengagement with Scripture along the lines I outline above will make a few things clear. First, we see that the ecclesia that is everywhere and always made up of human beings is a society of friends who wish to follow Jesus because God has acted, is acting, and will continue act in one way love directed at all creation. We strive to maintain a sense of grace and not perpetuate a moral society. The second hope is that our work helps us imagine a heavenly Jerusalem where all people flourish by virtue of being gathered in. I hope we can see the ecclesia as the spiritual Israel while at the same time accepting that, like human beings, the church is a fallen creature.

From here on out we will survey a number of themes: Jesus and love of God, understanding neighborliness, how Jesus is neighbor to people (where he goes and who he visits with), his invitation to go (not to colonize) but to be part of people's lives, his rejection of the culture of death, his vision of judgment and reconciliation. Then we must conclude by reclaiming the saints who have sought to call out the church and renew the prophetic tradition. For the church has not only stolen Jesus for its own purposes, but it has also stolen the saints and domesticated them lest we follow too closely.

Our task must be to open ourselves up. Not long ago while sitting amidst a circle of friends listening to poetry and speaking of Jesus, I was reminded of the story from Mark 7:31–37 of the man who was deaf and blind and had a speech impediment. Jesus engages him. He spits on the ground. He puts his finger in his ears. He touches his tongue. Jesus enters his life and meets him and he heals him. He raises his face to heaven and he cries out with the word "ephphatha." This means "be opened." We are participating in a church that is blind to the society around us (and in many regions wishes not to see or know their neighbors or know their stories). We work in churches of every kind that are enthralled by a consumer Christianity focused on attendance. These churches, this church, is listening but not able to hear the cries for mercy. We serve institutions that divide the sacred from the profane, institutions that perpetuate the idea of privatized religion, and so, because we know not our neighbor, we are deaf to their plight. We make hollow pronouncements.

Jesus come to us. Help us to imagine the ecclesia you intend. Help us to see again your ways. Help us to see that way stretch out behind and before us. Spit in the earth where our footprint lies, grab hold of your church, raise your head, and cry out and heal us. Open our eyes. Open our ears. Open our mouths.

CHAPTER SIX

BE ON YOUR WAY

This is true worship. Worship isn't vapidly stroking God's ego as though God has low self-esteem and created us to remind him how great he is. But real worship, true worship is to be the creature of God's creating living into the terrifying beauty of what's possible without what's possible being fettered by what's come before.

—Nadia Bolz-Weber, pastor and author[1]

I have been watching a show called *You, Me and the Apocalypse*. In one of the episodes God appears before a weeping pregnant nun to console her. The nun immediately grovels in the presence of the most high God—who, by the way, appears as an old woman. (I love this show.) God tells her to stop groveling and wonders out loud why we think this is so necessary. Of course this is a nod to the old Monty Python sketches, where God frequently speaks to people in a similar manner. Appearing before the knights of Camelot in *Monty Python's Holy Grail*, for instance, God says to Arthur: "Oh, don't grovel! If there's one thing I can't stand, it's people groveling."[2] I think we come by the idea that God wants us to grovel from our deep tradition of worship and stories like Moses and the burning bush (Exod. 3:1–2). We think that loving God is synonymous with worship. Or, put the other way around, when we worship God, we believe we are fulfilling our invitation to love God.

Let me be clear about our gathering as Christians and as Episcopalians specifically. We believe that what is essential is gathering weekly as the first followers of Jesus gathered. This is part of how the church remains tied to the society of Jesus followers. We also believe that when we gather we "unite ourselves with others to acknowledge the holiness of God, to hear God's Word, to offer prayer, and to celebrate the sacraments" (BCP, 857). I know the power of worship and the transformation of lives that does actually take place in worship of all kinds within my own denomination and believe this must be true elsewhere.

Our Episcopal Book of Common Prayer actually has very little description of our customs and what is to take place in worship. There is no mention of vestments or processional items, for instance. There is very little description about where people are to sit and how many hymns are to be sung. There is no mention of a building. Even in our service to bless a new sanctuary, there is not much to it. Yet we have overlaid the Prayer Book's very brief liturgical sketch with a whole host of inherited traditions. These inherited traditions have become liturgical and institutional narratives that define what makes us Episcopalians and Christians and our lens for reading Scripture. They cloud our understanding of what faithfulness actually requires. Our inherited traditions become what the church is about and some of us zealously defend our particular tastes as if they were ordained by God himself.

Jesus has quite a bit to say to those that lead worship about how worship itself can be a slippery slope. Like a Sinai prophet, he challenges the religious leaders of the day to see how they have lost the way—focusing on religiosity and practices within their buildings. Jesus indicts religious leaders who love titles instead of friends (Matt. 23 and John 15). We are not made to serve the religious order.

This is not an occasional assertion of Jesus. He constantly invites friends to sit at the table together. Jesus points out that the religious leaders will divide up traditions and separate the righteous from the unrighteous (Luke 11:42-44). Religious leaders will take pride in occupying the places of honor in worship. Have you noticed how this is physically made real in our worship space, with the altar area reserved for a few individuals? Jesus challenges the religious leaders of his day by calling into question their assumption that acts of worship make them better than others, less sinful, more righteous (Luke 18:9–14). In fact, religious leaders are likely to think their acts of piety have completed all that has been asked by God, meanwhile behaving horribly in the rest of their life (Matt. 23). Jesus reminds the religious leaders that their offerings actually belonged to someone else, the people who underwrite their religious system.

The story of the widow's mite is a great story about how the economy of religious organizations work. Then there is that great passage in Matthew 17:24–27, which describes religious leaders as earthly kings. They have replaced God and take up a tax for their sustenance like other kings of the earth. Jesus tells his disciples that God does not tax his family, but religious leaders always take from others. So, Jesus says something like, "Go to the sea, cast a hook, you will catch a fish and in its mouth you will find the money for the tax. Give that to them." Such a comment about the tax being found in the fish's mouth is not simply a literary device of the author or a sideways comment by Jesus.[3] This is no mere parable but a powerful message. Jesus is saying that those who follow him, who are "brethren," are a new order. They are free from the tax not because Jesus doesn't like the idea of the temple and its false suzerainty and dubious economy. He is saying quite specifically that this is not how God's society of friends is going to function. Jesus is clear that his ministry and the ministry of the community that comes after is to be free of such transactional systems of faithfulness.[4] The fish and the coin are a new and fresh perspective that held the religious priorities of Temple Judaism lightly, while inaugurating a new society with great sincerity and truth.

Those who follow Jesus will be the "last, the least, the lost, and the little, all of whom are key in the stories of grace he will tell."[5] These are not people who are somehow on the edge of the new society but central to it. The new society will divorce itself from the transactional society of the old temple ways.

Jesus constantly seems concerned that religious leaders are so busy with the work of worship and religion that they simply aren't with people (Matt. 9). This is especially true when it comes to sitting, eating, and being in relationship with those considered unworthy. Worship of God and the focus on the temple creates a number of assumptions about how we might respond to God for the mighty acts done on our behalf. The problem is that because of our church lens, we read these as concerns of Jesus about other people and not us.

Let's take the story of the transfiguration, for instance. This is a passage that appears in Matthew 17, Mark 9, and Luke 9. The story comes shortly after the revelation that Jesus is on his way to Jerusalem to die. Jesus heads up a high mountain with a few friends: John, Peter, and James. Jesus is "transfigured" there. He is changed and his face and clothes shine dazzling white. This is a mystical event of great power where the disciples see Moses and Elijah (two great Sinai prophets) standing there with Jesus. They are clear that this is a great sign, a revelation, about the person of Jesus. Peter says, "Lord, it is good for us to be here; if you wish, I will make three dwellings here, one for you, one for Moses, and one for Elijah" (Matt. 17:4). Immediately, their human nature kicks in to make a holy shrine because of their experience. They would build booths; people would come and visit. Here on this mountain people would come to worship Jesus, Moses, and Elijah. But Jesus heads back down the mountain. We don't get much from Jesus, only that the real work isn't happening on that mountain. He goes right down the mountain and begins a ministry of healing in the town. We see very clearly that the ministry is among the people who are in need of God.

In Matthew's Gospel, a man had gone to the disciples, but they couldn't help. Jesus says, "You faithless and perverse generation, how much longer must I be with you? How much longer must I put up with you? Bring him here to me" (17:17). It is as if Jesus says, "Look, you guys want to go around and replicate a new system of religion, build booths, and set up pilgrimages. The work of this community I keep teaching you about is in the midst of the people." This is right before the wonderful passage where Jesus rebukes the idea of a religious ingathering and sends Peter to go find a fish with a coin in its mouth. In every passage the disciples are to listen to Jesus, follow Jesus, and do what Jesus tells them to do. It has always struck me as funny that Jesus does not say, "Great idea. Let's build a building where people can come and worship God; after all that is the highest form of love." But instead Jesus takes them out into the world to be with people. So, I have always found naming a church "The Church of the Transfiguration" a bit odd given the story. Jesus's ministry of loving God is always in the midst of helping people.

I will talk a bit about the story of Jesus and the Samaritan woman at the well later, but I do want to pause here to point out what Jesus says specifically about worship. This is from John 4:19–23:

> The woman said to him, "Sir, I see that you are a prophet. Our ances-
> tors worshiped on this mountain, but you say that the place where
> people must worship is in Jerusalem." Jesus said to her, "Woman,
> believe me, the hour is coming when you will worship the Father
> neither on this mountain nor in Jerusalem. You worship what you do
> not know; we worship what we know, for salvation is from the Jews.

But the hour is coming, and is now here, when the true worshipers will worship the Father in spirit and truth, for the Father seeks such as these to worship him."

Jesus's words highlight the difference between the coexisting Sinai and temple traditions. But we might well ask, then where are we to worship? If loving God is not primarily done on Mount Zion in Jerusalem or on a high hilltop Sinai shrine, then where? Jesus is clear that loving God is done by being present in the lives of people . . . down the mountain. And worship is doing the work of God in Christ Jesus.

This last point is very clear when we examine how the word "glory" is used as a term for offering worship. In Matthew 5, glory is given in Jesus's work undertaken by the disciples. We are not to be like Solomon's Temple in Zion but like lilies of the field (Matt. 6:28). When the disciples want to sit and be worshiped on either side of Jesus, he tells them that they have misunderstood. Worship is found in the service to the least (Mark 8). Doing secret good things for others is appropriate worship and gives glory to God (Matt. 6:2). The devil offers Jesus people to worship him, to give him glory, but Jesus says worship God only (Luke 4:8). Good works are ways of worship. When Jesus raises Lazarus he does so as a work of bringing glory to God (John 11). In these instances the term "glory" is a form of worship or giving attention to God. Glory is attributed to God when mighty works are being done in God's name. The very incarnation of God in the world is an act that draws people to God. When the disciples actually do the work of the kingdom, they are making Christ present in the world and this is an act of worship.

The Book of Common Prayer says that this work of glorification or adoration is not done to gain something, but to enjoy God's presence. Jesus completely and continually reorients this work of love, glorification, and adoration to people and the relationships between them.

When we as Christians gather in God's name, we do so in order to be in the presence of God and to be in the presence of one another. And we must be very cautious that we do not repeat the idea that we are made solely for the worship part of this equation. About sixty years from the birth of the church, a great early church theologian, Ignatius of Antioch, wrote: "No longer observing the Sabbath, but living in the observance of the Lord's Day, on which also our life has sprung up again by Him and by His death."[6] Ignatius is clear that people should gather on Sunday, always with a bishop and priest, and in a building with an altar. The tradition around a building and altar and priest grew very fast. The people are to live for the high feast day of Sunday. Today we shame Christians who do not attend on Sunday—especially soccer moms and dads. We continue this very high tradition. I am not arguing that we shouldn't have church on Sunday. I am arguing that Jesus had something to say about what happens when humans become servants of religion.

You may remember the story. Jesus and his followers were walking in a field of grain on the Sabbath day. As they made their way, they became hungry and took some grain, plucked it, and ate it. The religious leaders of the day argued with Jesus, stating that his followers had broken the Sabbath law by working. Then Jesus says the opposite of what Ignatius says. Jesus says, "The Sabbath was made for humankind and not humankind for the Sabbath" (Mark 2:27). The Lord's Day, Sunday, is made for the people and not the people for the Lord's Day. Jesus is Lord of every day, all six days and twenty-three hours of the rest of the week in fact.

We easily turn stories about Thomas the doubter into symbols that shame people who miss Sunday worship. The disciples were gathered in the upper room for fear of the Jews (John 20:19–29). They are there on the first day of the week—Sunday. Jesus comes to them. Gives them his peace. Thomas is not there. They go tell Thomas about this. Thomas is there the next Sunday and gets to meet Jesus. Reading this story through the lens of the institutional church automatically reinterprets the story to be about gathering: those who believe are the good ones; those who don't believe and who aren't in church have something wrong with them that we must endeavor to correct. Thomas has a fault because he is not there. The disciples are good. Thank goodness they tell Thomas and he comes the next week to see Jesus. We are good because we can be like the disciples and bring others to Jesus in church. It gets very weird very quickly—and it is not the meaning of the narrative. The story of Thomas is not a story about getting people to come to church so they may believe. It is a story about a scared group of friends who are hiding in an upper room. Jesus appears and gives them peace so they can get on with the work Jesus gave them to do. A young layman recounts a very powerful sermon preached by the Rev. Martin Fields (now Episcopal bishop of West Missouri). In the sermon Fields quipped about this passage, "They were afraid of one Jew in particular: Jesus." They had denied him; they had not been present in his suffering; they were not out in the world doing what

Jesus had invited them and taught them to do. They were together on Sunday not because it was a feast but out of fear.

Not unlike Peter at the Transfiguration, we who serve and represent the institutional church have made the story of Thomas about something completely different. It is not a story about how Christians are to gather. Jesus came there, calmed their spirits, gave them the Holy Spirit, and literally kicked them out of the room. In Acts 8 we have a different story . . . but the same results. Whenever the disciples are content with following and hanging out together ("disciple" means "follower"), God sends Jesus or the Holy Spirit to kick their butts back out into the world. Every disciple is called to learn how to go and be an apostle. To leave and go out into the world. The only reason to come into a community is so you can learn how to leave it and do the real work of worship—being with Christ in the world around us. This is how we show that we love God—we go and love people, heal people, care for people, live with people, eat with people. We go and discover where Jesus is in the world and join his work there.

Paul, in his letter to the Philippians (2:5), writes, "Let the same mind be in you that was in Christ Jesus." Cynthia Bourgeault suggests that these words "call us up short as to what we are actually supposed to be doing on this path" of following Jesus. She writes, We are not "just admiring Jesus, but acquiring his consciousness."[7] This is both a consciousness and an outward living, both an inward grace and outward sign. Jesus says he is the vine, we are the branches. Jesus abides in God, and we abide in him. This oneness brings about fruit of relationships and ministry. This is about friendship between God and Jesus, Jesus and his followers, his followers with the people around them. God chooses us, to love us, to care for us, to call us friends. We are to choose others, not wait for them to choose us. We are to go out and be in the world and love it as God loves it. There is a very real sense in the Gospel of John 15 that God is one with Jesus and vice versa. Jesus invites us to have the same relationship with him and, therefore, with God. It is not enough for us to simply worship the one who abides with God, but we are to abide with God too. We are talking about more than simple imitation. Jesus is one with God. We are to be one with God. Jesus is one with us. We are to be one with others.

The incarnation itself is God's love. Our response, our embodiment of the incarnation in the world, is our love for God. Our incarnation of God's love continues God's outpouring of himself into the world. Paul writes in his letter to the Romans 8:38–39, "I am convinced that neither death, nor life, nor angels, nor rulers, nor things present, nor things to come, nor powers, nor height, nor depth, nor anything else in all creation, will be able to separate us from the love of God in Christ Jesus our Lord." This is the abiding that Christ invites us into—abiding with others. To abide is to experience a mix of God's love for us, God's love of Jesus, and Jesus's love of God (the Holy Spirit), Jesus's love for us, our love of Jesus. All of this is for the sake of the mission of God in the world, the grand gathering together of God's people into the bosom of Abraham as the Scripture imagines. All of this abiding and gathering happens so that the love of God and our love of God might be multiplied and amplified throughout all creation.

Bourgault says this isn't just some teaching. We are not looking at a text and seeing simple "proverbs for daily living" Jesus wants us to come and see. Jesus wants us to follow him out into the world. Bourgault writes, "He's proposing a total meltdown and recasting of human consciousness, bursting through the tiny acorn-selfhood that we arrived on the planet with into the oak tree of our fully realized personhood. He pushes us toward it, teases us, taunts us, encourages us, and ultimately walks us there."[8] To follow Jesus out into the world, we must recast our following as something much more than the fulfillment of the institutional church's dreams of flourishing: its idea of holiness and healthy church attendance. Such walking and living and loving and dying cannot happen within one hour plus some additional coffee time in a parish hall. I am not meaning to say that God is not present in those moments, acting in worship or healing the pains laid at the altar on Sunday mornings. I am saying that God does not limit the work and mission of the church to that hour and that space within a building's confines.

There is a very real fellowship intended here, and out in the world. There is a very real response invited. God intends this love to overtake the world and to be the core of the relationship of all who follow him. God intends for the work of "loving God" to be manifest in a way of living that is predominately found in the sacramental relationships of one human being in touch with another human being. Not for a moment or an hour, but over all of time. Theologian Katherine Grieb writes, "In response to God's love there is an imitation of Christ, not of just doing but of being with people in their own passion, in their own broken lives."[9] We are to be immersed in the life of others as God was immersed in humanity in the person of Jesus. God's mighty act of resurrection and the defeat of death will come as gift not for those who worship on Sinai alone or at its shrines, nor on Mount Zion; instead it shall be in the neighborhoods, around fires and with others, at table with bread and wine, on the streets of towns and the roads in far off lands. God loves us and we are forever linked. To love god will mean to love others, regardless of who they are. This is the most difficult part, I am afraid. God in Christ Jesus came for the ungodly . . . the very people we are afraid we might meet out there in the world if we leave our booths and sanctuaries. It is one thing to say that we as a church organization exist for sinners and the ungodly and trust that they will find us inside our abode. It is quite another thing to leave the safety of our building and property and to actually venture into the world and be with people we do not know. As one parishioner said without shame, "Why would I want to meet the people who live around my church?" Why? Because to do so is to risk the intimate love of Christ. It is to be seen with people who we are not comfortable being with. We may be concerned of what others will say or how this will affect our reputation.

Let us be clear though: Christ died for the ungodly.[10] Paul is clear in Romans 5:6 and 4:5 that Christ indeed dies for the sinner. God proves his love and unity with us by coming while we were still far off, while we ourselves were living imperfect lives, unrighteous lives. God acts on our behalf not because we have reached some kind of perfection but in order to grab us. This is a kind of "extravagance," says Grieb. Paul sees this love as an outpouring of God for all people. This is not some odd little piece of Scripture or theology. It seems that way only because we constantly hear about God's love in the midst of our community. So we easily transliterate the words to be about those present. Episcopalians have a Eucharistic prayer in our prayer book used when we share bread and wine together on Sunday:

On the night he was handed over to suffering and death, our Lord Jesus Christ took bread; and when he had given thanks to you, he broke it, and gave it to his disciples, and said, "Take, eat: This is my Body, which is given for you. Do this for the remembrance of me."

After supper he took the cup of wine; and when he had given thanks, he gave it to them, and said, "Drink this, all of you: This is my Blood of the new Covenant, which is shed for you and for many for the forgiveness of sins. Whenever you drink it, do this for the remembrance of me"(1 Cor. 11:25–26).[11]

We celebrate the memorial of our redemption, O Father, in this sacrifice of praise and thanksgiving. Recalling his death, resurrection, and ascension, we offer you these gifts.

Sanctify them by your Holy Spirit to be for your people the Body and Blood of your Son, the holy food and drink of new and unending life in him. Sanctify us also that we may faithfully receive this holy Sacrament, and serve you in unity, constancy, and peace; and at the last day bring us with all your saints into the joy of your eternal kingdom.[12]

We might well ask who are the "we" and the "you" and the "us." In the context of Sunday morning liturgy these words are very powerfully received by those in the pews as being about "them"—the faithful gathered. In our religious settings, the "we," "you," and "us" are narrowly focused. These words are not only about the them in the faithful "them" in the pews. These words are prefaced by this *very* important narrative: "He stretched out his arms upon the cross, and offered himself, in obedience to your will, a perfect sacrifice for the whole world."[13] We must read these words in the context of the whole world. The action of Jesus is an action for the whole world, for the goodly souls gathered on Sunday morning and the ungodly who are not. That is rather harsh, but it is exactly the point. We see everything within a bifurcated world organized by the needs of our religious institution, so all we see are the faithful and the ungodly. Paul reminds us, as does the whole of Jesus's own ministry, that God loves all. God intends unity with God's creatures. This is the ministry of Jesus and it is the way we are to respond to God's action and minister as Jesus. Moreover, if I am honest, there are many days when I am the ungodly one. Jesus, within the prophetic tradition of Sinai, reminds us that loving God is about being and living in the world. Living in response to God's love, it turns out, is what it is all about.

The model of Christian itinerancy I am sketching here could suggest and even provide unintended religious dressing for late capitalism's scorn of sacred sites. One of the fundamental indictments of modernity, by John Milbank, Charles Taylor, Catherine Pickstock, and Wendell Berry, among others, is the way that it atrophies and destroys our communities through the traumatic substitution of virtual (nonmaterial) space. The immanent frame and modern truth-speak is endlessly colonizing, schismatic, and violent in its destruction of sacred place. It leaves us like the damned in C. S. Lewis's *The Great Divorce*, hopelessly separated from each other by great distances, virtual and real.

So let us get clear about what I am proposing. I am not saying we should discard our spaces and buildings. I am saying that we must reclaim an itinerant mission and, in so doing, make more spaces holy by our presence as the body of Christ within them. Our goal is not to enter into and then leave community, but to expand and rescale the community until it encompasses the whole of humanity. So when we leave, we are taking what we had inside with us to the outside. These are false dichotomies, of course, but they are important in a world that claims privatized faith and religion. Our work is to make, with Christ, the whole of the outside and inside the same—spaces where people are at home in the kingdom of God, experience boundless love and genuine belonging, and ultimately find themselves for the first time in Christ. In this way, what we are doing then really is blessing and naming space.

The work of the itinerant church is to help people in the world come to concrete terms with their differences—rehistoried, rerooted, stewards of a specific, endlessly unique patch of soil. The old Anglican way of saying this was to know that the curate was the one placed for the "Cure of Souls" in a demarcated, geographic area, expressed through the liturgy of Beating the Bounds of the Parish. Anglicans have always practiced a spirituality of place, a sacramental localism, sprung from our agrarian origins. This is not a neo-dominionism or new colonialism, but is simply to see creation itself (cosmos and universe) as the sacred space of God.

Here is one final story in order to understand that Christ is inviting us to see that loving God means to be out in the world working as Christ. Jesus appears in Galilee on a mountain to his disciples (Matt. 28:16). Immediately they begin to worship him. I can imagine Peter saying, "Now, finally, he is risen, here is a great mountain, much better than the last one, here we should build a great shrine." But Jesus does not let them stay. In all of the resurrection accounts not once does Jesus say to them, "Stay here." Even when he says "wait," it is "wait until I send you." Jesus, who lived his life as a traveling prophet of God, always tells them to get moving, to be on their way. On this mountain there is no different message. They are to go out into the world. He does not tell them to go out and build little sanctuaries. He does not go out and tell them to build baptisteries. He tells them to go. Go and be with people. Teach people to go out into the world like I taught you. Teach them to love God by loving one another. Jesus promised them that no matter where they go, no matter what challenges they face, no matter their success, or their death—he would be with them. Jesus will be with them when they leave the mountaintop and go out into the world. Loving God means leaving our ideas of church-confined worship behind for an itinerant life on the road.

CHAPTER SEVEN

AN INVITATION

Our neighbors are starting to have faces, and that's crucial. We can't love in the abstract, at least not well.
—Jaime Clark-Soles, New Testament scholar[1]

Strange things are happening in our cities, suburbs, and towns. We have recently woken up as if from a dream and found that we are living together in mass (by 2040 over 85 percent of the world's population will live in cities). Yet we are living together alone. We are living the life of "buffered individuals." We live within an immanent order that is completely self-referential. Our experience entirely determines our decisions and walls off any outside "intervention," bidden or unbidden.[2] We are self-sufficient and individually focused. The faces of those around us are replaced by projections and stories of our own making. Charles Taylor, a Christian religious philosopher, writes, "We are no longer a porous self in an enchanted world as part of a cosmos."[3] This means we are cut off from our surroundings and the experiences and stories of our neighbors.

This great buffered identity, this "interiorization" of being, began during the Reformation. I am not going to trace this history here, though Taylor does it quite well in his book *Secular Age*. Ivan Illych does so in *The Rivers North of the Future*, and James K. A. Smith does in *How (Not) To Be Secular*. (Both Illych and Smith are a little more reader friendly. Taylor's work describes the emergence of "a rich vocabulary of interiority, an inner realm of thought and feeling."[4]) As Christians we look back and reinterpret our received theological history through this interior lens. We pull from our history bits and pieces of spirituality and story that amplify and sanctify this "interiorization," regardless of the damage this selective remembering does to the total context of our history.

This selective historicizing is occurring in the current explosion of popular texts on the exploration of the self. This obsession with mapping the topography of the self is analogous to other "genre explosions" across the history of literature, such as Montaigne's essays or the rise of novels that explore the inner depth of the human psyche. The resonant conversations of depth are no longer rooted in a cosmos or divine being outside of ourselves. Instead these conversations are carried on by the likes of Freud and Jung.[5]

I do not mean to say that this is bad in and of itself. But sometimes, inner exploration actually separates us from a God who is out there in the world. A spirituality of the self puts God inside of us. Moreover, it makes it very difficult for us to see God at work in the lives of others. Our society is composed of individuals, obscured from one another by their obsession with mapping themselves. The moral order facilitates this estrangement. We have become our worst fear: cogs in the machine. Our slots, our future, our place is already set for us and we have a role to play. This is the value of our society—find your place and fill it.[6] We ourselves are closed and so is the world. There is no room in our being or in our community for interruption from the outside—not "vertical, transcendent" interruption, and not even horizontal interruption by others.[7] We are constantly working on our insides without reference to the other, or even other stories of reality.

Reconciliation is difficult in this immanent frame, as is real community. Why? We have come to believe that our society itself exists for the good of all. Of course this belief is a lie and an oversimplification, as "society" encompasses many competing desires and expressions. Human freedom, even within a society that seeks the good of its citizens, brings harm due to this competition of desires. Hannah Arendt makes this very clear in her work entitled *The Human Condition*. What we have today in the West is a society full of individuals encased in a "closed spin of self-authorization."[8]

David Foster Wallace, in his commencement address at Kenyon College we discussed earlier, put it this way:

> Everything in my own immediate experience supports my deep belief
> that I am the absolute center of the universe; the realest, most vivid

and important person in existence. We rarely think about this sort of natural, basic self-centeredness because it's so socially repulsive. But it's pretty much the same for all of us. It is our default setting, hard-wired into our boards at birth. Think about it: there is no experience you have had that you are not the absolute center of. The world as you experience it is there in front of YOU or behind YOU, to the left or the right of YOU, on YOUR TV or YOUR monitor. And so on. Other people's thoughts and feelings have to be communicated to you somehow, but your own are so immediate, urgent, real.[9]

David Brooks, the *New York Times* columnist, called this phenomenon the "Big Me" in his book entitled *The Road to Character*. Marc Dunkelman in his essay "Our Tolerance Has Led to the Balkanization of Society" describes exactly how our individual lives are creating a society where all we do is bump into one another. We tell ourselves we are still a great "melting pot."[10] While our tolerance has grown, we are living in narrowly controlled environments. Diversity within our own lives is much smaller than it has ever been before. Society and the age of the internet have allowed us to not see and not hear the stories of our neighbors. We don't truly know the people we interact with. Sure, a diversity of people are only a click away but knowing them, truly knowing them, is actually more difficult today. So, Dunkelman argues we rely upon a very close knit family of friends and protect our individuality. Dunkelman argues that, where we do have the idea of neighbor it is built around commonality.[11]

We may think this is very different from the society and time within which Jesus lived. It really is not. Neighbor in the society of a tribe means those people who are part of your extended family. You can see the skeletal remains of this idea of neighbor in the city of Sepphoris in Galilee. In this Hellenistic metropolis from the time of Jesus, you can see the close quarters people lived in. Here is your neighbor who is very much like you, rooted deeply in your tribe and your culture. Certainly there was diversity, but this diversity was distributed by tribal pods. If you were one of those who worshiped at the temple in Zion and also participated in a local congregation, yours was a particular, closed kind of life. Anybody outside of that was a Gentile and not a neighbor. Neighbor was another word for brother and was narrowly defined as a member of your group. In fact, many were not neighbors: Samaritans, Syrophoenicians, Romans, Greeks. If you were not part of my tribe, then you were not my neighbor. This context is very important. If we do not understand it, we will miss Jesus's profound message for those who followed him, for the religious leaders of his day, and for those of us living in our isolated society of buffered selves.

Jesus's message is communicated most effectively in his parable about the "Good Samaritan," but before we talk about this well-known parable, we need to deconstruct the lens we typically use to read the text. It used to be that churches were composed of diverse backgrounds and histories. Even with the ever-presence of denominational sects, church communities were made up of a wide variety of people. This diversity was amplified in the wider culture as people would bump into one another at the one high school, one butcher shop, one coffee shop, and the bus ride across town that threw together in tight quarters every kind of person.[12]

As the church tribe has shrunk, it has become a place of conformity to the political and social values of its dominant members. Neighbor is articulated as those who are like us but may need our help. We automatically project that those in need must be like us in some way. Neighbor is the person we might do some good work for as a church. Neighbor is always an Other who is similar to me. People have confessed they don't understand why they should go out, why they should be with others, especially if there is no guarantee they will come to church. I have also heard, "They go to other churches, not ours." When we define neighbor as only those who are like us but in need, we cut off the reality of the world from our internal reality. We build buffered communities of like-minded people. Those not like us are not neighbors but untouchable others, the eternal "they" of the world. So it is that we have evolved in the West to being the most segregated when we are together on Sunday morning.

This idea that the neighbor is us is reinforced in the art used by churches, in the stained-glass windows, and in the children's art shared during Sunday morning classes. Everyone looks the same. You could literally take up any of the individuals and switch them around in the parable illustration and the parable would still work. The Samaritan looks like the man who is beaten, who looks like the lawyer and the religious leader. They all look the same. Of course you will argue that outer appearance would not have mattered much in the time of the parables telling, although the tribal clothes actually would have distinguished the individuals. Here is the real problem though: Today's neighbor looks very different from us. How we narrate and paint the storied picture matters if we want to truly get to a deeper meaning of Jesus's story about neighboring. Without changes in the presentation of our story, Christians in the West will be looking in a mirror that does not resemble the people in our communities at all.

The church also acts as if it is the neighbor's responsibility to come to it. Not unlike how the institutional church desires to remain with Peter on the mountain of transfiguration and build booths, the church is conditioned to receive initiative, not take initative. This places the onus on the neighbor to act on their own behalf and walk into the church booth for help. The ecclesia we have already shown is to be in the world. This means there is a particular proximity to the neighbor that is necessary for true Christian community, a proximity that is lost in many churches today. Churches are isolated from the people around them. This distorts their view of the other and keeps them from knowing the people made by God who actually are their neighbors.

The church also colludes with a culture of fear that is metastasizing globally. The fearful church believes that only good neighbors should be helped. There is a categorization of people into those who are good and those who are inhuman. Our obsessive fear of terrorism, and the negative behaviors and postures that this fear generates, are an example of the culture of fear. We also fear addictions and mental illness. Poverty and homelessness are the lot of some group of others who don't try or work hard. When the church participates in the culture of fear and shame, it steals Jesus from those who could use Jesus and from those who are trying to follow Jesus.

Churches that have become hostels for the likeminded shirk Christ's invitation to diverse community, which is the core of the ecclesia. The church that offers nothing but spiritual enlightenment for similarly minded individuals reinforces a religious consumerism that makes God, Jesus, and the other inner baubles to be probed and explored at leisure. The church that offers a vision of community as social sameness, racial sameness, ethnic sameness, and political sameness subverts the Christian meaning of neighbor, undoing the radical welcome offered by Jesus. The church that colludes with the powers of the world and creates an "us vs. them" narrative, where some are qualified to be neighbors and others are not worthy of our aid, rejects the breadth of the gospel of Good News for all people.

Jesus's society of friends is about something quite different. And, in the parable of the "Good Samaritan" Jesus discloses the key to the ecclesia's difference. The message of the parable of the Good Samaritan will consistently undermine any church that thieves the gospel. Jesus whittles away at any church that believes staying on its mountaintop within its booth is fulfilling the call of the gospel.

Other parts of the New Testament provide a few clues to what Jesus is doing in this radically subversive story about neighbors. Jesus continuously expands the Sinai law. He equates hate of the enemy with murder and even says that if you are going to the altar, you should make amends first. He equates sexual covetousness with adultery and declares remarriage to be adultery. Jesus encourages passive resistance and is clear that violence is not part of how we are to follow him. In Matthew 5:43–47, Jesus says:

> "You have heard that it was said, 'You shall love your neighbor and hate your enemy.' But I say to you, Love your enemies and pray for those who persecute you, so that you may be children of your Father in heaven; for he makes his sun rise on the evil and on the good, and sends rain on the righteous and on the unrighteous. For if you love those who love you, what reward do you have? Do not even the tax-collectors do the same? And if you greet only your brothers and sisters, what more are you doing than others?"

Jesus is expanding the law, beyond Zion even, but in a way that is faithful to the priorities of Sinai. Jesus is saying that living and loving goes beyond your tribe. With this in mind, we must retell the story of the Good Samaritan and see it again for the first time. We need to see how God wishes us to be and how that might be different from the current functioning of the institutional church.

The parable of the Good Samaritan is found in Luke. The question that gets the parable going in Luke is asked by a lawyer. Now, before we go any further, it is important to highlight that lawyers of Second Temple Judea and Galilee were not the lawyers of today. They were experts in the law—the Zion code. Jesus's interlocutor knows the commandments and is highly invested in their keeping. He is part of the wider circle of religious leaders. So, this lawyer might represent the institutional church. He is part of the religious establishment. The question he poses to Jesus is about eternal life. And he wants to know what one must do to inherit it. Jesus answers the question with a question, "What is written in the law? What do you read there?" The religious leader answered, "You shall love the Lord your God with all your heart, and with all your soul, and with all your strength, and with all your mind; and your neighbor as yourself." Jesus replies, "You have given the right answer; do this, and you will live." Now it is unclear if the leader was trying to trick Jesus or simply engage him. Jesus seems a little coy. The leader continues to press Jesus, though, and asks the big question, "Who is my neighbor?" Jesus, warming up to the conversation, tells a story.

There was a man going down to Jerusalem from Jericho. The trip from Jericho to Jerusalem is a downward trek, a descent from a high place to a low place. Having made this trek recently on a trip to Israel, I can personally testify that the journey is a radical decline across a significant distance. This drop is the first clue to our parable, according to theologian Robert Farrar Capon: this is to bring to our mind the descent of God in the incarnation.[13] Paul captures that ancient hymn in his letter to the Philippians 2:6–7, "Though he was in the form of God, did not regard equality with God as something to be exploited, but emptied himself, taking the form of a slave, being born in human likeness." The man destined to be robbed images for us the incarnation. Furthermore, the man is going down to Jericho. Jesus is on his way down to Jerusalem as he tells the story. He is going down where he will be tried and found guilty and the whole world will fall upon him and kill him. So, again the downward walk into the heart of darkness is for Jesus a personal revelation of what is coming. This man, Jesus tells us, falls among thieves. Capon wants to be clear the man is the Christ figure in this parable.[14]

The man, as the Christ figure, is taken into the hands of robbers, "who stripped him, beat him, and went away, leaving him half dead." Now two officials of the temple religion pass by. They are us, the church and the religious. Both of the men pass by on the other side. Now preachers often make a lot of this fact. The church exegesis of the parable, quick to make this about morality, wants to point out that "we" are not like "them." We want to be like the Samaritan. We even name him the Good Samaritan. We want to be like the Good Samaritan and not like those other religious people. Furthermore, the church wants to draw attention away from the man, God in Christ Jesus, and place the focus on a transactional act of mercy. When the church does this, it misses Jesus's criticism in the parable.

The religious leaders believe, because of their transactional faith, that they have done all that is required. They have kept the law. They have made their religious offerings that week. They have said their prayers. They have done this and they have done that. In fact, nothing else could possibly be asked of them. So it is that the religious pass the man on by. They have no need of him.[15] All is right with the world and with their faith. As Capon says, "Real messiahs don't die."[16] This man looks half dead already.

Jesus now introduces the Samaritan. Samaritans were not of the same tribe as the man or the religious leaders. The Samaritan is part of a group that worships in the same tradition but differently. They do not recognize the religious supremacy of Zion, so they have been cast out of the family. The Samaritan is an outcast in the Gospels; whenever you see them in a story or in conversation, Jesus is usually redeeming them. They were a Yahwist sect that followed the ancient Sinai tradition, and rejected the trappings of Davidic empire and temple religion. So it is that this sinner in the eyes of the religious establishment, this outsider, the Samaritan, stops to help. He actually comes near the beaten man. The Samaritan sees him. He is moved by what he sees. This is important. The Samaritan is coming along the road. He is not waiting for the man to find him, but instead he finds the man out in the world. He is not afraid of him but comes near him. He comes close enough to know him, to see him, to see his wounds and the damage done to him by the robbers.

The Samaritan enters into the passion of Christ by stopping to help the beaten, robbed man on the way to Jerusalem. The Christ figure is in the midst of his passion and the Samaritan comes and kneels with him. He is present in his passion. The Samaritan now takes up his own cross and follows down into the passion with the Christ figure. He stops his journey. He "bandaged his wounds, having poured oil and wine on them." This is expensive and precious. We are then told the Samaritan puts "him on his own animal." Capon points out that such an act of charity sacrifices convenience and time, as now the Samaritan must walk.[17] The Samaritan then spends money on the beaten man, and asks the people at a nearby inn to take care of the man. It is not enough to simply drop him off, but the Samaritan sacrificially offers money to care and feed the Christ. Moreover, he leaves it to the innkeeper to do all that is needed. He will pay.

Jesus then asks the lawyer, "'Which of these three, do you think, was a neighbor to the man who fell into the hands of the robbers?' He said, 'The one who showed him mercy.' Jesus said to him, 'Go and do likewise.'" Jesus flips the original question. He invites the lawyer to ask who was neighbor to the Christ? This is very different than seeing the answer about loving neighbor as some kind of legal requirement to be overly nice to someone. The person who is neighbor is the person who becomes an outcast like Jesus and enters into the passion of other outcasts. This is clear. It is not enough to leave the booth behind and reenter the world. We are to enter it in relation to the Christ and his passion. It is as if Jesus is saying to us, Capon writes, "Stop trying to live and to be willing to die, to be willing to be lost rather than to be found—to be, in short, a neighbor to the One who, in the least of his brethren, is already neighbor to the whole world of losers."[18]

Now, you may challenge me and say that I've slipped back into morality play. But the imitation of Christ is not about simple morality. To imitate Christ is to prioritize relationship and sacrifice over doing nice things out of requirement.[19] Humans want to codify this behavior and make it into a mandate—do nice things for others—and then to let it gradually slip into an economy—do nice things for others so you can get into heaven, or be loved by God. This codification is always dependent upon the individual and motivation and frequently rooted in the immanent frame or the tribal framework of one's own selecting.

Ivan Illich, an Austrian philosopher and Roman Catholic priest,[20] believes that the gospel offers a different way of engaging the world around us. It breaks open these naturally forming codes. The Samaritan's actions are not generated by a code outside of himself. Instead it is about a response to his humanness. Taylor digests Illich's thoughts on the Samaritan this way:

> He feels called to respond, however, not by some principle of "ought," but by this wounded person himself. And in so responding, he frees himself from the bounds of the "we." He also acts outside of the carefully constructed sense of the sacred, of the demons of darkness, and various modes of prophylaxis against them which have been erected in "our" culture, society, religion (often evident in views of the outsider as "unclean").[21]

In this way the Samaritan's actions show a new way of being in relationship outside of the boundaries of religious morality. The Samaritan is an extension of love and agape in the same way that Christ is an extension. Both the Samaritan and Christ create a new "kin" out of relationship and "enfleshment." In the Samaritan's actions we see a new kind of fitting together of people outside of their tribe, code, morality, and formed way of being.[22]

The Samaritan is surrounded by religious codes and he breaks them by involving himself in the man's passion. In this then he moves outside the tribalistic codes of his day and in so doing offers a different way, a code-breaking way. He models for the modern the opportunity to do the same, to reject the religious codes we have recreated in Christianity or the selfish codes of niceness and kindness. He invites us to dispose ourselves especially to the strangest and "least-deserving" folks we know.

We must remain focused on the Christ figure. Just as Jesus is going down to undertake the passion, to lose everything, the Samaritan does the same. Capon writes, "If you want to read his selfless actions as so many ways in which he took the outcastness and lostness of the Christ-figure on the ground into his own outcast and losing life—then I will let you have imitation as one of the main themes of the parable." Where do we find the passion? The passion of Jesus is always to be found in the "least of his brethren, namely, in the hungry, the thirsty, the outcast, the naked, the sick and the imprisoned in whom Jesus dwells and through whom he invites us to become his neighbors in death and resurrection."[23]

The passion of Christ invites the church to put aside comfort and enter the Way of the Cross. The passion of Christ invites the church to take up its cross and become more the ecclesia—a society of friends of Jesus who lay down their lives for others by entering into their passion and daily crucifixion. Theologian and preacher Fleming Rutledge ponders this parable and Capon's teaching and writes, "This is not a parable meant to inspire us to go out and do good and then feel good about ourselves because we have been good neighbors. This is about entering the way of Christ."[24] If the world could be fixed by nice people doing kind acts, then everything would be fixed by now. This is not the reality of Christ's sacrifice nor is it the reality of the world in which we live. Paul writes in his letter to the Galatians 3:21, "If a law had been given which could make alive, then righteousness would indeed be by the law." Rutledge reflects on this too and says, "Handing down a new law does not create new people. Something more is required than an exhortation to good works."[25]

Luke offers another story in Acts 9 that echoes the parable of the man who fell among thieves. The story is about Paul and Ananias and how the Lord sent Ananais to find Paul and restore his sight. We know from Paul's writing that he had a great experience at the hands of God. He had a conversion experience. We know that Paul has a huge influence on Luke/Acts. And we also know that Luke is keen to show the continuation of the tradition of Israel in the new Christian community. Who better as an illustration than brother Paul? Just like with the story of the man who fell among thieves, we have an interpretation bias that perverts how we read Luke's story about Paul and Ananias: we often make this story about the persecution of the flock, and thereby a persecution of Christ. This allows us to be on the Christ side of things. It automatically places us on the inside and those who are on the outside not one of us. This reading lets us off the hook for any bad behavior on our part. After all, we are on the side of Jesus.

Second, we make this about conversion into something, that is the flock of Christ, a holy people of God. This further complicates things because it makes us special and those outside of our clan not special. It creates a situation where those who are converted are our true neighbor and those who are not converted are removed from neighborly status.

We may even make this passage about Ananias's witness and his acts of kindness toward Paul as an implied action for Christians. In other words, we should be like Ananias. The problem with that is multidimensional. It is a problem because it reinforces that we are to be kind to those who are converted. It makes the gospel about good behavior. And, finally, it reduces the acts of Ananias to kindnesses.

Capon writes about the dangers of the model I have described in his book *The Mystery of Christ*: "In building this theological model you have also done something else. You have opened yourself to the idea that the church is the Fellowship of those who have the gift and that the rest of the world is just a crowd of outcasts who don't have it."[26]

To reclaim this passage from a churchly perspective or a perspective of morality, about good behavior, we must understand that Luke has told the story of Paul and Ananias within the framework of Jesus's teaching on the Samaritan (Luke 10:25–37). We must read as Jesus intended, with the passion at its center. So it is that Paul has been undertaking a war of passion on the followers of Jesus and upon Christ. He then undergoes his own passion—and resurrection (being stricken and having his sight restored)—and so Paul himself becomes not only an image of the man who fell among bandits but of Jesus himself. He suffers because Christ has revealed the truth about his actions. He experiences the passion of others as a passion of his own. Paul is converted by entering into the pain that he has caused.

Ananias is called to go and be with him. He is invited to go and find him and to help him. Here, then, we see that Ananias is not simply doing something nice as a neighbor. Ananias enters into the passion of Paul. Ananias goes through his own passion. He crucifies his desire to hate and dismiss this enemy as outside the family of God. Instead, Ananias embraces Paul. Ananias crucifies his desire to be somewhere else, anywhere else but with this enemy of faith and instead inconveniences himself to go and be with Paul. Ananias must crucify his assumption that God only chooses good people as instruments of his mission. Ananias must crucify his assumption that following Jesus was only meant for the Jews and not for the Gentiles. He must crucify his fear that healing Paul will harm his reputation with his fellow community members. He must crucify the part inside of him that does not wish to care for Paul. Despite all these powerful misgivings, Ananias cares for Paul until he regains his strength—further crucifying his convenience for the passion bearer. And we are told that they eat together, a most intimate act. Ananias must even crucify decorum: the strict rules of table fellowship.

The story of Paul and Ananias reveals that being in relationship with the mystery of Christ does not create some kind of churchly morality but pushes people into solidarity with those who are suffering their passion. The world sees this as folly. Strangers do not help strangers. Enemies certainly don't help enemies. The Samaritan, Paul and Ananias invite us to to help strangers and enemies alike. What is folly to the world is actually the wisdom of the gospel. The mystery of Christ pushes us to experience the passion with them—and in so doing, experience the passion of Jesus and our own passion. When we enter the lives of the other, we take up our cross. We are living into the death of self, to the death of the world, and in living into the passion, we discover Easter and resurrection. For in experiencing one another's passion, new life is had by both Paul and Ananias.

Loving God invites us to leave our self-made booths and our interior castles. We are to go out into the world in solidarity with our neighbor so that we enter into their story and their passion. The summary of the Law teaches us the meaning of taking up our cross and following Jesus. But in order to do this work well, we must know where we are to go and to whom we are to go.

CHAPTER EIGHT

A TABLE IN THE WILDERNESS

The dark night is God's attack on religion. If you genuinely desire union with the unspeakable love of God, then you must be prepared to have your "religious" world shattered. If you think devotional practices, theological insights, even charitable actions give you some sort of a purchase on God, you are still playing games.

—The Most Rev. Dr. Rowan Williams, theologian and former archbishop of Canterbury[1]

In his book *A Secular Age,* religious philosopher Charles Taylor narrates the move from an enchanted world to a world of disenchantment. In the enchanted world, meanings were not located purely in the mind as in the modern age. The enchanted world was composed "of spirits, both good and bad. The bad ones included Satan, of course, but beside him, the world was full of a host of demons, threatening from all sides: demons and spirits of the forest and wilderness, but also those which can threaten us in our everyday lives."[2]

The Church and even the ancient tradition of Israel connected the desert with unformed places. Colonizing such spaces helped to order emptiness; something done in partnership with God.[3] Certainly there are stories of saints like Anthony, Jerome, and Francis who are tempted in these wild places—repeating the story of Jesus.[4] The enchanted world was full of these empty spaces, where you might meet God but you jeopardize order and safety to do so. Time and space were imbued with meaning and powers outside of the self. The church was filled with magic too. The church was the arbiter of good magic that could save and protect the individual. Power resided not simply in the will of self, but in things and in others. So sacraments, candles, relics, and the host, among a plethora of real objects, contained in them the power of good church magic.[5]

The Reformation made a new secular world possible. This disenchanted world relocated power and meaning within the mind and self. The removal of the church's magic was key to the disenchantment of the world. God's power was no longer mediated by humanity or contained in things. This demagification would reform how the church thought about the relics of saints and the Eucharist itself.[6] Taylor writes, "Church magic was an illegitimate claim to control the power of God. Who made this claim? The hierarchical church. One vector of the revolt was directed at the claimants, who were often personally far from holy, wielding great power over ordinary people's lives, and abusing this power. The magic was discredited by the magician."[7] So the Reformation refocused on a personal faith mediated by Scripture. Power and authority was overseen by a moral elite in order to protect the other nonsaved sinners. This inner focus and personal mediation set the stage for a completely immanent society of individuals.

The Reformation unleashed a series of trends that have secularized society and privatized religion and Christianity. This is a far-reaching statement for this little book and I don't intend to go into this in depth. I am aware that the roots of the problems of the immanent frame lie earlier, in Franciscan breaks with Aquinas, and developments of late scholasticism. Mainline Christians and secularists see a culmination of a great axial movement in the Reformation—which is a time in which the pagan fetishes of the past were put behind us for a reasonable future. The Reformation "completed the axial turn" for Roman Catholics, Protestants, and secularists.[8] The same movements "which rid us of the relics of paganism and idolatry" jump a step forward using the same philosophical tools and rid us of religion and an enchanted world.[9] According to Taylor, Milbank, Bella, and many others, the Christian scholastic movement and its purge is clearly a watershed moment in our secular trajectory. Ironically, all of modernity is contained within late scholasticism; our secularism is naught but a perverted theology.[10]

Taylor argues that everyone in the West has this particular secular lens by virtue of living within the disenchanted world. So what of the institutional church in the midst of this emphatically closed, godless creation? In an ironic twist of fate, the church has, through the Reformation, actually brought its demise upon itself.[11] Western Christendom embraced and promoted the conditions of its own obsolescence. Its desire to order a world, to practice an "intense piety," to find God immanently present in the world around us, along with an abandonment of enchantment for the sake of reason has meant that, in the words of Charles Taylor, "the fruit of the devotion of faith, prepares the ground for the escape from faith."[12]

Today's institutional church sees the world in a particular way. The sacred has become "localized" and geographically focused.[13] The world outside the church is a godless world—a new wilderness. It is filled with unbelievers and a new science. The focus is on bringing people into the shelter of the geographically bounded community.

Inside, the church is a type of association for inwardly focused people. And each association of the postmodern church is trying to put the genie back in the bottle. Like the ancient cathedral bulwarked against the enchanted world, church today exists as a place where people can find a bit of respite and rest on the pilgrim way. Some churches claim the work of justice as their moniker—they are communities doing a bit of good in the world. Still others have become a kind of society that provides the resources to become a good person. Churches thus try to provide a structure for moral behavior. Instead of white magic to protect against the wildness of the world, some of today's institutional churches promise a safe environment for members to learn the spiritual skills necessary to navigate the wildness all around. Other churches are trying to return to a Middle Ages model, recovering the magic of high sacrament and symbol. They attempt to repeat a sacred time, within a sacred geography, along with a sacred hierarchy.

Many churches have become a kind of island or walled city looking backward into a premodern worldview, believing this to be the key to success for renewed growth. As a diaspora, the church has cut itself off from the world and is an inward-facing culture. Regardless of what churches we look at, what we see are islands in the sea of a culture that is quickly forgetting them. From the large denominations to the small nondenominational churches, we recognize that the world inside the church doors is vastly different from the world outside.

A peer in ministry once described his work as continuing the ancient traditions like the ancient Israelites who found themselves in captivity in Babylon. As for the ancient people carried off to a foreign land, the world outside is strange and irrelevant to the things that matter inside the church. To the people outside, the world inside these islands of faith seems odd and somehow disconnected from life. My fellow minister is correct; Christian communities exist today as diasporas. *Diaspora* is a term describing the Babylonian captivity of the Jewish people and today it describes the many Jewish communities that exist as islands outside of the Holy Land.

The Church is a diaspora community. It is a community that shares values and worldviews. Inside the diaspora, things are clear. It is clear who you are, what you stand for, and who you are not.[14] The Christian community large and small has an inward focus. Our communities are so unlike the rest of the world, it is difficult for people to look in and understand what we are doing and why. Things just do not make sense when you look out and things do not make sense when you look in.[15]

The church is being called into the future. It is being pulled toward the ecclesia. For the church to engage the pilgrimage to God's intended future faithfully, it will let go of past institutional models it previously used to buttress ministry. There will always be an appeal to continue past forms of church ministry, hoping for different results. Trying the same-ole-thing expecting different results is crazy. As Taylor emphasizes, all of these past forms brought about the present disenchantment. We, as the society of the friends of Jesus, must take a bold step out into the wilderness of the world. Only in the wilderness of the world will we discover what can deliver us. When we protect ourselves from the wilderness, we remove ourselves from the very space where mystery, enchantment, and God are to be found.

If we pause for a moment and think, we recognize that the wilderness is a place of danger. Nothing good happens in the wilderness. God is certainly not present there, we think. After going back and reading the Scripture, I see how the church has rehearsed across the centuries a false reality, where the church bears the standard for order, while the wilderness represents disorder. The city is order; the countryside is disorder. The Temple Mount is order and the world outside the walls is disorder. But if we truly desire union with the unspeakable God, then we must walk out from the safety of our churches into the wilderness and dark night where God is found.

It is true that there are a few passages in Scripture where the wilderness is given a pretty bad rap. The temple authors write that the wilderness is a "great and terrible wasteland" filled with "poisonous snakes" (Deut. 8:15). The authors are quick to remind the reader that it was the terrible misbehavior of Moses's flock that brought their long sojourn in the wilderness, a great redaction that favors good behavior prescribed by religious leaders in order to gain God's favor. Jeremiah, the prophet, speaks unfavorably about the wilderness (2:31). In the book of Ezekiel the prophet, we are told that the wilderness is a dry and futile land (19:13). Joseph is thrown into a pit in the wilderness in Genesis 37:22, which sets in motion the Egyptian captivity of Israel. Then there is the devil. Jesus is tempted by the devil in the desert wilderness. These really are the scant few passages that declare the wilderness to be a bad place.

Surprisingly, the overall picture of the wilderness is quite different. God invites Abram to leave the comfort of Haran in the land of Ur of the Chaldeans to go out into the wilderness and is present with him there (Gen. 12). God speaks to Abram in the wilderness of Sinai. God is with Abram's son Ishmael in the wilderness (Gen. 14). Jacob spends the night alone in the wilderness of Peniel and there wrestles with God, who puts his hip out of joint and gives him a new name (Gen. 32). Then in Genesis 36:24 we are told that the wilderness is a place of springs, life, and community. Moses meets God in the wilderness (Exod. 3:1; 4:27). God tells Pharaoh to let the people go out into the wilderness to worship (Exod. 5:3). We know that God makes bitter water sweet, manna from the dew, and brings water forth from a rock in the wilderness (Exod. 15; 16; 17). God tells the people to bring him gifts in the wilderness. It is in the wilderness that the people come to depend upon and receive from God. A whole new generation of people comes to love and respond to God's care in the wilderness. David is sheltered in the wilderness from those who wish to harm him (1 Sam 23:14). Elijah meets an angel in the wilderness in 1 Kings 19. The angel cares for him and ensures he is rested for his journey. Psalm 65 speaks of the wilderness as a place of joy and song. In Isaiah it is fruitful and justice dwells there (32:15, 16). The Maccabees, during the invasion of their homeland, find shelter and safety in the wilderness.

In the New Testament, the term "wilderness "comes from a Greek word that refers to "uncultivated land." When John the Baptist is in the wilderness, he is therefore not necessarily in the desert but in a land that is not filled with grown food, as stressed by Joan E. Taylor in her book *The Immerser*.[16] Furthermore, if you have ever been to the River Jordan, a desert is not what you find. Instead it is lush and green along the river's edge. Today it is all quite cultivated, but we can imagine it as a remote place where there is little habitation or organized civilization. Certainly, by the New Testament era, the wilderness is seen more for its positive aspects of being the place from whence the Word of God comes. It is a prophetic place. The wilderness is a geographic area more in line with the Sinai prophet than the civilization of Mount Zion. It harkens back to a time when God was understood to be dwelling among the people and not simply upon a mountain.

Josephus, the historian who wrote during the first century and chronicled the life of the Jews in Palestine, indicates that the early Christian view of the wilderness dovetails with other Jewish revolutionaries of Jesus's day. Jews, Samaritans, Egyptians, Theudas, John the Weaver, and others would use the powerful imagery of the promise of the wilderness for their cause. He did not have much good to say about these would-be pretenders. He did say John the Baptist was a good man though.[17]

Why is it important to rehearse these themes of wilderness? Because we encounter God there. God is at work in the wilderness. God's people are formed and learn God's character and come to depend on that character in the wilderness. I believe when we have a false idea about the meaning of the wilderness, we miss the work of Jesus and where he goes.

Yes, Jesus is tempted in the wilderness. But interestingly, Jesus is fully human there. He denies every attempt to make him something else. He does not use some kind of superhuman power to outwit the darkness that awaits him there. It is in the wilderness that Jesus accepts his humanness. He is given the opportunity to never want or hunger for anything and he says, "No." He is taken to the temple, where he is given the opportunity to be seen by all around as God—rescued on angel's wings. Jesus refuses. He is then taken to a high mountain and offered all the nations of the world. He declines. Jesus is completely human in the wilderness, a wilderness where he was baptized. Our humanity and our relationship with God are tied to the wilderness.[18]

How many times have we thought of Jesus and the lost sheep as a parable about serving others—going after the lost sheep? But what if the parable is actually a story about the sheep in the wilderness? The Shepherd gives up his shepherding and meets a single sheep in the wilderness, a sheep otherwise presumed to be dead. We meet the sacrificing Lord in the wilderness—this is where we are found and where we find the Lord.[19] The wilderness is where grace happens.

In his correspondence with the Corinthians, Paul takes a look back at the Old Testament and uses a form of typology to make a theological statement about God's presence in the wilderness. He writes in 1 Corinthians 10:4 that through the wilderness experience the people, "drank from the spiritual rock that followed them, and the rock was Christ."[20] Paul invites the Corinthians to find Christ in the wilderness like the Israelites. The prophet Nehemiah speaks to God and recalls that God was faithful in the wilderness, "you in your great mercies did not forsake them in the wilderness; the pillar of cloud that led them in the way did not leave them by day, nor the pillar of fire by night that gave them light on the way" (9:19). The light shines in the darkness, and the darkness did not overcome it (John 1:5). Joel says that the pastures of the wilderness are green (2:22). Jesus is the Good Shepherd and leads them to green pastures (John 10 and Ps. 23). Such a typological reading of Scripture may only go so far and only be so helpful. But here in this context, it should prick our ears to listen to where Jesus goes and how is he present in the world.

So let us begin where the Gospels of John and Mark begin—in the wilderness at the River Jordan. (Matthew and Luke will get there by chapter 3.) Jesus is at the Jordan for his baptism. This is most important because the Jordan is the place where Joshua entered the Promised Land (Josh. 1:2–3).[21] It is the place where Israel renewed their freedom from Egypt and the crossing of the Red Sea. Literally, the Jordan parted as they entered into the land of Abraham's promise (Josh. 3:15–17). Some scholars believe that this was a regular liturgy conducted at the river's edge.

The Jordan is the place where John the Baptist and others prophesied against the domestic and foreign powers. It is a place of great meaning, and on the last day, the Jordan wilderness would be the place from whence the fertility of all the land would come. As in the prophesies mentioned above, the wilderness of Jordan would be a sign of great abundance and give birth to fruit, and a great harvest (Isa. 35:6–7; 41:18–20; 51:3). Joan Taylor writes, "There was no one, ultimate wilderness that indicated these links; those of Zin and of Judea, the Negev and the Sinai—all carried the same associations:

the wilderness was the place of transition, of trusting in God, of being led towards liberation and security."[22]

It is this sort of wilderness that contextualizes the beginning of Jesus's ministry. This wilderness is where the liberation begins, a liberation to come for all people.[23] Oppression is thrown off as the great prophet begins from this starting point. It is here then that the associations of fertility, of the kingdom of God, of knowing God, of deliverance, and the theme of reform converge in the ministry of a man who rises out of the water. Make no mistake, when God pronounces Jesus as his Son with whom he is well pleased, this is not simply a nice gesture of recognition. It is a sign that in the wilderness, from the wilderness, the shackles of both the state and the state-sponsored religion are thrown off the people.

The wilderness is not simply a geographical place in the mind of the reader, but it is a sacramental symbol, a place where God is encountered and from whence God in Christ Jesus will make his journey to his passion. There is no Jerusalem or cross without the journey that begins in the wilderness. There is no mission without the complete dependence upon God that is fostered in the wilderness.

Jesus does go to the temple early on in the narratives as well. In Luke he is presented there, as was the custom by his parents (2:27). This is long before his baptism and the time when we meet up with John the Baptist. On Zion's mount, Jesus is brought where all the faithful are taken after birth, to be presented before God and have all appropriate offerings made to secure his well-being. The holy life of faithfulness begins with a presentation. You become part of Zion's ways. You begin to live to bring about the faithfulness of Israel so that the Davidic reign might be restored. When Jesus is presented, however, something different happens. When he is presented, he is proclaimed as a light to all those who do not worship there. Jesus, the old man Simeon prophesies, is the light for the Gentiles. So from the wilderness (where the prophets have spoken a harsh word against the Gentiles), Jesus enters the temple and is proclaimed as the one who will break open the religion of the temple to all people—to the Samaritans, Romans, Greeks. Jesus is the light through whom all people shall come to know God and shall inherit the reign of God and the promise of Abraham (Rom. 4:13; Eph. 1; Gal. 3:9).

Again Jesus is found in the temple in Luke. He is lost after a pilgrimage to the city of Jerusalem as a young boy. His parents find Jesus teaching at the temple (Luke 2:46). But this story is another prophesy: this is his father's house—he proclaims. He is here to claim it, but not as the expected Davidic king. Instead, Jesus will claim the temple by cleansing it, tearing its religion down, and rebuilding it in God's image.

In the last days of his ministry, Jesus, in all four Gospels, goes to the temple and finds a disordered house (Matt. 21:12). He calls it a den of robbers (Matt. 21:13). He proclaims that God will raise up the temple in three days—relocating the cult of the temple around the person of Jesus himself, declaring himself to be the center of the future faith (Matt. 26:61, also in Mark, Luke, and John). Jesus continually angers the religious leaders by undertaking his disruptive work without requiring sacrifices. He heals people (John 9 and 11). Eventually he is tried in the temple by the leaders of the day for healing and raising the dead.

We do not know how many times Jesus went to the temple—though there are many theories out there about this based on trying to figure out what kind of a leader, rabbi, religious person Jesus was. What seems important though is that in the Gospels, for the first followers of Jesus, the movement was itself not primarily about Jesus being in the temple. We find this to be true when we look at Jesus in relationship to the synagogue.

He goes to the synagogue in Matthew 9:18, where he restores a girl and heals a woman. In Matthew 12:9 he heals a man with a withered hand in a synagogue. He is rejected by people in the synagogue in Matthew 13:57. He heals a man with an unclean spirit in Mark 1:21. He teaches at the synagogue in both Mark and John. During one of his teachings at the synagogue (Luke 4:14–30), he is filled by the spirit and speaks of his own ministry: "The Spirit of the Lord is upon me, because he has anointed me to bring good news to the poor. He has sent me to proclaim release to the captives and recovery of sight to the blind, to let the oppressed go free, to proclaim the year of the Lord's favor." This is quite a nonreligious mission. It is not focused on synagogue or temple. It is about people.

When Jesus enters a synagogue or the temple, they are merely backdrops for proclamation and prophecy, places where Jesus declares himself to be of God and invites us to follow him. If we are to understand what it means to love God and love neighbor, then we must leave the confines of these geographical places and enter the wilderness of life away from these religious centers. The vast majority of the narrative of Jesus is spent out in the world with people. The presence of God stretches from the Jordan wilderness throughout the countryside and into the hearts and homes of people.

Jesus spends the vast majority of his time in the midst of life. His work and ministry takes place in Galilee (Matt. 4:23). He teaches on the mountain (Matt. 5:1). He heals men on the road (Matt. 9:27). He goes to all the cities and villages and into the fields (Matt. 9:35, 11:1, 12, 19:1). He goes to the water—sea and lakeside (Matt. 21:16, Mark 4:1). He is in Gethsemane (26:36), where he prayed. He went to the mountaintop where he was transfigured and to the River Jordan, where he was baptized. He was at the Decapolis (Mark 5:20) and in Tyre (Mark 7:24) and in Capernaum (Mark 2). He goes to people's homes, like Peter's, the tax collector's, and a synagogue leader's (Matt. 8:14, 9:10, 9:23). He goes to Bethany and to the home of Simon the Leper (Matt. 26:6). He goes to Jarius's home in Mark 5:38. He is in a centurion's home and the house of a Pharisee. He visits with people in the dark of the night and over dinner. He goes to Nazareth (Luke 4). These are the places of the Jesus story. Some accept him and his teaching and others reject him. He goes to be with them all as their neighbor.

In his book *Binding The Strong Man*, a book about the Gospel of Mark, Ched Myers writes that it is in the wilderness of Galilee that the great things of ministry happen in Jesus's life. It is here that the gospel takes root. Myers argues that the temple and the synagogues are places of confrontation with a religion that no longer does the Father's work or cares for the Father's people. Jesus's temple and synagogue work is casting out demons and freeing people from the oppression of a religious system that is burdensome.[24] On the other hand, the work that Jesus does in the midst of the people is freedom work, grace work, and merciful work. After the resurrection, Jesus also appears to the disciples in a home, by the seaside, on a mountaintop, and on the road. As if to echo the reality that this is where he is to be found—in the midst of life. Eternal life is woven together with real life. The gospel of the Good News of salvation is proclaimed and rooted in Jesus's actions within the religiously uncultivated world that surrounds Zion.

Jesus lived the majority of his life outside of the temple and synagogue, engaged in ministry with people as part of their daily life. Jesus declared the prophetic witness of a Sinai prophet, but he also lives it out by being part of the people's lives. He entered the passion of their lives. He met them, named them, healed them, and cast out their demons. He was present in their lives in a powerful way. Jesus entered the wilderness of everyday life. Jesus met them as neighbor. He first saw them as neighbor and then he acted as neighbor to them.

If the church organization is to become the ecclesia of God's dream, then it must go out into the world and be present in the wilderness where strangers can be found. This will mean giving itself over for the sake of the world. This is just it—our walk into the wilderness will be sacrificial. Jesus's body shakes with fear in the Garden of Gethsemane. Friends abandon the body of Jesus as he is taken into custody. His body is beaten and bruised. His body is forced to carry his cross, except when Simon of Cyrene picks it up for a while. His body is hung and crucified while the faithful few watch; all others having gone home to attend to their Sabbath. Only a few will take his body down and lay it in the grave.

To do this work as ecclesia, to be the body of Christ in the world, is not a mission of comfort. Make no mistake, it will sound glorious, but it will bring bloody sweat and tears. To be the church is to enter deeply into the passion, willing to be abandoned. To be the ecclesia is to be bloodied by the world. To be the church is to do more than be a nice place to go where nice things are done for the right people. To be the ecclesia, Christ's body in the world, is to be broken by the world. It will mean suffering, abandonment, rejection, and mockery. To be the ecclesia will mean to carry our cross, though we will be joined by others, and they will carry the cross as well. We are to be crucified and laid in the grave. Here is the ecclesia's work. Here is the work of all who seek to be friends in the society of Jesus. We must manifest the life, ministry, and mission of Jesus in the midst of the suffering of the world—to suffer with and for the world. To enter into the passion of the world as Christ did and to be buried as Christ was buried. Only in going all the way is there resurrection. There are no half measures for those who claim the body of Christ as their moniker.

There is great cost to this leaving and wandering with God in the wilderness. Much will have to be left behind for much to be gained. Like the people who followed Moses, we are going to complain and say things like: Why are we out here? Could we not have died in peace inside the church? Why did you bring us out here, were there not enough tombs in Egypt (Exodus 16)? The text tells us that a whole generation dies in the wilderness. So the answer to the question, "Why did you bring us out here? To die?" is "Yes." You have been brought out into the wilderness to die.

CHAPTER NINE

AN UNCOMFORTABLE NONSENSE

The more one respects Jesus, the more one must be brokenhearted, embarrassed, furious, or some combination thereof when one considers what we Christians have done with Jesus. That's certainly true when it comes to calling Jesus Lord, something we Christians do a lot, often without the foggiest idea of what we mean. . . . Has he become (I shudder to ask this) less our Lord and more our Mascot?

—Brian McLaren, theologian and author[1]

We long for a Jesus that is greater than a mascot. We know that Jesus invites us to go and be neighbors in the world. He invites us to do this out in the wilderness in relationship with people. Jesus himself spent most of his time doing this wilderness relationship work. It isn't just that he is geographically located in the context of the world and humanity. He is constantly in relationship with others. We have to recognize that his invitation puts pressure on us individually, communally, and as a church.

We are deeply motivated by a sense of wanting to love God and love neighbor. I rarely meet anyone who isn't interested in helping other people. In the West, we are prone to being a bit smug about how helpful we are compared to other societies. We also feel shame when we don't live up to this standard. Feeling good or feeling shame around our desire to love and care for others is not a sustainable cycle. Somehow our institutionalization of the story of the Good Samaritan has sapped away the gift of folly intended in the original. We have removed the joy from the work of crossing boundaries. Instead, such leaps of faith are viewed with anxiety, fear, and concern for our own well-being. In this way our view to the mission isn't very motivating. This cycle causes us to bleed stamina. It makes us fickle. Tragedies capture our attention briefly, for a day or a month.[2] We have seen this multiple times in the South with hurricanes, fires, and tornadoes. The public attention quickly shifts to the next awful emotion-capturing event. Emotive motivations for doing what Jesus asks of us may capture our imaginations for a short while, but eventually these motivations fade.

We are also deeply motivated by a sense of our shared humanity itself. I am human, you are human. We may acknowledge some measure of shared dignity in this. I can reject the notion of being a miserable sinner and embrace the value and worth of being created by God. Charles Taylor invites us to consider that we as human beings have a tremendous potential, there is an ever present opportunity to achieve this potential, and the project of assisting one another is a worthy one. Here lies the great experiment of humanism and community. The problem with this motivating narrative is that humans are bound to disappoint. Again, Taylor believes that we cannot actually live up to our potential. Modern history is littered with the tales of progressive hope undone by the greed of humanity for power and wealth. We will continue, no matter how hard we try, to "fall short of, ignore, parody, and betray this magnificent potential; one experiences a growing sense of anger and futility."[3]

In the face of these failures to motivate, we fall back upon some moral framework to help us. Humanism, our immanent frame and secular age, offers us a choice between one of two positions, two internal centers of gravity that suit our circumstances. Even the church models these perspectives.

One of these positions revolves around the self and the preservation of the self. It is a humanism focused on the individual over and against the other. This is a kind of rugged "pull yourself up by your boot straps" individualism. It creates a world that orients everything around itself and believes that it can do anything it puts its mind to. It believes that if it works hard enough, it can perfect itself by sheer will. It demands that the world, society, and all things bend to its personal arc of super human trajectory. This position is key to the old Protestant work ethic—it is the individual human flourishing that is important. This is how the West was won and the great society built. Within this framework, action is the serving of others for the sake of service—fulfilling the duty of the individual. This is how we have overcome the evil that has faced our nation. This individualistic frame of reference is particularly suited for a kind of national Christianity.

This individualistic humanism turns faith into a transaction of sorts. You work hard, you are a good moral creature, you get God's love, and you get into heaven. This narrative is not very tolerant of the weak and those who are less inclined to the demands of perfection. It tends to root out sinful, broken, and sullied human beings in order to manifest political, religious, societal purity. It criminalizes the "other." Charles Taylor describes this perspective as Neo-Nietzschean in his essay on "A Catholic Modernity."[4]

When the church acts out of this paradigm, it places itself at the gravitational center of the faith, displacing the body of Christ. As the center, the church bends the world to its cause. It wants everyone to come to it. It chooses what the community needs—most of the time without asking. It does good work by giving but not by relating. It desires many things and hopes for good, but at the end of the day measures the success of its work by determining whether or not more people are in the pews. What is worse, it believes in this try-harder gospel that orients around an individual will to power. It invites its members to work harder to be good moral people for the sake of gaining God's love and approval and a place in heaven. It believes that if it keeps doing the same things over and over again it will eventually grow and thrive again. It believes in a kind of accumulated notion of church—it has arrived at its logical orientation—no more change is needed. Furthermore, it is reticent to acknowledge that mistakes have been made along the way.

An individualistic church will read the Scripture as if Jesus was a super human. He was super powerful and super religious and super good. If we will just emulate him, then we will be super Christians like Christ. Churches caught up in this individualistic narrative also take on an orthodoxy that is not helpful. They keep out the sullied, the marginal, and the poor. They treat those who do not believe as an "other" to be avoided. They are slow to apologize and not eager to explain. They are chock-full of boundaries that render them hard to map and even harder to join. There is a lot of inside talk and all the pressure of belonging is placed upon the newcomer.

The second way we respond to our failures of motivation is also rooted in humanism, but this humanism is rooted in an appreciation for community.

Instead of the self as the organizing motif, communal well-being becomes the organizing motif. All humans and their flourishing is the goal. This orientation foregrounds justice concerns in order to promote a new loving society where all people are welcome. When the community of humans is at the center, diversity and inclusion become the most important issues. This orientation always focuses on the individual in relationship to the "other." It is rooted in the Enlightenment values of equality and egalitarianism. This perspective also promotes a transactional way of being in the world. People are judged by how well they think and act on behalf of others.

These judgments create a "who is in" and "who is out" society. If you are not accepting, you are "out." This way of thinking excludes the powerful on the grounds that the powerful are themselves exclusive. This perspective promotes the binaries of the activist and the soldier: you are with us or you are against us. Because this perspective is laser-focused on distributive justice, its proponents will reflexively demand that the powerful be removed from power and their resources dispersed. Liberation theology is rooted in this kind of humanism. Unfortunately, when "liberation" has been gained and the revolution is over, a new group of elites emerges. There can never be an elimination of "the powerful" because society always tends toward order. A new oppressor will always emerge.

Churches that have embraced this community-centered perspective make everything about doing good works for others. These churches tie themselves in knots creating a more and more egalitarian society that becomes so fractured that very little can get done. Structures and policies governing behavior are key and help protect the community and its identity. In its worst manifestation, this kind of church supplants Jesus in favor of being together, being open, and welcoming all. Like its Neo-Nietzchean counterpart, this perspective marginalizes Jesus, so it can create another humanist society that does some good things.

Neither of these contextualizing narratives resembles the work of Jesus that we have been describing. Neither of the churches created by these perspectives promote the love and work that Jesus has in mind and so they fail at making people who actually follow Jesus. Both of these churches claim Christ as a mascot, and little else. Quite simply, Jesus is not at the center of either of these humanist narratives. At best, he plays a minor supporting role. The humanist roots of these stories mean that value is only found within the realm of creation and the life of the individual or community. The real actors in both stories are the church and the individual. It's also important to note that both narratives bisect liberal and conservative churches alike. Liberals can be neo-Nietzschean. Conservatives can be communally oriented. Because this is part of the immanent frame that constitutes us all, there is no real escape. Unfortunately, both of these mascot churches inevitably promote social and physical violence.

Charles Taylor reminds us that humanism in both of these forms always regresses and transgresses due to a meaning-fatigue inherent to the immanent domain itself. Eventually humans "gradually come to be invested with contempt, hatred, aggression. The action is broken off, or, worse, continues but is invested now with history of despotic socialism."[5] Both strands of humanism tend toward power play, as do the churches these humanisms manifest. Over the last fifty years, the church has been endlessly fragmented by this power play. Denominational and nondenominational churches have both suffered from this kind of conflict. Some studies show that, at any given time, some 75 percent of congregations are in conflict. The growing diversification, will to power for the individual, and the drive for ever-greater justice are rooted in humanism and have caused a rolling collapse that has cascaded across decades.

I do believe that God is interested in individual and corporate human flourishing and interested in our mutual care of one another. I think this is a true statement. Whatever we do, we should not cast aside humanism (as some who wish to put the genie back in the bottle and return to an enchanted world of magic so often attempt). Humanism has helped us become better in many ways. Humanism has helped us hear voices we would not otherwise hear. Humanism has helped us see how we might share power and how unjust our societies are. Humanism has opened us up for advances that are good for our society in science and technology. Humanism has resulted in bringing new, diverse leadership into play. So humanism and its desire for human and societal flourishing (with all its faults) has been good and we don't want to get rid of the good it has brought with it. But human flourishing, regardless of being oriented around the individual or society, is not the end purpose of God in Christ Jesus. Emotions, good thoughts, doing things for each other out of our pure sense of shared humanity and our moral devices are not enough to overcome the self-centeredness that plagues our various humanisms.[6]

The end purpose of God in Christ Jesus is to gather all of humanity into God's self. Here is the good news: God in Christ Jesus came into the midst of this brokenness to found a new humanity. In her new book *The Also Life*, Barbara Cawthorn Crafton brings hope to those of us caught in this violent double-bind, the malaise of humanism. This includes the whole church, as we too are imprisoned!

She speaks of how God has the amazing power to pull us forward. In all of our brokenness, our yearning to self-protect and win, in all of our desire to be good and our frustration with this desire, God pulls us forward. God beckons us. This action of being drawn forward is taking place even now in this life and it will continue in what she calls the "also life."[7] It is God's love that is pulling us forward. This is not a kind of affection where our spirit swoons over God as though he were a boyfriend. Crafton does not promote an emotional love as the solution to our problem. She also does not promote a conquering, possessing, or overpowering love at war with our human selves. We are not drawn forward by an erotic love either.[8]

The love that draws us forward is a transformational love based upon God's giving of God's self to the other. She writes that it is "the nature of love to transform the lover into the object loved." God becomes human that we might become a part of the divine. As Athanasius said, "God became man that man might become God."[9] Crafton is one in a long line of orthodox Christians like Athanasius who have had a way of troubling our imaginations. As we open ourselves up to Christ Jesus we discover that we are invited into this transformation. To set our hearts and minds upon Christ alone brings about this transformation, by God's loving, which begins to turn us into that which we love, and vice versa. Just as our love begins to transform us into Christ, so too God's love works on us, transforming us into God. We call this *theosis* and it is an ancient teaching originating in the earliest Greek theology.

God is remaking humanity. We are to become more the human being God intends. This is not something that happens solely in the "also life." It has happened and is happening in the life around us now. It is a love that takes the center space from the willed self. It is a love that takes center space from the pure human community. This love is none other than the Holy Spirit of God. It is deeply rooted in otherness and the nature of God's embrace of otherness. Both the love of God for Son and Son for God, and the love of God for humanity and humanity for God are rooted in the Holy Spirit as love.

This is the meaning of the 1st Letter of John, chapter 4, verses 7–12:

Beloved, let us love one another, because love is from God; everyone who loves is born of God and knows God. Whoever does not love does not know God, for God is love. God's love was revealed among us in this way: God sent his only Son into the world so that we might live through him. In this is love, not that we loved God but that he loved us and sent his Son to be the atoning sacrifice for our sins. Beloved, since God loved us so much, we also ought to love one another. No one has ever seen God; if we love one another, God lives in us, and his love is perfected in us.

This is the meaning of God's incarnation. God loves the world and the creatures in it. As Paul says about Jesus in his letter to the Philippians, "though he was in the form of God, [he] did not regard equality with God as something to be exploited, but emptied himself, taking the form of a slave, being born in human likeness. And being found in human form, he humbled himself and became obedient to the point of death—even death on a cross" (2:6–8). It is the folly of a God who overcomes God's own godliness to reach across the divide of heaven to earth and become human. God in Christ Jesus becomes human—that which is completely other than God. God in Christ takes on humanity in order that through the uniqueness of the incarnation in human form, we might become more human. Out of love, God becomes the creature—the lover becomes the object of its love. There is something power-ful, hopeful, and true in this message. It is mysterious and it is absurdity (I Cor. 1:18–31). It is foolishness to the wise and wisdom to those willing to be like the Samaritan and foolish enough to live in this way following in the wake of Jesus.

Christ is the lover; we are the beloved. And in this love God beckons us to become him, to become Christ in the world. This love moves us beyond ourselves, and Christ Jesus, our mascot, becomes our center. Here the center of the church is not the church but instead Christ Jesus, who came, who died, who rose, and who will come again. This Christ beckons us to be Christ in the world and beckons us on. What we learn from our relationship with Jesus is how to give up ourselves to God and God's mission. We do this in our world, in the midst of our society and creation not in order to benefit from some kind of moral transaction that gets us into heaven, but as practice. We practice in this world, giving ourselves as the beloved over to our lover so that we might be ready to give ourselves over to God in the world to come. Moreover, this Jesus who comes into the world comes for all people: the sullied, the broken, the abused, the thief, the poor, the suffering, the rich, the hateful, murderers, liars, victims, the possessed, the sick, and the mournful. This Christ Jesus loves and calls all these lambs God's beloved.

Jesus offers a better way than either of the two humanisms and their corrupt parodies of Christianity. Jesus offers himself and human flourishing through the multiplication of himself in everyone. God in Christ Jesus offers a full life and human flourishing by becoming us through love. And in so doing, Jesus moves us beyond human flourishing and the self to unity with God. The good beyond life is the union of God and creature, the church and God. This God comes for all of us—the long list of the least of these and the lost and the other.[10] This God gives his life for all of us—even the church.

Let us go deeper. The language of the Gospels is clear regarding God in the person of Christ Jesus as defender of, voice for, and advocate of the lost, least, and other.[11] The Old Testament, all of the Gospels, and most especially the Gospel of John are clear that God is the defender and even avenger of the weak and powerless. Our God is the God of the people—all people. God is the one who raises Jesus, the victim, after first raising the people of Israel, the victims, out of Egypt. René Girard, in his work entitled *Job: The Victim of His People*, makes clear this is deep theological language and juridical language used in first-century legal discourse.

Of course we are immediately drawn to Matthew's Gospel (chapter 25), where we are reminded that our service to the least of these with whom we live is always service for and to Christ. God appears in the person of the other. When we do this work, we do it for Christ and on behalf of Christ and as Christ—Christ's love in us works out God's purposes. God is a God who rescues us in our darkest night. This too is clear in the Gospel account. God stays the stormy sea, rescues Peter from the waves, and he defeats death. This is a God who heals those imprisoned by their illness: the man possessed by legion, the woman who bleeds, the mother-in-law, the daughter, and the servant. Luke's Gospel attests to a God who is present and involved in the life of the living and part of the miraculous work of the body in need of healing.

God cares for and advocates for the lost, the least, and the other. And yet, as Girard recognizes, if God is only the God of the victim, then what we are envisioning is no God at all. Girard writes, "A God of victims cannot impose his will on men without ceasing to exist. He would have to resort to a violence more violent than that of the wicked. He would again become the God of persecutors, supposing he had ever ceased to be."[12] Girard believes that the victim will quickly reestablish the same victimizing behavior. God is intent on breaking up the system of oppression whereby the victim becomes the victimizer. Girard and so many others are quick to remind us that the persecutor believes he knows the true God of victims: for them he is their persecuting divinity. Girard reminds us that God is God of both the victim and the victimizer—God (if he is to be any kind of God at all) is God of all. Here is the scandal of the gospel—God in Christ Jesus loves and beckons all. Perhaps you are thinking, "That is not right, that is not God at all. God cannot be for victim and the victimizer!"

The argument of the vast majority of church preaching begins to go downhill at this point. Conventional church preaching argues: if God is the God of the victim, God must judge the persecutor guilty and sentence him. Justice at the quantum and Newtonian level, at the microcosmic and cosmic level, is always, from the perspective of the victim, an injustice "mixed with vengeance" and this in itself is an imitation of a god but not our God. This is merely the humanist mascot god.

Girard deals with this perspective when he speaks of Job and his friend Eliphaz. Eliphaz's primary argument against Job is that the faithful, the righteous, the good do not perish. Instead, it is only the wicked, the victimizer, the oppressor, and the sinner—the wicked—who suffer. Furthermore, their suffering is a measure of their sin (Job 4:7–9).[13] What is revealed in Job, according to Girard, is that God's justice does not work as the world's justice works.

God's justice is not of this world nor does it apportion the misfortune that plagues the world we live in. Here we might well remember the passage from Luke regarding those Galileans and the poor people upon whom the tower fell:

> Do you think that because these Galileans suffered in this way they were worse sinners than all other Galileans? No, I tell you; but unless you repent, you will all perish as they did. Or those eighteen who were killed when the tower of Siloam fell on them—do you think that they were worse offenders than all the others living in Jerusalem? No, I tell you; but unless you repent, you will all perish just as they did. (Luke 13:1–5)

While Luke is reminding us that we should learn to give ourselves over to the most high God through repentance lest death come calling like a thief in the night, the point for our argument is also clear. Evil that seeks to destroy the creatures of God is real. Persecutions are real. Accidents are real. All manner of genomic bodily weaknesses and cancerous trials are real.

God, Girard explains, is also a God who refuses to parse out injustice and justice or the pain that we experience. Girard and Capon alike remind us that the God that Jesus speaks about in the parables is a god who is always gone. God is always the absent master of the house, the property owner, and the ruler who has gone away. God in the parables leaves the work to the servants, and tenants, and workers. They in turn are either "faithful or unfaithful, efficient or timid."[14] While other gods in myths allow the judgement of those who are left behind to rule, the God of the parables always returns and as the Scripture is quick to remind us, he makes his sun shine and his rain fall on the just and the unjust alike (Matt. 5:43–50). God refuses to be the arbiter of human disputes for he knows our ways of justice all too well.[15]

This is not to imply that God is lazy or inattentive. In fact, the gospel tells us that God gives completely of God's self for the victims of the world and in fact for all of us. This is most profoundly offered in the witness of Jesus himself as he offers a way, a movement forward, away from victim and victimizer to a common humanity. Girard writes:

> Jesus enjoins men to imitate him and seek the glory that comes from God, instead of that which comes from men. He shows them that mimetic rivalries can lead only to murders and death. He reveals the role of the scapegoat mechanism in their own cultural system. He does not even conceal from them that they are dependent on all the collective murders committed "since the beginning of the world," the generative murders of that same world. He demands that they recognize the sons of Satan, devoted to the same lie as their father, the accuser, "murderer since the beginning."[16]

In placing God above the small petty schemes and "little systems" of humanity, Jesus himself is found guilty by challenging the system. Like Job, he is innocent and yet found guilty. Like all the prophets before him, like Abel, Jesus's own passion and trial is a replay of the bloodshed that constitutes human society. But here is the Girardian switch: in the trials of the world, the victimizer is judged guilty and the price paid. Here in this world Jesus is found guilty and pays the price.[17] As God of the victims, it is God's right to overturn the reason, logic, and sentence of this world and to overturn the victimizing power. This is the way this world works. The victimizer is guilty, the victim receives the just demand, and the victimizer pays, becoming himself victimized. Girard's point is that this is not how God works.

Instead, God in Christ Jesus, the advocate, the Paraclete, the one who is justice, who is judge, the one who is the God of the victims, chooses differently. Our identity is found in this crucial difference. According to Girard, the advocate of the Father chooses to suffer instead of act against the victimizer. Girard writes, "Christ is the God of victims primarily because he shares their lot until the end. It takes little thought to realize that nothing else is possible. If the logic of this God shares nothing in common with that of the God of persecution and its mystifying mimesis, the only possible means of intervention in the world is that illustrated by the Gospels."[18] This means of intervention is most clearly represented in the crucifixion and resurrection.

Here is a gospel in which the Christ remains unsupplanted by the Jesus of the church. God is the God of the victims because "he shares their lot until the end." There is no false sacrifice here. There is no Adoptionism, Apollinarism, Arianism, and Docetism. These are the heresies that make the action of giving of Christ's self no sacrifice at all.

The complete victimization of Jesus is exactly that—complete. "The failure is total," says Girard.[19] This failure is itself an action and not a nonaction, Girard is quick to point out. This is not an idle God, or a God of the deists, this is not a God who does nothing. Instead, this God is a God who chooses loss as intervention. This God in Christ Jesus is not the God of the victim. This is not Eliphaz's God at all. This is not our mascot to cheer us along to victory nor is it a puppet master.

This God transcends the victim by entering into victimhood totally; God in Christ Jesus is the victim. God experiences the pain and estrangement of victimhood. God is not some distant legal advocate for the victim but is experientially present in the cruelty and suffering of the rape victim, the abused child, the family of the murdered husband, the conscripted child pulled from the mother's arms in Africa, the addict, the son or daughter killed by a drunk driver, the woman sexually taken advantage of by her counselor and priest, and every possible human suffering. This is the God of the one who has cancer. The God of the one who survives. The God of the one who is lost to her family. This is the God of the dead man, woman, child, and the God of the dead church.

Unfortunately, oftentimes the mascot Jesus of the church is much more the god of Eliphaz. When individual and communal human flourishing is at the center, the church must adopt a god of Eliphaz. The institutional church's god has a strong hand, who acts and intervenes for the righteous. This god is promised for those who follow and believe. This is the god that funds the prosperity gospel. At its worst, this god is a god humanity enjoys worshiping. This is not a divine god, but rather a human-shaped god. This is a god who brings persecution in one hand and blessings in the other. This is a god of nations who fights the gods of other nations. These are gods of our own making whose name is no higher than any other name. These human gods rule on behalf of the victimizer and the powerful, the authorities and rulers of this world. This is the god of populism and tyranny and autocracy. These gods will always have followers, but they will never have love or bring love. They will only have adoration.[20]

Turning to the opening words of the Lord's Prayer, Girard reminds us that this god of the powers, the church, and Eliphaz does not reign. The God of Jesus will reign. "He reigns already for those who have accepted him. Through the intermediary of those who imitate him and imitate the Father, the Kingdom is already among us. It is a seed that comes from Jesus and that the world cannot expel, even if it does all it can."[21] Charles Taylor says this is the "Thy will be done" God that cannot be reduced to human flourishing alone.[22] This God is much more than a human-made advocate.

Edwin Muir in his poem *The Incarnate One* reminds us this is no "ideological argument." As Malcolm Guite says, we're warned against "the dangers of theological abstraction and urges us to try and stay with the Incarnation, with flesh and blood, to drop our 'ideological argument' and look again at the cross in 'ignorant wonder.'" Further, it is this shameful truth that the Church rejects and which we try to "unmake." The church can't stand a God who chooses to be victim as the central role to overturn power, authority, and the ways of humanity. So it is that the church refuses the actual gift of solidarity with us in our flesh, his closeness, and instead push him back to some infinite distance of abstraction. In so doing we "betray the image," we prefer the "bloodless word," the "cold empire" of the abstract man. In this kind of church, "The Word made flesh here is made word again."[23]

One of the ways we do this is to espouse the idea that Jesus was sacrificed because his Father demanded it. This is simply not the reality. It may have made sense as a theology in a context where kings ransomed relatives to go and live with their enemies for the sake of peace, but it has no merit theologically. It doesn't even make sense given the story of Abraham and Isaac. It is the lie we perpetuate in our poor Lent, Holy Week, and Easter theology. It is this poor theology that makes, as Girard points out, the true incarnation invisible to the world and makes "Christianity only one among many religions of violence, and possibly the worst of them."[24]

The Easter message, the message of the ecclesia, the message of the society of the friends of Jesus, is one that does not deny the failure, or victimhood; instead it confirms it—and reveals it for the solidarity and victory Christ's victimhood is. Here we are made children of God, citizens of the family of God. In our death, in his death, in the drowning death of baptism, we affirm God's solidarity with us. All human beings rejected by humanity join in Jesus's own rejection and participate in the "beginning of the end of the 'reign of Satan.' "[25]

What separates this from some Greek myth and false Christianity is that the victory does not take shape in the afterworld but in our world. It is in this life and the also life beyond. We live in a very real world where the passion narrative is reenacted over and over again. It is part of the human genome. It is our model of life of the powerful who consume the weak. The victim is the perpetual scapegoat. In the experience of Jesus, in the experience of Job, we see, as Girard would say, "the satanic principle on which not only this community, but all human communities [are] based."[26] Furthermore, because this is ALL of our human natural behavior, our go-to behavior, we have a difficult time going even deeper. We have a difficult time not replicating in our own Christianity, in our own religion of self, in our religion of celebrity, the religion of persecution. Taylor makes it clear that all humanism, all false church Christianity, will lead eventually to despotic fascism.

What we are saying is this: true faith of Christianity and the ecclesia is not some illusion or metaphor of imaginary hopefulness. This is the incarnation—this is redemption—this is resurrection. Here is the full meaning of "Christ has died and Christ has risen." Here is the God who is greater than the temple, greater than we see, and who will not dwell in booths on mountaintops. Here is the God who is neighbor to all and who comes alive in the wilderness. This is the God of Golgotha and this is the God of Easter morning resurrection. This is our end and it is our beginning too. God in this victimhood is gathering us all in. God is our gravitational center pulling us ever to the also and beyond life.

John Heath Stubbs writes in his poem "Golgatha" that the cross is our nexus at the center of our new life: "In the middle of the world, in the centre, Of the polluted heart of man, a midden; A stake stemmed in the rubbish."[27] Malcolm Guite reflects on this poem, "One key to the mystery of the Gospels is the truth that everything that happened 'out there in the back then' also happens 'in here and right now.' "[28] What happened back then happened to both Christ and to us and to all whom God has made. As we plunge into this deep theological well, we discover that our center is the God of Golgotha and the empty tomb. With this God we are both freed and reborn as Christ. We participate in his death and resurrection. This is the God at our center, not the mascot who legitimizes our empty humanisms.

CHAPTER TEN

WALKING TOGETHER

See Jesus standing in the lowly place. He is not pointing at the lowly place. He is not saying, Would you get over to the lowly place please? No. He is standing in the lowly place and he is not saying anything. You just see him in the lowly place. Which is the place of humility, it's also the place where the poor, and the voiceless and the powerless, and those who live outside the camp, that is where they stand. So he stands with the demonized so that the demonizing will stop. And he stands with the disposable so the day will come when we stop throwing people away. He stands with those who are outside precisely so the circle will widen. You don't erase the margins except by standing at them. Then you can look at your feet and see that they are being erased. That's the only way to do it. And that was the strategy of Jesus.

—Greg Boyle, founder of Homeboy Industries,
Jesuit priest, theologian, and author[1]

A Sinai people are icons of Christ through the power of the Holy Spirit in the world around us. To live the wilderness life results in a very real participation in the passion experiences of others. In 2016, I made a trip to China. I went there to visit friends of a particular mission society with which I am involved. We traveled together to Nanjing and while there it was important for them to take us to the Nanjing Massacre Memorial Shrine. The shrine, similar to Holocaust museums, was a powerful witness to the atrocity and efficiency human beings demonstrate in killing one another. The massacre took place in 1936 and over 300,000 Chinese were killed by the invading Japanese army in Nanjing (then called Nanking). A city that was the cultural center of China would never be the same again.

I slowly made my way through the museum. It was haunting, powerful, and terrific—as in terrifying. I prayed and I forced myself to see what was rooted deeply in my hosts' hearts. This was their story. I was invited to know their crucifixion. I was allowed the great privilege of knowing their pain, their suffering, their Golgotha.

As I came to the end of the memorial museum portion of the walk, I suddenly beheld the features of a Westerner in the chiseled bust of an American Episcopal priest. John Gillespie Magee stood before me. My hosts told me, "Oh! Yes, the Anglican! The Anglican!" Magee was a priest serving in Nanjing. He would survive the massacre and later returned to serve at St. John's Episcopal Church, Lafayette Square, in Washington, DC. He officiated at the funeral of President Franklin D. Roosevelt in April 1945. He also served as chaplain to President Harry S. Truman and as chaplain at Yale Divinity school. While in Nanjing, Magee served as an Episcopal missionary, sharing the gospel, celebrating the Eucharist, creating a school, and building relationships with the people in the community. At the time of the massacre, he was also the chairman of Nanking Committee of the International Red Cross Organization.[2] Magee disregarded his own safety during the reign of violence and sought out every living soul he could, helping to rescue over 200,000 Chinese citizens. Magee did not stand by, but entered the suffering of the people whose culture he lived in, becoming a neighbor to them. He also shot several hundred minutes of film.[3] He took rolls and rolls of pictures of the events surrounding him.

His films were smuggled out of Nanjing and used politically to call attention to the abuse and killing.[4] Magee was fearful that the film and photos would fall into the wrong hands and so he kept them safe. Upon his death, he passed them to his son David. In 2002 David gave the film and photos to the museum in Nanjing—without charge.

What I realized in that moment as I came to the end of the museum is that in large part much of what I had seen in terms of pictures and film was due to the witness of a fellow Episcopal priest. He was invited in to be present at the foot of the cross of the Chinese people in Nanjing. Like many before him, like many after, he was invited as a friend of Jesus to bear witness and to name the victimhood of his fellow man. He was invited to see, to hold the sin of some, to free the sin of others, to see the cross and to proclaim resurrection and hope. He was given the opportunity to make Christianity incarnational through his witness and his actions. Today many Chinese know him simply as the "Anglican." That man that did not flee before the massacre but instead ministered and saved many.

Those who choose to follow Jesus are invited to enter into the suffering of others. It is too easy to discount their witness or to separate ourselves from the other who suffers. Like Job, Girard argues, we are too easily "neutralized" by our own human will to violence and the distractions of false religion to stand with the victim at the foot of their cross. Girard writes, "Many things divert us from the crucial texts, deforming and neutralizing them with our secret complicity."[5]

Only in reading the passion into the story of the person sitting across from us do we unearth the truth. If we hear in the other's story the story of Jesus and the passion, we quickly see them as Christ and Christ's own. Only when we hear the other's story in the context of the passion and Gospels do we see that God and we now stand as the advocate, the Paraclete, the God of the victim and his healing followers. In this, then, victims and others are revealed as Job and as Christ. This is not some illusion but instead deep revelation. Here we are not saying that somehow the other, the victim, like Job, is some "prefiguration of Christ" because of "his moral goodness and his virtues, especially for his patience, even though Job in reality was the personification of impatience."[6] This is not allegorical or metaphorical. This is not some theodicy—a story where divine goodness is vindicated and providence revealed in the midst of evil. No. All those who dare to listen to the story of the other see Christ.

In our care for the other or the victim we are not saying to them, "See God is good and you are vindicated, despite the evil that has happened to you. After all, what do you really know about the one who set the heavens and earth in motion? What do you really know about pondering the depths of the God of the universe? Yes, bad things happen but providence and the goodness of God is still before you. Be faithful, you will find it." NO. God as the crucified victim experienced your murder, rape, beating, hunger, defeat, suffering, and starvation. You are victim and God is victim. Your Christ likeness hides in God's victim experience.

In this witness, you and I, Magee and many others, reveal human violence for what it is—evil. We lay bare the truth that violence and war are not the ways of God. Satan, and all the pretend gods of this world, are the first murderers. When we dare to witness the other's crucifixion and suffering we "[strike] a death blow to a world system that can be traced in a straight line back to the most primitive forms of violence."[7]

Our oneness, our unity, is in making this witness. We are to know this particular God of love and suffering and to make him known. The prayer of Jesus in John 17:20 invites us to be witnesses to these things and to be unified with the world. As God in Christ Jesus becomes one with the suffering world, so do we. In the words of Henri Nouwen, we are invited to drink the cup of this unity. We are prayed for and invited to become one with Jesus in his work of sharing the suffering of the world—to drink the suffering of the world.[8]

Jean Vanier, founder of the L'arche communities,[9] believes it is more nourishing to our human relationships when we share our weakness and difficulties than when we share our qualities and successes.[10] When we bear witness to the cross in one another's life, we recognize that "to be lonely is to feel unwanted and unloved, and therefore unloveable." Vanier continues, "Loneliness is a taste of death. No wonder some people who are desperately lonely lose themselves in mental illness or violence to forget the inner pain."[11] The work of Jesus is the work of seeing one another for who they and we really are. We must quit the illusions of success and perfection. Instead we must own our brokenness, our starvation, our suffering, our struggles, and our deep poverty of spirit. In doing this, we are Christ to the other; we are genuinely present for the other.

Vanier writes, "Jesus is the starving, the parched, the prisoner, the stranger, the naked, the sick, the dying. Jesus is the oppressed, the poor. To live with Jesus is to live with the poor. To live with the poor is to live with Jesus"[12] This is a tragedy of course. That there is suffering in the world is tragic, and that they should suffer alone is horrific. God in Christ Jesus upon the cross steps into the suffering lives of people to bring about great healing. This is the paradox of Christianity and the cross. So too when we step alongside the lost and least. This living as Jesus, this being, and doing as Jesus is how we are to make our way in the world. Rather than some kind of moral law, Jesus offers us life with one another. In this there is something beyond a life of agony for all.

I believe that if we look at Jesus and his relating with others, we see this very different way of living, moving, and being in the world. The church that is challenged to be the ecclesia must learn to stop pretending righteousness in order to enter the world as Jesus does. Furthermore, we can't expect anything in return—no butts in pews. We enter, witness, and are present at the foot of another's cross. There is no bait and switch. We are simply giving up our safety and walking into the streets of Nanjing, come what may. We are giving up our safety and entering the fray of the world. After all, Jesus never promised safety. He did promise a cross. We walk into the wilderness with Jesus and we are going to do some things that will make our righteous friends raise eyebrows.

Let us begin with what we know first about Jesus as he looks at humanity. I have always been struck by the passage from Matthew 9:36 where it says, "When he saw the crowds, he had compassion for them, because they were harassed and helpless, like sheep without a shepherd." This Greek word for "compassion" has a bodily root—it describes being moved in the gut. Jesus was moved in his gut by what he witnessed. He had a physical experience of solidarity with those who suffered before him. He was moved, and in Luke 13:34 Jesus says, "Jerusalem, Jerusalem, the city that kills the prophets and stones those who are sent to it! How often have I desired to gather your children together as a hen gathers her brood under her wings, and you were not willing!" It is as if he knows that while the need is great and laborers must be sent out, there is a cross waiting for all who are moved in their gut to bear witness. Jesus longs to gather all in.

The lesson here for those who have ears and want to hear is that to follow Jesus is to get your heart broken. It is to be moved in your gut. It is to care and love the other. In that work—in that living with the other—we may go down. We may be dragged down like a lifeguard pulled to his death by a drowning man he wishes to save. Let me say very clearly that if we aren't moved by poverty, violence, death, murder, suffering, psychosocial madness—then we aren't following Jesus well.

We are sent out. It isn't as if Jesus is sending someone else. We are the ones who have been given the Holy Spirit to go out and to be the messianic ecclesia. We are to be the church proclaiming a Sinai gospel. We are to manifest the identity of Jesus as Messiah in our actions and work. And I promise you when we do this well, we are going to cause ourselves, as the institutional church, some trouble. We in the church will naturally feel nervous. We will have to lean into and work through our anxiety. When any organization or group within an organization attempts this work, it will make the conventionally religious very nervous, as did Jesus.

First of all Jesus did not hang out with righteous. So, if you are spending most of your church life with the righteous, you know right away that you are not living the life of Jesus. God help me! Theologian and author Philip Yancey reminds us that those outside the church think the church is for those who have already cleaned up their act.[13] We are short on Paul's Gospel of Grace and heavy on the law. We would do well to spend more time with those who are outside our comfortable, protective church walls. If you dare to follow Jesus and want to be his friend, then you are going to have to hang out with the friends that he makes.

This is the first thing we must learn in our way of the cross. We are going to have to learn to hang out with all those people we think aren't worthy of receiving the gospel because they haven't repented, sought forgiveness, amended their life . . . or whatever excuse we want to make. Jesus goes around and hangs out with those that "no proper Messiah would have any truck with," says Robert Farrar Capon.[14] We so overidentify with the heroes of the story of Jesus that we turn the sinners into the righteous. The church cleans up the saints of God to make them palatable to the social institutions of our time. Trust me: fishermen, tax collectors, and all the rest of them were not considered pleasant people, esteemed as the righteous in the eyes of the religious leaders of the day. We need to come to terms with the fact that Jesus hung out with those that society does not deem as good. Not only did Jesus have the audacity to visit these people, he invited them to spend time with him. He invited them to live in community with him. And he ate dinner with them right out in the open for all to see.

This may be clearest in the case of the tax collector/toll collector called Levi (Mark 2:13–17). Levi was a customs official and a complete outcast. This position was normally held by a Jew employed by the administration of Rome and Herod. They were viewed as complicit with the oppressive occupying powers. They were seen as collaborators with Herod, who was corrupt. They were known to be dishonest and they often times added to the tolls/taxes to make up their own income. The hierarchy of taxes included up to seven different levels and was seen as an oppressive system all on its own. These collectors were so maligned by their fellow community members they were seen as ritually impure and denied basic civil rights.[15] Jesus, as Capon reminds us, was intimately involved in the lives of the least and the lost. Normally we think of this category as the poor. Levi was not poor, but he was considered an outcast by the society in which he lived. He was considered the lost and not worth spending time on.

When challenged by the religious leaders on this point (because religious leaders always think you need to hang out with other religious people so we know you are okay), Jesus says that he didn't come to hang out with or call or spend time with the righteous (Mark 2:15–17). This is an affront to the religious leaders of the day and I believe Jesus does this on purpose. Yes, I think Jesus likes hanging out with the sinners (victims and victimizers) and he likes to do this in the face of the religious.

Some of you will say, "Yes, bishop, of course you hang out with the sinners in order to convert them." Notice though that Jesus, in Matthew 9:13, seems little concerned with the sinning and more invested in the hanging out.[16] I believe that Jesus loved them, was moved in his gut to be with them, and hung out with them—the end. How they responded to his presence was up to them. We in the church, every church, must admit that this kind of radical behavior is not like any respectable messiah that we have heard about. This is not the Jesus we have been preaching for ages. This crazy, un-Messiah-like, misbehaving Jesus is the Jesus that is hidden from church-going folk. He has been stolen, trusting that we won't read the Bible too closely or that we will at least read it with our church lens on.

Jesus has no intention of fulfilling our messianic expectations, or being a good upstanding citizen. Jesus's actions are innocent because they are the actions of a loving God who convicts the world of its lack of grace, love, and forgiveness. But in the eyes of the righteous, the religious, and the courts of the day, Jesus was guilty of upending society. Jesus was killed because he broke the social conventions of his day, and literally sat at table and ate with those considered unclean. Jesus intentionally broke bread and spent most of his time with the walking dead of his society.

Not only did Jesus eat with the riffraff, Jesus fed them. The earliest scriptural record in Mark tells us that the crowd that followed Jesus is described by the Greek word *ochlos*. The *ochlos* is a particular kind of crowd: the unwelcomed members of society. This group of people is mentioned some thirty times in Mark—they are ever-present in the ministry of Jesus. Most people (preachers and teachers) assume that this is a generalized term for people—in Greek *laos*. Mark wants to make sure that our lens of insider/outsider is broken down. The term itself is particular and often times refers to a "confused" group of people. It also refers to those who travel with soldiers, who follow along and clean up after the soldiers. They are a mass of people who follow along, a motley crew, stragglers and the disorganized. The Rabbis would call them the 'am ha'aretz.[17]

As scholar Chad Myers puts it, "After the time of Ezra [the term] came to mean specifically the lower class, poor, uneducated, and ignorant of the law." The religious leaders of Israel made it clear that the faithful were not to "share meals nor travel together" with this group. Jesus travels with them openly. They are constantly with him. He goes even further; he calls them his family.[18] In Mark 3:32 we read: "A crowd (the *ochlos*, the 'am ha'aretz, the people of the land) was sitting around him; and they said to him, 'Your mother and your brothers and sisters are outside, asking for you.'" (Remember his family thought his behavior was crazy and they wanted Jesus to stop embarrassing them and breaking the law.) And Jesus replied, "Who are my mother and my brothers?" And looking at those who sat around him (the crowd), he said, "Here are my mother and my brothers!" Jesus calls them family, and he feeds them.

The feeding of the five thousand is recorded in all four of the Gospels. Jesus looks at the crowd and is moved in his gut. He has compassion on them and sees them as sheep without a shepherd. The outcasts are his family and he will feed and sit and eat with them. Jesus and his disciples are surrounded by the mass of undesirables and the unclean. They are pressing in upon Jesus and his disciples constantly. The disciples in the stories want Jesus to send them away to buy food (Mark 6:30–44).[19] Jesus instead invites them to feed the people with what they have. There is a great multiplication. Many scholars go too far in deconstructing the story into a story about sharing. I don't think that is what is going on here. This story reinforces the principles at the core of Jesus's mission.

Jesus is in the midst of a great desert—a famine. His deeds here echo the Sinai prophet Elisha, and the many food miracles that Elisha did while there was a famine in Israel (2 Kings 4:42–44). It is a reminder of how God provided during the desert wanderings and fed the people with manna from heaven (Numbers 11:4ff). Lastly, the shepherds of Israel were the leaders, the kings, the Herodians; the sheep were the people. So Jesus sees them as leaderless. Jesus is making a political statement here: the people are not being cared for by those who have been given charge over them, to make sure they are fed and cared for. The expectation of the Sinai prophet Ezra is clear: those who shepherd Israel are not to feed themselves but their people. Shepherds, religious leaders, are to actually see to the caring and feeding of their people. They are to give strength to the weak, heal the sick, bind up the injured, and to be merciful. Instead, Ezra prophesies that those religious leaders have instead scattered the sheep, allowed them to be consumed by others, and to be lost. God will in the end gather them up into God's arms, but it will be quite a different kind of gathering (Ezek. 34:2–10).[20]

I believe that Jesus's feeding stories do two things. They make it clear that to follow Jesus means to dwell with and live among the outcast, the least and the lost. It also means that we must sit with them and eat. To eat with them means to feed them and to feed them with dignity—note in Mark 8 he refuses to send the hungry away fasting. So people must be fed. If we are to follow Jesus, we are going to have to sit and eat and feed those outside of our comfort zone. Capon points out that it is only after the experience of eating with the crowds and feeding them that Jesus begins to be openly clear about his impending death.[21] In some way the feeding of people, the caring for people, will mean a dying to our comfort. We must enter the passion of the least and the lost. Eating and feeding is an intimate event. When we eat with others, when we serve them, feed them, clean up with them, participate in their lives in this way—we cannot help but be transformed and changed. The institutional church is challenged to change in this way, to be more the ecclesia God dreams will mean living and moving and being with those who are unclean, unrighteous, unchurched, or the nones—or whatever the term d'jour is. We are called to be family with the despised other. This deep relating is punctuated by sitting at table preparing, serving, eating, and cleaning up together. Table fellowship is also marked by intimacy and the sharing of one another's passion. All the feeding episodes in the Scripture and all the meals shared with sinners and outcasts, whether they be five thousand plus or a tax collector or intimate friends like Mary and Martha, are a prefiguration of the Last Supper, Jesus's final meal before the crucifixion. The stories of feeding are about family and sharing in one another's hunger. To be the society of friends of Jesus means sitting at table to eat and to listen and be present in the breaking of the bread and the breaking of the heart. Here at our tables, with fellowship binding the outcast, least, and lost, we stand at the foot of each other's cross.

God in Christ Jesus looks across the fields, across the tables, and rooms where he sits and beholds his beloved. The incarnation is the outflowing of God and God's love into the creation and to the creature. In the Gospels, Jesus is more than an ethical shepherd or shepherd king who is generous and forgiving. The Christ is the lover of humanity. Jesus sees with the eyes of the creator—and he always sees something beautiful.[22] In all of the stories of Jesus, the value of the person, their nature, or their forgiveness is never based upon their actions or faithfulness. Instead they are given value by the "beholder, shepherd, fisherman, and judge."[23] Jesus beholds us and loves us, values us, and finds worth in us. It is from an awareness of our worth and value that Jesus reaches out and gets messy. Standing at the foot of our crosses, our passions, Jesus does not choose to be a bystander but a participant. Jesus literally becomes ritually unclean (not only by sitting, eating, and associating) by touching humanity. God becomes lower than the angels and does not stop there but instead becomes human. This is scandalous and made all the more scandalous by the love Jesus demonstrates for those he beholds in all their weakness.

Jesus touches the unclean and the sinful. Jesus spits and makes mud and rubs it into eyes, remaking them as God made Adam from the earth. He prays and raises the dead. He heals lepers and cures all manner of illness. He unbinds the bound whether literally by their lack of faith, mental illness, or oppression. Jesus's healing breaks down the typical boundaries of a God who remains in heaven and a society bisected by class, health, access to food, and wellness. The religious do not and will never (without their own personal conversion) come to see Jesus as more than the authenticator of their rules. Jesus "unwinds society" by breaking down order and boundary, and reaching across the open space that protects us from God to touch the unclean.[24]

Not only does Jesus do this work, but he does it in the face of the religious establishment and on special days set apart for worship. All social convention is set aside as Jesus reorients those who would follow him around their relationships with one another and their shared need. Capon writes, "Healing on the Sabbath . . . is a crime against civility, against decency, against common sense—against, in short the revised wisdom about how life should be lived."[25] Jesus, and any one who would come after him, breaks with the boundaries of social conformity. To heal, to raise the dead, to give the blind sight, and enable the lame to walk is all ok if it happens in the confines of the hospital—and the right hospital—not the hospital where the poor go—but to conduct such healings in living rooms is another matter entirely. The point here is simple: just as Jesus breaks barriers by hanging out with, feeding, and eating with the wrong kinds of people, he also breaks the same barriers by raising those we wish were dead and undeserving of God's love and healing instead of those who we believe have somehow earned their lot in life.

When the church does the same, it whittles away at the calcified edifices of organized social religion, revealing a bit of the ecclesia God imagines. When the society of friends who choose to follow Jesus spend time with the socially outcast (especially the socially outcast by standard religious circles), we show the world that the body of Christ is not only unafraid of death, we are unafraid of the dying. We are determined to liberate the sin-sick soul with a message that is foolish. The church, if it is to faithfully stand at the foot of another's cross, will have to be revived like Lazarus.

Lazarus was a friend of Jesus's and part of the family circle with Mary and Martha. Jesus hears of Lazarus's death and is moved to travel to Bethany at some risk, and see where Lazarus is now buried. The Scripture says that Lazarus has fallen asleep, and that Jesus is going to wake him up. His disciples don't understand and so Jesus has to explain that he is dead but that they must go to Bethany (John 11:14).[26] Upon his arrival Jesus is overwhelmed by emotion. He is sad that Lazarus, his friend in ministry and in life, has died. Capon says, "Jesus approaches the tomb angrily upset again (*embrimóme-nos*)."[27] Martha is upset that Jesus didn't come sooner in order to prevent her brother's death. She fusses at him. Jesus tells her that he will raise Lazarus. She says, "Yeah, yeah, on the last day." Jesus emphatically explains that as resurrection and life he will raise Lazarus in the here and now. This is everyone's potential. To be raised in the future—sure. But everyone also has the amazing potential to be raised here and now. Lazarus had been in the tomb three days and according to the conventional wisdom of the day, his body and soul had already separated. All that was inside Lazarus' tomb was a rotting corpse.

F. D. Maurice and Robert Farrar Capon bemoan the fact that neither the Israelite teachers of Jesus's day, nor the modern church have gotten people to the brink of Martha's theology. Reflecting on Maurice, Capon writes, "Only a handful have ever gotten past the point and made the leap of faith that Jesus got Martha to make: the leap to resurrection now—to resurrection as the fundamental mystery of creation finally manifest in his own flesh." Ephesians 2:5–6, Colossians 3:1–4, and in fact all the Gospels make it perfectly clear that "Jesus never meets a corpse that doesn't sit up right on the spot." Jesus raises them because, quite simply, Jesus "has this effect on the dead."[28]

Jesus calls out for the stone to be removed. This is how John 11:43–44 describes what happens next, " 'Lazarus, come out!' The dead man came out, his hands and feet bound with strips of cloth, and his face wrapped in a cloth. Jesus said to them, 'Unbind him, and let him go.' " We are told immediately, from that moment on, the religious leaders plot and meet to kill Jesus (John 11:53). I believe that Jesus has never met a church corpse that didn't respond positively to Jesus's call to roll away the stone, and be unbound. Today's church is Lazarus. We have already been in the tomb three days, but it is not too late. Jesus invites us to come out.

In his life of associating with the unclean and castaways, Jesus gives life. In making them his family, he gives life. In feeding them and in sitting at the table with them, he gives life. In touching them, spitting on them, and healing them, Jesus gives life. By resurrecting those who have died in this world and the next, Jesus gives life. All things are made through Christ and not one thing is made without Christ.

God acts in the world. The body of Christ, the ecclesia, acts in the world precisely because God is alive within it. In our action a new Sinai covenant is proclaimed—a new testament. After delivering the people of Israel out of slavery into freedom, the people responded and they made a covenant together. The wilderness God came and dwelt among the people. In the incarnation Jesus becomes a manifestation of this wilderness God's love in the world. Those who respond to God's love by sharing his associations, family, and feeding habits will embody God's love in the world. God's dream is that the ecclesia remember itself, remember the relationships between the friends of Jesus and their relationship with others, as the replacement for the mountain of God's dwelling, the burning bush, the pillar of fire, the tabernacle, and the Sinai shrines. The resurrected ecclesia of God's making, like the family in Bethany and the disciples, is a network of relationships in which the Spirit of God dwells. We are resurrected now, healed now, fed now so that, as God lives and moves within us, we bear witness to the world.

Come out church, and live! Come out church, and be unbound! Come out church, and meet your maker, your creator, and the one that sustains you! Come out and be remade—Christ within you, and Christ within the world.[29]

CHAPTER ELEVEN

CONVERSION

Evangelism is intrinsically relational, the outcome of love of neighbor, for to love our neighbor is to share the love of God holistically. The proper context for evangelism is authentic Christian community, where the expression of loving community is the greatest apologetic for the gospel. Holiness—being given to God and God's mission in this world—is a way of life that is expressly concerned with evangelism.

—Elaine A. Heath, theologian, dean and professor, missionary[1]

I believe that Jesus did not see humanity as the object of his mission and ministry but rather the subject of it. Jesus saw people with eyes of hope, resurrection, growth, and transformation.[2] Jesus saw the human heart and its wilderness as a place where the kingdom might take root. Jesus wanted people to be converted, to have an experience of God through him and the power of the Holy Spirit. Moreover, Jesus hoped that such an experience would create an infinite loop where people are drawn into community, and then in turn draw others into community.

Greg Boyle, a priest and missionary in LA, reminds us of the Sinai prophet Jeremiah, when he ponders those he encounters in the midst of life and on the margins (Jer. 33:10–12). Through Jeremiah, God describes a wasteland without life. When you look at people on the margins, community on the margins, and families hanging on, you see a wasteland. You see the other. But God says, "Here [in this wasteland] shall once more be heard the voice of mirth and the voice of gladness, the voice of the bridegroom and the voice of the bride, the voices of those who sing, as they bring thank offerings to the house of the Lord: 'Give thanks to the Lord of hosts, for the Lord is good, for his steadfast love endures forever!' "[3] Jesus, looking at those who come to him, those he meets on the roads, and those he converses with, sees not wasteland but soil in which the kingdom of God might take root. Sure the land may be filled with weeds and wild birds, the bones dry and bleached, but Jesus looks upon humans and whispers the words of Jeremiah, "In this place that is waste . . . and in all its towns there shall again be pasture for shepherds resting their flocks."[4] Nothing is wasted.

As I travel around and welcome people into the church, as a bishop I am conscious that conversions are rare indeed. One is led to ask why? Conversions happen for many different reasons, but only people convert other people. Confusing God with church, people often believe that they must gain converts in order to create some kind of sustainability. The "Church Growth" ideal is built upon a number of fallacies but one of the most insidious is the misunderstanding that conversion is the aim of the church. After several decades of ministry, I have come to realize that most churches want new members to join their community in order to stave off economic collapse. Churches want new members to boost their average Sunday attendance, or to bolster their financial health. Others reject these as valid markers of health, and adopt a laissez-faire "convert if you want to" attitude. Neither of these is the ecclesia at its best.

There is another reason the institutional churches are concerned with conversions—the belief that a high number of conversions indicate that we are doing Jesus's work. This is "notch in the belt" evangelism. It is about power, pride, and control. Sometimes this syndrome is also a way of proving we are good Christians. The institutional church can make conversion into an exchange program. You get to be considered a good Christian if you will bring people to Jesus. Unfortunately, this was not what Jesus meant when he invited people to go into the world and "make disciples of all nations, baptizing them in the name of the Father and of the Son and of the Holy Spirit" (Matt. 28:19).

The church has also undertaken evangelism and conversion through violence, both spiritual and real. The church has fed people a steady diet of fear and anxiety about their eternal soul. Many churches promise that faithfulness will keep you out of the hands of an angry God. Not only is this not a gospel of grace, it has created generations of religiously abused individuals. Religious wars of a colonizing faith aimed at converting native or nonbelieving people contribute to the culture of violence that Jesus rejected. Religious Christianity combined with nationalism has killed millions in the name of purity. Interreligious civil wars where reformers and traditionalists shed blood trying to bend one another to their will have killed hundreds of thousands. Such wars are the outcomes of national machines and promoted by individuals who hunger for power and earthly authority. Such violence has truly made a mess of the gospel work.

We followers of Jesus underestimate the skepticism of those who know the history of how often the church has been moved by motives that are not gospel motives. The church must separate itself from these misaligned desires for conversion. It must also reread the Gospels and the work of Jesus through the eyes of the new hermeneutic we have been developing here, to see what Jesus does and how he invites people into the life of God. I have become convinced that the church isn't really about the same kind of conversion as Christ. As we reread the Gospels with new eyes, we should pause and think about conversion—both its meaning and the way it happens.

An essential preliminary for this conversation has already been established. We are clear that Jesus is in the midst of people and that he is willing to enter into their own passion and suffering in a particular way. He is willing to be with people who are not normally religious and he is willing to act with them and on their behalf for the betterment of their lives. With this in mind, we turn our attention to the Scriptures to see how God through the person of Jesus engages people regarding God. Jesus's conversations about God reveal how the society of Jesus's friends might go about their work of sharing the gospel.

Jesus does initiate some conversations about God (eight by my count). But the vast majority of his conversations are started by someone else. There are inquiries, challenges, arguments, desires, hopes, and puzzlements all placed at the feet of Jesus (twenty-three invitations by others). And there are a number of examples (though not nearly as many) of conversations where people engage Jesus because of a third-party relationship. The first significant feature of all these conversations is that they do not take place in religious settings. They take place in workplaces, streets, and people's homes. Rarely are they actually in seats of power or religious centers. Jesus's very presence in the world, the wilderness—that desolate place called the secular and profane by the church—means that he is approachable. To have the kind of conversations that Jesus has, the ecclesia must be out among the people. In order for the work of conversion to begin, people must be in relationship with non-church people. The conversion process hinges on our willingness to engage people, mostly through others and passively. This means that we should be aware that every chance opening, journey, meeting, or relating with another can be an opening for such conversations.

The next significant feature of Jesus's conversations is the number of questions that Jesus asks. He asks way more questions than he gives answers. Jesus is curious. A quick Google search reveals that Jesus asks 100+ questions. He asks things like: If you love and are in community with people who already love you what good is that? (Matt. 5:46–48). Do you think anxiety helps you? And why are you afraid? (Matt. 6:27; 8:26). Why are you so judgmental when you have faults of your own? (Matt. 7:3). Is it easier to forgive people or cure them? (Matt. 9:5). Why do you break the commandments to love each other for the sake of tradition? (Matt. 15:3). Who is my real family? (Matt. 12:48). Why did you doubt? (Matt. 14:31). Who do people say I am? (Matt. 16:13). What is it you want? (Matt, 20:21—he asks this one a lot). Can you drink the cup I am going to drink? (Matt. 20:22). Is it the temple and its altar that makes sacrifices sacred? (Matt. 23:17–19). What is the kingdom of God like? (Mark 4:30). What were you arguing about? (Mark 9:33). Where is your faith? (Luke 8:25). Why do you judge what is right? (Luke 12:57). You are a religious leader, why don't you understand? (John 3:10). If I talk about earthly things and you don't get it, why do you think you will understand the heavenly things? (John 3:12). If you don't believe the Sinai Moses, why do you think you will believe me? (John 5:47). Did I not choose you? (John 6:70).

These are just a few. There are a huge number of questions that arise out of the parables, but we will come to them later. And many of these questions are responses to challenges. Of course the Gospels are synchronous so there are many repeats. What this means is that part of Christlike conversion work is being curious about others and what they are thinking and feeling, what they want and what they are interested in. So let us examine two stories of conversion where Jesus asks questions as part of a conversion narrative: the woman at the well and Zacchaeus.

The story of the woman at the well is narrated in John's Gospel chapter four beginning at the fifth verse. Jesus comes to the Samaritan city called

Sychar, to a well. The story doesn't begin with a great evangelism sermon on water. All Jesus needed was a well and a woman, and many people were converted. Jesus does not go to the well to meet people. He goes to the well because he is thirsty from a long trip. He is traveling in a country where he is not particularly welcome. The Samaritans were the tribes of Israel who settled in the north. They were problematic for a number of reasons, including the fact that they didn't recognize the temple and chose instead to worship at the shrine on Mount Gerazim instead of in Jerusalem (John 4:20). They were also racially mixed because of resettlement after the Assyrian invasion of the north. Jesus's people despised the Samaritans. They were the lost and the least in the eyes of Israel's leaders, if they ever considered the Samaritans at all. Jesus comes to the well—Jacob's well we are told—and he is thirsty. He sits by the well. It was the heat of the day. Jesus doesn't have any way to get water. A Samaritan woman comes by to fetch water. Jesus asks if he might have a drink. She is shocked because it was highly unusual for a Jew to speak with a Samaritan. She was despised and invisible to the temple religious of the day.

Jesus answers her in a quip, I think. He says, "If you knew who I was and asked me for living water I would give it to you. Why not give me water?" She misunderstands and says partly, "You don't have a bucket to get the water." And "You are no Jacob!" (It was likely that the well was situated near Shechem where Jacob settled and later a Sinai covenant site [Gen. 33:19].) Continuing the banter, Jesus then decides to use an image that has significance for the woman—water. Note this is in response to the conversation, his presence, and her curiosity. Jesus says, "Everyone who drinks of this water will be thirsty again [indicating the well], but those who drink of the water that I will give them will never be thirsty. The water that I will give will become in them a spring of water gushing up to eternal life." So in this moment Jesus offers her an experience of fullness. She desires it.

They begin to speak about her family and husbands. She realizes that this man is a prophet. She brings up the fact that people argue about where to worship—the Samaritans on Mount Gerazim and the religious in Jerusalem on Mount Zion. But here you are, she points out. You are here at this well and you have revealed much to me. Jesus responds, telling her that in the future people will not worship on mountaintops or require such religious sites because of the work he is doing. Those who follow him will worship everywhere and will recognize God's presence everywhere. Jesus says, "The hour is coming when you will worship the Father neither on this mountain nor in Jerusalem. . . . The hour is coming, and is now here, when the true worshippers will worship the Father in spirit and truth, for the Father seeks such as these to worship him. God is spirit, and those who worship him must worship in spirit and truth." In this he reveals himself. He tells her he is the one who is promised and he is bringing about a religious shift whereby people will worship God through the Spirit wherever they may be. This is an amazing conversation. Jesus's followers are shocked that he is speaking to a woman, shocked that he is speaking to her alone, moreover that she is an outcast and he is speaking with her.

The woman on the other hand has such an experience of God's fullness at that well that she goes into the city—leaving everything behind. She goes and tells many other Samaritans at Sychar about her conversation. Notice she isn't even sure who Jesus is. She had an experience and she wants to share it, because she is curious about what it means. She even says, "Come and see a man who told me everything! He cannot be the Messiah, can he?"

We are told that many Samaritans believed in Jesus because of the woman. They even wanted Jesus to stay with them. So it is that Jesus continues to break down barriers and move across lines. He does so with the woman and then stays in the city with the Samaritans for two days. During this time, even more of the Samaritans believe in him. They listen to Jesus and experience God in the same way as the woman at the well. Jesus was present. He was curious. He taught by analogy to water and the famous well of Jacob, which were part of the local context. He didn't premeditate this event. He used what presented itself in order to talk about God. Furthermore, Jesus was not interested in converting these Samaritans to Israelite temple worship. Jesus was solely focused on the woman having a full experience of God-with-her. In time he did the same with the whole village. His presence, curiosity, conversation, and relationship brought about the fullness of God, who was present in the Spirit and in truth outside the religious prescriptions of the day.

The second story is the story of Zacchaeus, from chapter 19 of Luke's Gospel. Jesus is passing through Jericho, the same Jericho that makes a cameo in the parable of the good neighbor. It is a steep walk down to Jericho. Jericho is an oasis compared to Jerusalem. In 2 Kings 2:4–5, Elijah is taken up by God into heaven by a chariot of fire in Jericho. The walls of Jericho, in particular their falling, is a major dramatic moment in the book of Joshua.

In Jericho, Jesus meets a man named Zacchaeus. Zacchaeus is another one of the lost and least. He is a tax collector. We have already discussed how despised they were. This tax collector is even more despised by the people because he is rich. It isn't enough that he took a share of the tax to live on. Nope, Zacchaeus has actually made a profit off of the backs of the people. He is a rich man and, just like in today's political climate, he is looked upon with disgust from many of the temple faithful. There is a little song that children who grow up going to Sunday school learn about this encounter. The words are: "Zacchaeus was a wee little man, and a wee little man was he. He climbed up in a sycamore tree, for the Lord he wanted to see. And when the Savior passed that way, he looked up in the tree. And said, 'Zacchaeus, you come down! For I'm going to your house for tea! For I'm going to your house for tea! Zacchaeus was a wee little man, but a happy man was he, for he had seen the Lord that day. And a happy man was he; And a very happy man was he." As an Anglican I learned that Jesus was going to Zacchaeus's home for tea. People always look at me funny when I sing it that way—but that is the way we Anglicans learn it. The Bible actually doesn't tell us if Zacchaeus was small or Jesus was small—that is the funny thing about this song. But this tax collector did want to see Jesus so badly that he climbed a sycamore tree to do so. This is one of the few instances where Jesus makes the first move. He sees Zacchaeus in the tree and says to him, "Zacchaeus, hurry and come down; for I must stay at your house today." We are told that Zacchaeus was happy to have Jesus stay with him. We are also told that the people were not! Why? Because they don't like Zaccheus. We don't really like him either. Despite the song we are neither happy with the rich religious who put a pittance into the offering plate compared to the poor who by percentage give more. We are also upset by the rich who don't give at all. They are both losers in the sight of the religious.[5]

Zacchaeus is profoundly changed by Jesus's visit to his home. Zacchaeus immediately responds to Christ's presence by pledging to reform his life. He says to Jesus, "Look, half of my possessions, Lord, I will give to the poor; and if I have defrauded anyone of anything, I will pay back four times as much." This is wonderful, but Jesus is quick to ensure that Zacchaeus understands that he did not come there because he hoped to provoke Zacchaeus to reform. Jesus did not choose Zacchaeus because he was in Jericho to make a rich man repent. Jesus reminds Zacchaeus, and all of us, that we experience the fullness of God only in our brokenness. Salvation comes to the household of Zacchaeus not because he repents but because God chooses him to be a son of Abraham. He is saved because God is about finding the least and the lost.[6] I can only imagine the even greater conversion that stirs in Zacchaeus's mind and heart as he hears Christ's words.

Zacchaeus experiences conversion because he is chosen by Jesus. He is literally picked from a tree and chosen. Conversion isn't just God's presence, or the conversation alone. Something much more is occurring in the life of people like Zacchaeus. They are claimed as members of God's family and when Jesus eats, drinks, and is present with them, they start to belong to God. God is present in their midst. The conversation and the journey are just the vessels the divine Spirit is using to act.

What I believe happens is that through presence, engagement, and conversation, Jesus makes space where people are able to experience the love, mercy, forgiveness, and grace of God. Conversion happens because people come to an experience of the fullness of God. The woman at the well begins by seeking fullness through her understanding of places of worship and life lived within a particular community. We might easily read that Zacchaeus comes to seek fullness by believing that it rests in achievement—doing good works. Both of them have an experience beyond this and are converted.

Charles Taylor reminds us that it is typical for humans to seek out a place where this fullness can be had through our own means.[7] We deny that this fullness is beyond us—that it is a *mysterium tremendum*. Figuring out exactly how to game God with religiosity is a much safer game. Getting God "right" is a lot harder than entering the holy of holies naked and exposed.[8] The conversions of the Gospels or conversions like those of St. Francis, Teresa of Avila, or Mother Teresa are great epiphanic moments. There is a sense of great fullness that places the human in their place before God. Taylor says it is the "heightened power of love itself which God open[s]" up to the individual.[9] This is not some great personal power. This is not a magic spell that enchants the heart or enthralls these individuals.[10] They experience something much greater than themselves. Nothing less than "that than which no greater can be thought" comes into contact with them.[11] Theirs is an experience of being raised into the life of God. It is much more than a faith that brings transformation by enacting particular accepted norms—like Zacchaeus giving to the poor. No, his transformation is much greater than this.

Ivan Illich helps us with this idea a bit more. He argues that we lose something when we make this conversion simply about following a set of rules. Illich, who was Orthodox as can be, understands clearly that, as Taylor says, the "actual development of the Christian churches and of Christian civilization (what we used to call 'Christendom') are a 'corruption' of Christianity."[12] By contrast, the authentically converted come to this fullness and find that they are "fitted together" by the very incarnation of God.[13] The Samaritan woman and the villagers belong in God because of Jesus. Zacchaeus belongs in God because of Jesus. The Samaritan and the tax collector and the religious leader and the people are all now "fitted together" because of Jesus. This kinship is beyond "tribal" relationships. Kinship is set together instead by the being of God in Christ Jesus.

Taylor writes, "The corruption of this new network comes when it falls back into something more 'normal' in worldly terms . . . a church community becomes a tribe." The belonging becomes too easily a conversion into the tribe. "We are led to shore up these relations; we institutionalize them, introduce rules, divide responsibilities. In this way, we keep the hungry fed, the homeless housed, the naked clothed; but we are living caricatures of the network life. We have lost some of the communion, the 'conspirator,' which is at the heart of the Eucharist. The Spirit is strangled."[14]

We have all been converted into a Christendom that is rooted in the immanent frame. The French philosopher Charles Péguy described the conversion that takes place in a beautiful paragraph from *Un Nouveau Théologien*: "One is not Christian because one is at a certain moral, intellectual, or even spiritual level. One is Christian because one belongs to a race *which is reascending*, to a certain mystical race that is spiritual and carnal, temporal and eternal; in other words, because one is of a certain *blood*."[15]

The spiritual, that which is outside of ourselves, is always connected to the carnal. Conversion happens because of the very connectedness with the other that the fullness of God reveals. Conversion requires one person reaching out to the other. One conversation opens the door to another. One ventures to speak and the other listens attentively. The one reaches out and the other receives the reach and grabs hold of the hand for help. Jesus and the woman, Jesus and Zacchaeus, Jesus and all those who come into contact with him join hands, just as the ecclesia does through its own relationships.

One person holds the hands of the other and so there is as Péguy says, "a chain of fingers that can't be disconnected."[16] In this holding of one another is the conversion moment, the epiphanic experience. This happened in the Gospels between Jesus and others. It has happened since that time in mystical experiences and in the experiences between humans who chose to follow this Jesus without agenda other than presence, listening, and conversation built upon curiosity of the other. We must be careful to understand that this is neither the idea of getting some past tradition correct nor is it getting the present church idea correct.[17] This is to say that the rich path to God and the conversion of another is rooted deeply beyond time and the immanent frame in which we exit. It is an actual participation in a unity that stretches out beyond the present community.

Taylor is clear that the saved cannot be "identified with those of any one age."[18] No. The converted, the saved, are always participating in the great chain of human oneness that is rooted in God's unity, and this is part and parcel of the fullness experienced. We realize by watching Jesus, his engagement, his presence, his listening and questioning posture, the images and themes he conjures from the immediate context of his conversations, that the work of conversion is a work of conversational theology. William Stringfellow said rightly that all biography is itself theology.[19] It is the narrative telling of God's acts in the lives of people. Leonardo Boff in his work on the Trinity describes all creation as a vessel for God as Trinity.[20]

What is important is that conversion does not come from a scientific proof of the "truth" of Christianity. Conversion does not come from propositional arguments. Conversion does not come by memorizing texts or believing correctly in catechisms. Conversion is the process of coming into being. Rachel Held Evans, author and theologian, writes in her blog that her continuing faith is less a moment of conversion than a long series of conversations that have grown. Each tradition has helped to form her in her relationship with God and has helped her along the way to discover more of God's fullness. She writes, "Faith has never been a matter of conversion; it's been a matter of evolution, of gradual change over time. I carry traits from every season, every age."[21] This is what seems present in the gospel—God in Christ Jesus connects to people in the very intersection of the incarnation where God, alpha and omega, meets humanity.

Taking the lead from Hans-Georg Gadamer, philosopher, we say that conversion by this fullness of God is not about meaning or understanding as objects to be grasped, but instead such a conversion is the "inevitable phenomena" of human experience.[22] The Gospel conversions, like our own, occur because of the fusion of the horizons of our potential; a new "belongingness"[23] is opened up. In this belongingness a whole world, experience, and relationship becomes possible. Certainly this is what happens between Jesus and those he comes into contact with in the Gospels.

Moreover, this unity is brought by Christ in the relationship with the Father. This unity is provided only by Jesus. As in John's Gospel, if you know Jesus, you will experience God (John 14). Jesus asks God that those who follow might mimic this unity. He prays, "that they may all be one. As you, Father, are in me and I am in you, may they also be in us" (John 17:21). There is a "fusion of horizons" here wherein those who come into contact with Jesus are deeply opened to the unity he shares with the Father.[24]

In treating the other before him as subject instead of object, Jesus takes seriously the truth claims of that person. It is in the question and answer, it is in the touch with those who are ill, it is in the presence in home and hearth, that we see the joining together of the two horizons. The most important dynamic of the conversion is the relationship bound by presence and conversation.[25]

Let us take another story of conversion, that of Nicodemus, the religious leader found in John 3. Nicodemus begins with a lot of praise, "Rabbi, we know that you are a teacher who has come from God; for no one can do these signs that you do apart from the presence of God." Jesus uncharacteristically responds with a statement and explains that in order to be converted Nicodemus must accept being "born from above." Jesus invites him to understand that the ways of religion are not ways of heaven. Jesus is telling him it isn't in the things that he does that one shall come to truly understand the fullness of God, but it is in the experience of the fullness itself.

Nicodemus does not understand and asks a question about flesh and birth in the world. Jesus explains that the power of rebirth happens because of the spirit. Nicodemus still doesn't understand. Jesus reminds him that this is not a new idea but instead is deeply rooted in the Moses tradition from Sinai. Jesus reminds Nicodemus of a story when Moses enabled people to live. People were dying in the desert because of snake bites and Moses made a totem and when the people looked at the snake as it was lifted above them they had life. In this way as people come into contact with Jesus, prefiguring the crucifixion, they have life. Conversion and life comes in relationship with Jesus in the wilderness.

Jesus goes on to say that his purpose is to gather people into God, to keep them from perishing. This will be undertaken not by rule, or code of law, or judgement. Instead, religion shall die as death dies upon the cross. Only those who refuse this conversion of God and man in Christ shall perish.

We don't know Nicodemus's immediate response to this conversation. Yet the rest of the story in the Gospel of John tells us that Nicodemus, who like Joseph of Aramethea was a disciple of Jesus, comes and brings spices. Together they wrap Jesus and lay him in the tomb (John 19:39).

The church often has a lot of nice things to say about Jesus and his work. The church is eager to make converts to itself to mimic the work of Jesus. At the same time, the church has a difficult time recognizing that God in Christ Jesus through the power of the Spirit is at work in all conversions, including its own.

The church is invited to be converted as Nicodemus is converted. The church is given the opportunity to not perish but have life as the ecclesia. It is invited to be converted and to be at one with Christ. The opportunity is not to convict the world through persuasion, nor to colonize the world with its theology. It is not the work to judge the world or condemn it. It is not the work of the church to seek conversion for the sake of attendance, or economies. Instead, the church is to be the body of Christ in the world—the ecclesia and motley crew of Jesus followers who are present in the world engaging in conversation and through presence in the lives of its neighbors.

Here the church, like Nicodemus, makes way for God to do the work of resurrection. Like Nicodemus and Joseph, the church is present in the life and death of individuals—helping people down from their crosses, anointing them with spices, caring for them in their death even as the Spirit of God is uniting them with God.

CHAPTER TWELVE

THE POWERS

In a quip that makes the rounds, Jesus preached the coming of the kingdom, but it was the church that came. . . . All these years later, the way many of us are doing church is broken and we know it, even if we do not know what to do about it. We proclaim the priesthood of all believers while we continue with hierarchical clergy, liturgy, and architecture. We follow a Lord who challenged the religious and political institutions of his time while we fund and defend our own. We speak and sing of divine transformation while we do everything in our power to maintain our equilibrium. If redeeming things continue to happen to us in spite of these deep contradictions in our life together, then I think that is because God is faithful even when we are not.

—Barbara Brown Taylor, priest and author[1]

Jesus challenged worldly power and authority, and so found himself crosswise with religious institutions as well as political ones. It is very clear that he is going to be trouble for each institution, when he is tempted in the desert to be king of each.

In Matthew, Mark, and Luke's Gospels, Jesus is led out into the desert, where he makes his own personal wilderness journey. Of course this recalls the Sinai wanderings with Moses and Joshua, wanderings that taught the people dependence on God. Jesus is in the desert for forty days and forty nights. He is hungry and we are told in Matthew's Gospel, chapter four, that the "tempter" comes to him. We tend to imagine this encounter as a Faustian bargain, but there is more than a simile here. In this encounter with the tempter, Jesus's entire ministry is refocused on distinctly Sinai priorities.

The tempter says to Jesus, "If you are the Son of God, command these stones to become loaves of bread." And, Jesus answered, "It is written, 'One does not live by bread alone, but by every word that comes from the mouth of God.'" Jesus cites the Sinai responses to God's deliverance. From Deuteronomy 8:3 Jesus reminds the tempter that God's promise to provide will prevail. God's love and deliverance, whether with manna or any other sustaining gift, will endure. Jesus rejects the notion that earthly goods will make heavenly stores. The desire for the fullness of God will not be quenched with earthly possessions—not even food. Then the tempter took Jesus to Jerusalem and placed him on the pinnacle of the temple, saying to him, "If you are the Son of God, throw yourself down; for it is written, 'He will command his angels concerning you,' and 'On their hands they will bear you up, so that you will not dash your foot against a stone.'" Jesus said to him, "Again it is written, 'Do not put the Lord your God to the test.'" Jesus recalls Deuteronomy 6:16 when the Israelites were frustrated and tested God by cursing because they felt forsaken in the desert. They cried out, "Is the Lord among us or not?" Jesus is mindful that God is always present. Even in these temptations God will deliver Jesus. Finally, Jesus is taken to a very high mountain and shown all the kingdoms of the world and their splendor; and the tempter says to him, "All these I will give you, if you will fall down and worship me." Jesus replies, "Away with you, Satan! for it is written, 'Worship the Lord your God, and serve only him.'" This passage recalls Deuteronomy 6:13, "The Lord your God you shall fear; him you shall serve, and by his name alone you shall swear."[2]

Jesus's three responses to the temptations are very clear: the God of Sinai shall deliver us, we shall have no other God but him, and we shall rest upon his providence. In this passage we see Jesus striving to fulfill the Sinai covenant. Faithfulness includes a rejection of the ways of the world where you scramble for goods, you test God by acting and living as if God is not present, and you make yourself your own master and serve your own needs.

Matthew scholar Daniel Harrington writes, "Understanding this text against the background of Deuteronomy 6–8 allows one to go beyond the narrow themes of fasting and temptation to the level of Christology. As in the case of all the material in the opening chapters of Matthew, the focus of attention is the identity of Jesus. Understanding it as the testing of God's son allows one to see the nature of Jesus's divine sonship and its relation to Israel as God's Son."[3] God in Christ Jesus rejects the would-be powers of this world that tempt and destroy the creatures of God. God rejects all forms of domination and power that aggrandize the individual. God rejects all religious, social, and political powers that demand allegiance. Jesus's faith is summarized in Deuteronomy 31:6: "Be strong and bold; have no fear or dread of them, because it is the LORD your God who goes with you; he will not fail you or forsake you."

Walter Wink, scholar and author of *The Powers that Be,* captures this moment well: "Jesus is being nudged by God toward a new unprecedented thing, for which no models existed. No one else could have helped advise him. Scripture itself seemed loaded in the opposite direction—toward messianic models of power, might, and empire. . . . Satan is offering him the kingdom of David, grown to the proportions of world empire. Scripture was rife with this hope."[4] We cannot remove this hope from the religious leaders of the day and the centuries of movement toward a centralized social, economic, and religio-political power far from the idea of the Sinai God. Again, Wink writes, "Israel seethed with longing for some form of its fulfillment. Jesus could not but have internalized that desire: freedom from Roman oppression, restoration of God's nation, the vindication of Yahweh's honor." These are nothing less than the "highest goods known to the religion of the day."[5] In point of fact, these temptations are the key motivating factors at work in the church today.

The church longs for a great conversion of society. Liberal Christians and conservative Christians both have ideas about what this conversion is to look like. Yet such systems of domination and power always come attached to death, oppression, slavery, and extermination. Wink reminds us it is always easier for us to be "pliant, docile, and obedient" Christians. He writes, "Is it not easier to let Jesus do it for all of us . . . rather than embark on the risky, vulnerable, hazardous journey of seeking to find God's will in all its mundane specificity for our own lives?"[6] This is the challenge for those interested in the society of the friends of Jesus.

If we have not yet understood God's handiwork in our previous chapters, we see it clearly here. Jesus, God incarnate, is creating a new order out of God's very nature of love: the challenge to enter the lives of our neighbor, to be neighbor, to venture into the wilderness where God is present, and to be converted into communion with God both at the foot of his cross, our own cross, and our neighbors' crosses. None of this works if, like new wine in old wineskins (Luke 5:37), we try and fit it all into the institutional church bent on dominion.

The rejection of the powers of this world begins in the very nature of the incarnation and continues throughout Jesus's life. The story of the incarnation itself is often "demythologized" to the point that the power of its nonviolence escapes the church. God in Christ Jesus is born in nonviolence and transcends the power of violence that is the hallmark of domination.[7] All worldly systems are systems of violence and domination. Christ himself, René Girard argues, is the only one who is able to "escape from these structures."[8] In our unity with him, through conversion, we are freed from their dominance as well.

God gives a sign of his presence to the creatures of this world by casting out the violence that is their inheritance. The Gospels speak the truth that violence is not intended for creation. Their proclamation both in the incarnation and in the ministry of Jesus rejects the mythology that violence is a necessary part of the world.[9] Girard writes, "Every man is the brother of Cain, who was the first to bear the mark of this original violence."[10] Yet we pass from this mark of death into life precisely because of the abiding love that is made known in the incarnation of Christ (1 John 3:11).

Mythical stories of gods copulating with mortal women abound, each resulting in the birth of the hero. Yet each of these involves violence. These Girard calls the "monstrous births of mythology."[11] They are violent oppressions of a dominating system of powers undertaken by the gods and repeated in the social orders of humanity. The story of the incarnation and the virgin birth does in fact parallel this story and yet it is precisely in its divergence that we see the rejection of violence by God. Girard writes, "No relationship of violence exists between those who take part in the virgin birth: the Angel, the Virgin and the Almighty. . . . In fact, all the themes and terms associated with the virgin birth convey to us a perfect submission to the non-violent will of the God of the Gospels, who in this way prefigures Christ himself."[12] There is no violence to Mary. She is the lost and least and is raised up. There is no scandal. Mary does not resist her calling. There is no rape or sexual power that overtakes her.[13]

Furthermore, the demythologizing of this story, which is a way of making Mary's story derivative of those other, more monstrous mythologys, misses the point.[14] The story of the incarnation is significant precisely in the ways it differs from the pagan stories of monstrous birth, in the ways that the incarnation narrative departs from the domination culture of antiquity, and of modernity. The story's rejection of violence is only one of the many reasons the early church struggled to achieve renown with the Romans. God and the birth of Jesus adhere to no mythic tropes known to paganism. Furthermore, our own sexually oriented culture, also consumed by violence, rejects the story of the incarnation as not reflecting the present ideals. God in the incarnation soundly refuses to appease the violent expectations of either epoch.

From the Gospel perspective, Jesus is defined as a second Adam. This notion, found in the writings of both Luke and Paul, reflects the great truth that Jesus is completely "alien to the world of violence within which humankind has been imprisoned ever since the foundation of the world."[15] Beginning with his birth, however, Christ will have the same struggle as Adam and Cain, the human inclination to revert to violence as the primary means of moving the human story forward.[16] Girard writes, "All men share in this archetypal state of blame, but only to the extent that the chance of becoming free has been offered to them and they have let it slip away. We can say that this sin is indeed *original* but only becomes actual when knowledge about violence is placed at humanity's disposition."[17]

The very incarnation of God in Christ Jesus is an act of peace and itself rejects the mythological predecessors. In Jesus's birth God begins to rewrite the narrative of global violence. Jesus's confrontation with religious and political leaders, and with his disciples, makes clear that the way of Christ is tantamount to a rejection of the powers of this world. In Luke's Gospel (22:24–27) Jesus makes plain his continued rejection of the systems of domination. Finding his followers arguing about who among them is the greatest, Jesus answers with these words: "The kings of the Gentiles lord it over them; and those in authority over them are called benefactors. But not so with you; rather the greatest among you must become like the youngest, and the leader like one who serves. For who is greater, the one who is at the table or the one who serves? Is it not the one at the table? But I am among you as one who serves."[18]

In John's Gospel he makes clear that religious domination is not God's way either. In John 15, Jesus remarks that the key to righteousness is abiding in God's love. This "abiding" makes the society of friends of Jesus different. Jesus says, "I do not call you servants any longer, because the servant does not know what the master is doing; but I have called you friends" (v. 15). Jesus demonstrates through his actions that he envisions something different from the dominating hierarchies that peopled the world then and now. In the Beatitudes and elsewhere, he makes clear that systems that are based upon "power, wealth, shaming, or titles" do not reflect the reign of God.

Religious systems are also indicted by Jesus's criticism. The church lens used by our institution and its preachers marginalizes these criticisms and interprets the Scripture as Jesus talking to some other "them" rather than "us." In Matthew 23:1 and following, Jesus says that those who follow are not to be called rabbi because God is the teacher. That no one is to be called father because there is only one Father who is the God who creates all things. Jesus is the humble beggar who has no place to lay his head, who serves his followers by washing their feet, must borrow a place for the Passover, and even a ride into the city. Jesus has nothing, and serves all. He is the lowliest of individuals who dies on a dung heap as an outlaw and refugee. It is his complete defeat that marks his ministry and highlights the abuse of political and religious systems rooted in structures of this world. No institution with power and wealth can stand against the servant of all who is condemned. There is no hero here, no Jesus action figure.

Walter Wink argues that the second way Jesus reveals systems of dominion and powers is by reversing economic barriers. Economies of this world lead to "rank, status, and class."[19] Jesus to the religious says, "you cannot serve God and wealth" (Matt. 6:24). Those who follow Jesus are confronted with the reality that his order is a mendicant one. Jesus sends them out, telling them "to take nothing for their journey except a staff; no bread, no bag, no money in their belts; but to wear sandals and not to put on two tunics" (Mark 6:8–9). They are to depend on the hospitality of strangers and live amongst the people. The mission is to be undertaken in community with the people. They are freed from the constraints of temple and shrine and are to be focused upon the people. The society of the friends of Jesus, Wink argues, rejects the way of religious leaders who wear beautiful robes that are fashionable. This new society is one where his followers are not to seek out notice by the powers and people in public—they are not to seek out fame. They are not to have the best seats in church or take places of honor. Jesus also instructs them not to make long prayers![20] The kind of community that Jesus teaches about is VERY different from the institutional church.

Jesus further rejects the religious and political marriage of the day by giving parable after parable with images of a reign that happens among the people. Wink writes, "[The kingdom] is established, not by armies and military might, but by an ineluctable process of growth from below, among the common people. He is, in sum, not looking for a kingdom for himself or anything else where God imposes the divine will on the world. Rather, he is inaugurating God's domination-free order."[21]

Jesus further rejects the domination systems' power over women by relating to them, serving with them, and openly conversing with them. He rejects the purity and holiness codes by openly eating with sinners, healing on the Sabbath, touching the unclean, and being touched by the woman who bleeds. The domination system of family in society where everyone had its place is undermined by Jesus's teaching about his own family, brothers and sisters, and squarely places such convention only to be honored in relationship with God.[22] Jesus correlates the family with the society of friends. Jesus does not see the family as "intrinsically evil," says Wink. "The goal is not the eradication of the family, but its transformation into a nonpatriarchal partnership of mutuality and love. As such it is exemplary of the new family of Jesus."[23]

The society we live in demands violence and we even will go so far as to make Jesus justify our behavior. This is how it works. We believe that we are "good/ordered by identifying a contrast case from which we separate ourselves."[24] We also give ourselves permission; in the case of Christians we quote the Bible and point out our faith ancestors' habit of participating in death, killing, and revenge. Or we tell ourselves that our anger is justified because of Jesus in the temple and that violence can be used because Jesus used a whip. (According to Wink, reading the story carefully Jesus drives out the animals with the whip in order to spare the lives of the sacrificial victims.[25]) What this really does is enable the church to participate in the continuation of a mythical tradition of violence justified by God or the gods.[26] Placing these two strains of violence together is powerful enough, adding religion makes them supreme. What happens is that the institutional church scapegoats the impure—"the other." That other can be gay, straight, bi, conservative, traditional, liberal, male, and female. The point that Wink, Taylor, Girard, and so many others are trying to make is that there is always a crusade. There is always a war where we must "turn on, kill, or expel an outsider."[27] Living by these purity codes enables the rise of the warrior culture. We are the warriors battling out in the name of our religious purity. Those who fight the good fight deserve our highest praise. This leads to the nonsensical idea that we wage the battle in the name of the prince of peace so that the peace of God may be brought to this church, nation, land, and society.[28]

This also works in the secular world and its areligious humanism. Here "morality rationalizes." That which is good and related to the human's individual highest potential or the society's highest potential is to be pursued at all cost.[29] It quickly becomes necessary to cleanse the evil doer and the terrorist from inside our midst. There is an "identified threat" that must be expunged from within and without globally.[30] Both the religious and the nonreligious are united in the state's campaign to put down evil and purge the wrongdoer. Hate for the aggressor is permitted.

The modern narrative of violence even coopts seemingly charitable acts, like demonstrated concern for victims. In our society, believer and nonbeliever are continually united in various cleansing wars. Taylor describes the nature of this twist: "There is a narrative of the modern world, like and parallel to that of the growth of freedom, democracy, which sees us as redressing all the historical wrongs and inequalities. We rescue and recognize all the victims. But this is connected to the moralism of meting out . . . punishment/ vengeance on them. So another powerful engine of destruction is born; and an equally paradoxical one."[31] When we grasp purity through victimhood, we move into a campaign against the other, a domination licensed by our need to root out those who knowingly and unknowingly participate in the system that victimized us.[32]

Today's church is complicit in the cleansing wars of our culture, because its leaders involve themselves with issues of state and politics by taking sides in tribalistic liberal and conservative ways. The church has offered a "just war theory" for the culture wars. It has supported the death penalty and slavery. We must come to terms with a very real truth: regardless of political flavor the state will always "embody the meaning of death," as William Stringfellow writes. "[E]xile, imprisonment, slavery, conscription; impeachment, regulation of production or sales or prices or wages or competition or credit; confiscation, surveillance, execution, war" are the hallmarks of the state. Every political leader is sullied with the countless histories of their involvement.[33]

Our culture of violence resonates well with the Hellenistic culture of violence proliferated in the age of Jesus.

Jesus flatly rejects such violence. His followers often had a hard time with this fact; just as we struggle with his categorical rejection of violence ourselves. In Luke 9:51–56, Jesus and his disciples enter a Samaritan city. Unfortunately, things don't go as well for him there as they do with the woman at the well and the village of Sychar. He is rejected. Jesus continues to make his way toward Jerusalem. His disciples, though, say to him, "Lord, do you want us to command fire to come down from heaven and consume them?" Jesus "rebukes" them. And when the religious and political leaders come for Jesus in the garden and Peter raises his sword and cuts off the ear of one of the slaves there to arrest Jesus, Jesus rebukes him. The disciples are instructed to not even take staffs for self-defense in their missionary journeys.[34]

Jesus makes clear that violence is to be met with peace and nonviolence. He refuses to raise an army to defend himself. In his crucifixion, he rejects the "redemptive" power of violence. So powerful was this image of the Lord of peace and nonviolence that it is captured in Paul's Second Letter to the Corinthians. Paul makes clear that the way of the world, the way of flesh, is one of war and violence. The way of the society of the friends of Jesus will avail themselves of different weapons: presence, conversation, and humility. Such nonviolence is memorialized in the first three centuries of the church and throughout reform movements. Alas, with the emergence of a Christian empire, nonviolence was discarded.[35]

The institutional church must take seriously the call to oppose the systems of domination in this world. It must realize that it is tied to them both philosophically and structurally. William Stringfellow had very little to say that was good about the church as it engaged the world; he saw only an organization fully enmeshed with the culture. He wrote:

> With these and similar principalities, the churchly enterprises are much engaged in elaborate worship of death. They are vainglorious about reputation, status, prosperity, success; they are eager to conform, solicitous of patronage from the political regime, derisive of the biblical witness, accommodated to American culture. In fact, the American churchly institutions, for the most part, are not truly involved in apostasy—that is, in betraying the faith—or even in hypocrisy—that is, in practicing something other than what is

preached. There can be no apostasy, if that faith has not been upheld; there could be no hypocrisy, if the gospel has not preached.[36]

Robert Bellah, in his essay entitled "Civil Religion in America," argues quite clearly that Christians have often confused their own idea about a "Christian nation" with the very real American civil religion.[37] This civil religion draws on biblical archetypes: Exodus, Chosen People, Promised Land, New Jerusalem, and Sacrificial Death and Rebirth. But the American civil religion is very different from the one we have been outlining. Bellah argues that the American civil religion "has its own prophets and its own martyrs, its own sacred events and sacred places, its own solemn rituals and symbols. It is concerned that America be a society as perfectly in accord with the will of God as men can make it, and a light to all nations."[38] Yet this nation state has at its core not God's intent or God's vision but rather its own prosperity. America is everywhere and always America's ultimate concern.

We must carefully parse what Bellah is telling us. Our civil religion asserts America's success is the will of God. The will of God is that America be the light to all nations. The center of the civil religion is that God works for the cause of America. America does not work for the cause of God. Those are very different things and we, the resident aliens who live within this nation's borders, must get clear that we are living in foreign territory. Dwight Eisenhower supposedly said, "Our government makes no sense unless it is founded in a deeply felt religious faith—and I don't care what it is."[39] The secular nation we participate in is very clear that the perpetuation of this Enlightenment political experiment, and the community it has birthed, are the center of nation's concern. What is at play is an understanding that "religion is partially disembedded from the traditional social structure of kinship and village life [and] comes to serve as an expression of a larger social identity, namely the newly emerging nation state."[40]

Here you and I must ask, "What do we do?" How do we live if we must live in the midst of a fallen and violent world? To begin with, we need to admit that there is no other kind of world for living out our faith. The Christian, a citizen of the heavenly Jerusalem, is always simultaneously a human in the midst of a fallen, imperfect, and violent society.[41] The individual Christian and the ecclesia stand in opposition to the powers of domination.

The first task is to reject idolatry. There is no human system, no human form of government that is not dependent upon domination. There is no us and them, no evil other, no liberal or conservative political theory that is not idolatrous. Our nation is not our Lord. Christians may love America, but we are not its citizens. We are first and foremost citizens of God's kingdom and members of Jesus's family. This means we are always discerning, from our experience of the fullness of God, how we are to live.[42]

William Stringfellow captures this in his discussion on discernment as the key to the Christian way of life. I believe it is further amplified when we consider Taylor's claim that we live a life of experience. Our ethic must come from that place where the newly visible Jesus, unmoored from the false gospel we repeatedly tell ourselves, touches daily life. What emerges from this encounter is not a false morality or a code of values that supports the system of domination. Our "imaginary," in the words of Charles Taylor, must move us beyond intellectual schemes. We must move out of the realm of syllogisms and into the world of human interaction and art. The togetherness of community itself, the nature of being human and living in human community, will organize itself through our eyes into a narrative of lived experience. This "cultural repertory" will inevitably lead to shifts and new understandings.[43]

As ethicist Willis Jenkins proposes, we must give "an account of culture in which theological creativity can make a difference for social reform even when Christian practices no longer determine the social imaginary of a culture."[44] We must also see the problems that face our society as problems that are central to the practice of faith. At the point of engagement, our lens cannot be church-centered. Our lens must be Christ, the kind of Christ I have attempted to describe in this book. The system of domination is overturned by an incarnate Christ who practices a Sinai love of God and love of neighbor, and makes this love-practice the foundation of a new community.

The Jesus society begins in peaceful incarnation and offers a different narrative than the old institutional church. Instead of supporting the institution, the purpose of following is reimagined as making relationships the center of all piety. This occurs, not within the walls of sanctuaries, but instead in the midst of life and wilderness. It engages real community issues as the ecclesia of Christ and is willing to stand at the foot of the cross and in the midst of the passion of any and all who would be "other" in the world of domination and violence. A community of so-called followers of Jesus stands with dehumanized people against domination systems, including the church, and brings about conversion by its presence in the society.

Such a community can never be, however, if Christians continue to mimic the immanent frame of reference, the culture of violence, and the culture of domination. Such a community will never be as long as the church sees this particular messy and unclean Jesus of the Gospels as an enemy to the mission and loses him in the mad scramble to shore up the trappings of bureaucratic religion.[45]

In Luke 15 Jesus tells two stories. Jesus has befriended the unclean sinners and tax collectors and the authorities are "grumbling" about his choice of friends. Jesus addresses two parables to them. The first is about a sheep that is lost and how the shepherd leaves ninety-nine and goes after the one. Robert Farrar Capon argues that this parable is not about the one vs the many. Instead it is about "lostness."[46] We might say that this parable is about lostness outside the religious institution. God is the shepherd, but not the kind of shepherd that an institution wants to follow. Capon argues that a lost sheep is a dead sheep.[47] Furthermore, we have one lost sheep. Then when the shepherd leaves the ninety-nine, they are lost in turn. Then the shepherd who behaves this way is "lost to shepherding."[48] Jesus is blaming the religious authorities, those who are so offended by the company he keeps, for losing God's sheep.[49]

The second parable that Jesus tells in Luke 15 is again directed at the religious authorities. Here is a woman inside a house. Is it possible that the woman represents the religious leaders who have lost something within the house? Jesus intimates that they have indeed lost something inside. She lights a lamp and completely turns over the house. Perhaps Jesus is inviting the religious leaders to see that they must turn over the house to find what they have lost. Night has fallen and that which is lost is now unclean according to the Torah.[50] Parables always have a way of challenging us. Combined with the shepherd story, Jesus throws a two-punch combo. The religious authorities have lost inside and outside. They have wandered from the freeing purposes of God and they have lost their way.

The parables are about lostness. God in Christ Jesus is about being part of the world of lostness and by virtue of its lostness, a world of death. It is into the world of violence and domination that Jesus comes. It is in the world of lostness and death that his followers are to live and move and have their being—in and among the lost, the dying, and the dead.

The good news for the institutional church is that it is lost like the sheep, like the shepherd, like the woman, like the coin. It is lost and it is dead. It is precisely in its lostness that it receives grace. Grace is a gift for the lost and the least. Capon makes clear that "confession, contrition, and absolution" don't get you found.[51] Grace is not a response to a good and believable "I am sorry" or a better lived ethic.

The church can only become ecclesia if it accepts its own lostness and death. Only in doing this can the church truly participate in the society of Jesus. Only in confession can the church discover its integrity, standing in the midst of the global community of the lost. Only in the confession of the church's death does Jesus raise us up to new life. Jesus doesn't say, "It's ok, church. I understand your weaknesses." It isn't as if Jesus makes allowances for the church's wrongdoing. No. Jesus "disposes of, he finishes with, the whole of our dead life and raises us up with a new one. He does not so much deal with our derelictions as he does drop them down the black hole of Jesus' death," writes Capon. Jesus "finds us, in short, in the desert of death, not in the garden of improvement; and in the power of Jesus' resurrection, he puts us on his shoulders rejoicing and brings us home."[52] The invitation to the church is not simply to hear the parables and story of Jesus as a story about a savior and those out there who need saving. Instead, the invitation to the church is to accept its own lostness and be found.

CHAPTER THIRTEEN

CHRISTIAN BABEL

There is one story, which contains all others; and the center of that story is the perpetually displaced God who addresses us from the edge of human affairs, who has chosen the place of the excluded. Culture is not to be rejected or given theological legitimacy; it is a fact with which we have no choice but to engage. However, our engagement as Christians must be determined by the question of who or what the culture is currently forgetting, since it is there that we are likely to find God waiting for us. This cannot therefore be a prescription for liberalism or for conservatism. The more fashionable a cause, the more likely that the crucified God has moved on; the more embedded a practice or trend, the more likely that God is elsewhere. There is nothing to be recommended except the daily development of the mind of the crucified.

—Rowan Williams, theologian, author, and
104th archbishop of Canterbury[1]

The God in Christ Jesus found in the Gospels is quite a different God from the one promoted by the institutional church. His work on the margins, against systems of hierarchical domination, and his relationships with men and women who are the lost and the least will always make the conventionally religious ill at ease. This "displaced God" is at the edge. Williams challenges us to rethink our work through the presence of this God on the margins. If we are to be the society of friends of Jesus, then like the Sinai prophet himself, we will have to abandon our civil religion and be disbursed to the dubious edges of our common life. This is the way it has always been. God is in the midst of the scattered.

Take the story of Babel, for instance, in the eleventh chapter of Genesis. The story of Babel is one of the best-known stories of the Bible because it captures our imagination. Typically, in Christian church contexts, it is told this way: Once upon a time there was a people and they built a tower that would reach to heaven. In doing this they became like gods. They made a name for themselves—the story says. God is displeased with them because, like gods, they will be able to do many things. "Nothing will be impossible for them." So God scatters the people. Most of us aren't even aware of the ambiguity in this passage. We read this story as a cautionary tale about human sin and God's judgment, a lesson learned in Mrs. Irving's fourth grade Sunday school class. But something more is going on here.

Let us look at the actual story, which is an origin story about creation that repeats the narrative of how God populated the earth with people. People are being scattered. Just before the Babel story we are told that Noah's descendants are scattered. They are sent out to populate creation. There is great debate about this very short origin story, and whether its verdict on the populating of the earth by the scattering of the people is positive or negative.[2] But I want to focus on the disbursement itself.

One of the issues in the story is that the people want to stay together. They don't want to be scattered. So they build a tower. The purpose of the tower is to reach to heaven. God, on the other hand, wants the people to be scattered. It seems that in the scattering, regardless of its causes, God is present. God is present in the scattering after Eden, God is present in the scattering after Babel, God is present in the scattering after Egypt, and after the fall of the first temple in Jerusalem. God is present at the edges, on the margins, in the scattering. God is not particularly interested in towers that reach up to heaven and make names for those who build them. A very large number of Jewish and Christian scholars believe that humanity's want to cohere is directly opposed to God's desire. It displeases God when people are all in one place where they are comfortable, avoiding being scattered.

The church has a Babel quality to it. It builds towers that are gates to God. It especially likes big ones. The church attracts people, and holds them in place so they aren't scattered. In my own tradition we joke about how there is effectively assigned seating on Sunday morning. The institutional church creates a holding pattern, a safe routine. Every year in liturgical traditions of Christianity, fifty days after Easter, the feast of Pentecost is celebrated. The institutional church celebrates Pentecost as its birthday. We never stop to think about the absurdity, the contradictory themes of the Bible passages read on this day every year, read to people sitting in thousands of shrines that boast to be the gates to heaven, or gather inside rooms to hear about God disbursing his followers into the world. The lens here is wrong. We can imagine a lot of things about the story of Pentecost and what God intended and imagines will take place as a society of friends of Jesus. But one of those things is not that some two thousand years later the followers of Jesus would be sitting in a room listening to a story.

In the beginning, shortly after the resurrection, the disciples had a custom of getting together. We already talked about this in a previous chapter. Every time they gathered, Jesus appeared and told them to get out. In Matthew they are on a mountaintop and Jesus appears and they are sent out into the world (Matt. 28:16–20). The shorter ending of Mark tells us they were sent out to the east and west (Mark 16:8). In the longer version of Mark, Jesus appears to them in a room where they are all sitting at a table. Jesus "upbraided them for their lack of faith and stubbornness" and then sends them out to do the work (Mark 16:14–20). In John's Gospel he appears and gives them the Holy Spirit by breathing on them. Then, in a series of visits, Jesus explains that they are to love as he has loved, and they are to follow Jesus in the way that Jesus lived—including his suffering and death (John 20:1–31). Each of these stories makes clear that the work of the gospel is living in the world just as Jesus lived.

Now, most people who know the story will tell you the story of Pentecost that matches the one found in Luke's writing. So let us ponder the Christian story of Babel found in chapter 2 of Luke's second book, Acts of the Apostles. We are told that, as in the other Gospels, the disciples have a habit of meeting together. They get together, men and women, for prayer. It happened that they were together on the day of the religious festival called Pentecost. Pentecost was a pilgrim festival in Jerusalem—it was a holiday from work—and people from all around would make their way to Jerusalem for special observances at the temple. Pentecost was also called the Feast of Weeks, and it happened fifty days after the festival called First Fruits. So the disciples are together. There is fear and anxiety about what has happened to Jesus. They are trying to figure out what they are supposed to do. They are worried that they will be taken away, scattered, and killed. In this setting, the disciples experience a mighty epiphanic moment: they have an experience of God's presence. I like Eugene Peterson's telling of this story in his well-known biblical paraphrase called *The Message*. He writes that there is a sound that fills the whole house. The sound is like a great and mighty wind. It is a gale-force wind, a knock-you-down wind. Then there is a wildfire that comes upon them. Some translations say tongues of fire. I prefer Peterson's imagery of a wildfire. A fire that is wild comes upon them. It is madness.

This moment is a recreative act. It is an image that recalls God's mighty acts in history, including Babel. We are reminded of the book of Genesis when the mighty wind moves over the waters of the earth. We are reminded of the creation story of Israel, when God appears to Moses in a burning bush that is not consumed. The inauguration of the freeing of Israel happens before Moses, and a pillar of fire leads them away from Egypt. These images and words are intended to capture our imagination and show us the remaking of the disciples.

Like Babel, God does not intend for them to be sequestered in upper rooms. God does not intend for them to make spaces that are the gate to heaven. God pours out God's recreative fire that they may be disbursed, that they may go out. God disburses the disciples so that the gospel story of God in Christ Jesus might be shared with all the people. And so those who followed Jesus, who were praying together so they would not be scattered, who were taking care of widows and orphans, who were in a holding position, are sent out into the world. The doors burst open and they go out. And they speak in many languages.

Those disciples who had previously been known only as followers—that is what "disciple" means—were turned into apostles—people who are sent. That is what "apostle" means—people who go. All the disciples were made apostles; all disciples are to be made apostles. There is no place for Christian towers of Babel among the friends of Jesus. We are set free. We are the laborers sent out on the fiftieth day for the harvest. We are the laborers that God in Christ Jesus has been praying to be sent (Luke 10:1–20). Christ's resurrection on Easter is the first fruit; it happens on the festival of the first fruit. Jesus is the first fruit of this re-creation and new Genesis. The Christian Babel story is the harvest story that falls fifty days later in parallel with the religious feast. God is at the margins; God is disbursed. God's people are to move to the margins and be disbursed.

So these laborers of the harvest blunder out into the streets. Not in a reverse Babel, but in a parallel Babel, as if enacting the great disbursal of the gospel to all nations. The people we are told are "amazed and astonished, they asked, 'Are not all these who are speaking Galileans? And how is it that we hear, each of us, in our own native language? Parthians, Medes, Elamites, and residents of Mesopotamia, Judea and Cappadocia, Pontus and Asia, Phrygia and Pamphylia, Egypt and the parts of Libya belonging to Cyrene, and visitors from Rome, both Jews and proselytes, Cretans and Arabs—in our own languages we hear them speaking about God's deeds of power.'" The power of this story is in the going out. Like Jesus, the church has left the building—not entered it. The rest of the book of Acts is the story of how they go, who they go to, and how they share God's love. It is a story about how they love others and do work where God's love profoundly changes the lives of those who come into contact with these individuals. I believe in this moment the disciples have such an experience of God that they are converted to see their work differently.

We are told that this community of followers goes out and they challenge the domination system of powers as Jesus did. Men and women work together creating new families and new communities. So radical is this transformation that Paul writes in Galatians 3:27–29: "As many of you as were baptized into Christ have clothed yourselves with Christ. There is no longer Jew or Greek, there is no longer slave or free, there is no longer male and female; for all of you are one in Christ Jesus. And if you belong to Christ, then you are Abraham's offspring, heirs according to the promise." People were a commodity and a good for the family in terms of labor. People's bodies belonged to the Roman emperor. But for this new community, living as members of Christ's family broke all these bonds. This new family further challenged the domination system by caring for the widows and orphans, the lame and the sick. People of no value were cared for by the society of friends. They shared everything in common, reversing the commoditization of money, power, and authority.

By their going out, other people had experiences of God and believed because they experienced God's love. We are told that when the apostles go out on the day of Pentecost, some three thousand people are profoundly changed. Through Philip's ministry, Samaritans are transformed. The Ethiopian eunuch believes. Cornelius learns of God's love from Peter. In chapter 13 of Acts, a whole city is transformed by the witness of Paul and Barnabas. Lydia, a woman who made a great deal of money selling purple cloth, experiences a conversion because of God working through Paul in Thyatira. A jailer, Dionysius and Damaris, Crispus and the Corinthians, Aquila and Apollos: these are only some of the names mentioned in the book of Acts. They all had conversion experiences because the apostles went out. Imagine the many more who are transformed because on that day the mighty wind shook the building and pushed the followers of Jesus out into the world.

Make no mistake, these conversions put pressure on the accepted norms of the Christian community, just as Jesus put pressure on them. The notion of worthiness and control in the falling of the Holy Spirit is challenged by the Ethiopian eunuch, who asks Phillip what prevented him from being baptized. The ministry of Peter with Cornelius challenged the purity codes regarding food, an inherited concern that the early church brought over from Judaism. The understanding of circumcision as a key sign of participation in the Jesus movement was challenged through the spread of the gospel among the Gentiles. The friends of Jesus were unwilling for the gospel to go unheard because of tradition. They were continuously challenged by the mission they had been called to undertake, and for which they were kicked out of the door.

These people who were sent bore witness to people's suffering; they stood at the foot of many crosses. They entered into the suffering of the lame and blind. Miraculous things happened as Peter, Stephen, Philip, Ananias, and Paul became witnesses of Christ who is present in the brokenness of people's lives. Many were healed and thus restored to their communities. By their witness, those who were unclean were made clean. Those who had no value were made well and given value through the love of Jesus Christ, all because the followers of Jesus went out. Those who are sent suffer with people. They not only follow Jesus, but they drink the cup of suffering that he drinks. They are jailed, imprisoned, beaten, stoned, and crucified. This is no mission of mere words or kind thoughts. Those who are sent out die to their own comfort in the wilderness and participate as victims of the systems of domination. They reject comfort and security, and by their holy dying, witness against the culture of death.

The early church didn't happen because the disciples received super human powers on Pentecost. They are not given secret magic spells to control an enchanted world. This is nothing less than an experience of the "heightened power of love" itself, which God opened to them and to others through them. This was an encounter with God's fullness, an encounter that propelled the disciples into the world sharing that fullness, so that others could experience it as well. It is not a fullness found in the whole or perfected self. It is not a fullness of perfect community. It is not found in the contours of human life, feelings, or achievements.[3] Instead it is fullness experienced as communion with the other, a solidarity with difference that stretches beyond conventional human boundaries.

All of the stories in Acts occur because the Holy Spirit, the experience of God's fullness and love, sent the people who were inside out into the world. Those who sat in darkness saw a great light. They saw the light and were broken free and sent. It took a wildfire and a mighty wind, but they left the building.

There is an encounter in the Gospels sometimes referred to as Jesus's conversation with the "rich young ruler" or the "rich young man." You can find the story in Matthew 19:16–30 and Luke 18:18–30. The story goes like this: Jesus was traveling in the wilderness near the Jordan. Crowds were following him. He is teaching some very difficult things about the way God works, who God sees as family, and how everyone should have access to Jesus. These are teachings about who is part of Jesus's new family and that is clearly the least and the lost. In the midst of this walking and teaching a man comes to Jesus. The man wants to know how to be part of the next life—part of this kingdom Jesus is speaking about. Jesus wants to know why he is focused on the "good." We must attempt to see this man as Jesus sees him. Capon argues that the problem lies in the fact that the man cannot accept his lostness. Spiritual success lies beyond his reach because he thinks it is something to be earned. He had done this and that. He is good—though Jesus jabs him with this comment early on. "Jesus," Capon writes, "has his number. 'Nobody's good, and nobody's going to be. Maybe I'm good; but my goodness looks so much like badness that people can't even stand the thought of it. And God, of course, really is good, but not in any way you can hope to imitate. So just knock off this goodness routine and listen to what I'm trying to tell you.'"[4]

Jesus offers the law as an exercise for responding to God's love. But it can't be earned; that is not the Sinai way. The law just isn't going to save you. God is the one who saves. To this the young man says, "Blah, blah . . . been there done that. What else must I do?" Of course he misses the point. Jesus then tells him that he has to let go of everything. Jesus said to him, "If you wish to be perfect, go, sell your possessions, and give the money to the poor, and you will have treasure in heaven; then come, follow me." Jesus is trying to help him understand that we are all lost, we are all losers, and the only way to inherit is to be a loser. You have to lose your life, lose your stuff, lose what is valuable to you, lose it all. It is only in the losing that you discover you have gained something else.[5]

Unfortunately, the man cannot hear what Jesus has been telling him all along. You can't win by winning. You only win by losing. In death all this man's winnings and losings would be washed away. Everything he had gained in realized wealth and perceived as spiritual wisdom would be lost. All of his sin, all of his sinlessness, all of the good love and bad love, the anger, hate, and the joy would be lost. Death was going to claim it all. The young man could have started living that day if he had understood that losing is everything. Losing is living.[6] It is in fact upon the losers that the kingdom is set.

One of the great misfortunes of Christendom is that the institutional church believes that the kingdom is built upon winning. The church is like the rich young ruler. It believes that it must keep the moral code in order to inherit eternal life. You have to perform and do all the things. You must be a winner—a spiritual, religious winner. The church—like the rich young man—doesn't get it. Why? Because the church has many possessions. The church is responsible for them, and struggles with the very core of the gospel message that every earthly gain is to be lost. Comfort, safety behind closed doors, it is all lost. The church remakes the gospel out of its struggle. It will even try and make Peter out to be the winner of the great church lottery. Jesus after all says, "You are Peter, and on this rock I will build my church, and the gates of Hades will not prevail against it" (Matt. 16:18). Of course, the reason Jesus says this to Peter is because Peter stumbled upon the truth of the gospel, the truth that Jesus had to die. Jesus had to become the lost son. Furthermore, despite all the church's efforts to make the case that Peter is a winner and that is why he gets to be the rock, the truth is that Peter isn't a winner. He is a loser and he loses quite spectacularly. And it's only in his losing that he is found.

You may remember that at the Last Supper Jesus predicts that his favorite follower will fail him three times (John 13:38). And Peter does. Peter denies following Jesus, Peter denies loving him, he denies believing in Jesus's mission, he even denies being Jesus's friend. Peter denies Jesus three times (John 18:17, 18:25–27). He loses. He loses his friend. He loses everything he thought he had been working for. He loses faith in Jesus's words and teachings. Peter is a big loser. Why? Because in the end, like the young man in our story, Peter valued much and feared losing much. Like the young man, like the church, Peter denies the gospel and in so doing is lost.

But it is precisely to the lost and the least that Jesus comes. He comes to Peter on the seashore and asks three times if Peter loves him. In this way Peter realizes that when you are lost you are found. Jesus declares Peter to be the kind of lost leader he needs, and orders him to take care of Jesus's sheep. He tells Peter that he is destined to follow Jesus faithfully and experience what Jesus experienced. Peter will lose everything, including his life, but will have gained everything in the losing of it.

This is good news for a church that is ready to follow. It is never too late to lose and to love and to be loved and to follow. All we have to do is admit our failure and our lostness. Like the blind man in John's story, we have simply been born blind. Jesus looks at us and sees us and spits on the ground and makes mud. Then he puts it in our eyes. Once we have a little mud in our eyes, we learn that we are just as lost as all the rest. In our lostness, we are found.

EPILOGUE

*Iconoclasm always sides with the doubters of perfect faith; so for my part,
I will be quite content if all I have succeeded in accomplishing is to supply this century's best candidate for a book-burning.*
                    —Edwin H. Friedman, rabbi and family therapist[1]

My guess is that there are a variety of reasons readers have reached this
point. Some of you have decided that the institutional church must
come tumbling down. Others have decided to oppose any mission agenda
that flows out of the pages above. Still others were my "predetermined
adversaries" as Friedman might say. I am not seeking political allies or
friends. I am hoping to foster an open conversation about the great work
that is before us as a church that believes the gospel, the good news of God
in Christ Jesus, will not be satisfied by organizational strength or deterred
by bureaucratic weakness. I am not interested in survival. I am interested in
the mission of Jesus and how that mission calls the church to faithfulness in
this time and in this context.[2]

I believe that we are stuck. We are stuck in a civil religion more faithful to
the cause of our self-perpetuation and the accepted social politic than the gospel.
We work harder and harder, but we only worsen our stagnation. As Friedman
points out: "There exists a connection between the stuckness that leaders experience and the stuckness in the thinking processes of those who would get them
unstuck."[3] I have hoped to reveal in the pages above how the nature of our stuckness is deeply rooted in the lens we use to read the Scripture. This stuckness has
constructed a simulacrum of the gospel, a social construct, that has drifted far
from the original mission of Jesus.[4] The institutional church barely resembles the
ecclesia of God's dreams. This poor resemblance to the original mission causes
us to become expert diagnosticians of people within and without our church. I

do not believe that our way out of this box can be found by "tinkering with the mechanics." Therefore, I am hoping to offer a different lens to help us engage Scripture and the church, its organization, and its mission. The way forward is back into the mission field. The way forward will require a shift in the way we think about relationships with Jesus and others.[5] We must change how we, as church leaders relate to God, and how the church as a whole relates with God, and how the people outside of our organizations relate with God.

We have reached a moment similar to the guests in the parable of the banquet in Matthew 22. Nobody has the right to attend God's party. Attendance is always by means of grace. And God, we are told in the parable, is intent on having the party. God is even now drawing us into the great wedding banquet. People can choose not to attend, but it won't be because God didn't invite them. Nobody has the right, or has achieved enough merit, to earn the privilege of attendance. It is always by the work of God that we are invited. The lost, the least, the undeserving are all invited. The real problem for the church is the same as the one faced by the guests who choose not to attend the banquet: the invitations went out to a list that the church did not approve. The wedding banquet is made ready for the church too. The problem is making our way. Will we choose to put on our wedding garment and go, even though we are lost and undeserving? Or will we find our own way in the outer darkness?[6] In the Gospel of Matthew, the religious leaders hear the story and plot to undermine the gospel in the hopes no one will receive the free invitation.

As a bishop of the Church of God, this has been a difficult book to write. In conversations I have been asked if I intend to keep my vow and undertake the work of the church. The answer is, yes. I understand full well that I am to lead the church. But the vow continues beyond leadership of an organization, a bureaucracy, or a hierarchy. Certainly the church is an organization that demands fiduciary, legal, and canonical responsibilities as its bishop and executive officer. My heritage though is more than this. My heritage is the faith of patriarchs, prophets, apostles, and martyrs, and those of every generation who have looked to God in hope. My joy is to follow Jesus. I am to boldly proclaim and interpret the gospel of Christ. I am to stir up the conscience of my people and encourage them in their gifts. There is nothing in the vow that says that I will uphold the institutional church when it fails the gospel. Instead, I feel challenged by the Scripture I study, and that challenge makes me invite the church to mission in its various contexts. Such an invitation means a provocative rereading and pondering of the Scripture. How can I see that the church, like Jonah, has set sail for Tarshish instead of being discomforted by the call to Nineveh, and not speak out?

I imagine, after reading this book, you must feel like you've tumbled down Alice's rabbit hole. We have been trained to see the church and the world a certain way. You might be feeling that something isn't quite right and you are wondering what is next now that the book is done. You see that the perverse lens, the immanent frame and the churches it has created, are everywhere, affecting everything, and so much of your conventional approach to the church and your life is implicated.

You see your place in it all. You see that you have been bound to a particular gospel. But at this moment you also have an opportunity. Like Neo, you have the opportunity to put the book down and go right back to doing what you were doing before. You can go right back to working harder and harder and expecting different results. Or, like Neo, you can take a step into the messiness of the kingdom of God all around you. You can stay in the church matrix or you can come with me and walk out the doors of the church into mission and discover just how deep this kingdom goes. It is your choice. It is your invitation to the banquet. It is your invitation to lose. But as we have discovered, it is in the losing that you will actually gain freedom from that which binds you.

While you ponder the choice, let me tell you a little story. "Cousin Judy" and her family had just moved to a small town in Scotland. Work had torn them from their American home and they were in a new culture. They sought out points of familiarity in order to make the transition less stressful, to find their place, and make connections. Having grown up in Texas as an Episcopalian, Judy sought out a local Scottish Episcopal Church to make friends. She was welcomed, and became part of the church family. All was going well until one fateful day in December when one of the members asked Judy whether her son Jeffrey would participate in the live nativity that Christmas.

When they came to her, Judy knew that if she said yes, the live nativity would not end well. Her son Jeffrey had always been a handful and a delight, but mostly a handful. Judy tried to explain that this wasn't a good idea. But the woman was so nice, so convincing, and pleaded, "We really need Jeffrey to pump up the numbers of our shepherds this year." Judy returned a smile, that motherly smile, that knows more than it projects. So she said yes against her better judgment. She wanted to belong. So Judy sat there in that small church north of Inverness, warming her hands, wringing her hands, and nervously watched Jeffrey's every move.

All of the children were sparkling and cheery faced. Angels, shepherds, Mary and Joseph were all neatly pressed and perfectly poised. And there was Jeffrey, a completely disheveled shepherd, a perfectly disinterested shepherd. He looked completely bored. Judy listened as the story of Jesus's birth was retold. The images of the shepherds and the angels washed over her as she imagined that first Christmas Eve. Then she was snapped back to reality as her motherly sense was pricked. She immediately focused in on Jeffrey, and she noticed he was looking at the baby doll Jesus. His eyes were now gleaming. He was interested. He was scheming. Judy tried to figure out how she could jump over the pews and the family in front of her and reach her son. How could she stop him? But it was too late. Jeffrey jumped down and pushed Mary and Joseph aside. He reached down and grabbed that baby doll Jesus and sprinted out of the church. He took that baby and ran with it.

I imagine the saints and angels cheering him on. I imagine God cheering him on. Go, Jeffrey, go! I marvel that the priests and parents and all the good faithful church people could not stop that little boy from stealing Jesus. Every Christmas Eve I can't help but think of that little Scottish Episcopal Church north of Inverness. There the locals gather and sit and watch the next generation take the stage for the same rehearsed precious and holy live nativity. And, they whisper to one another, "Do you remember the year that little American boy stole the baby Jesus?"

Of course, when we leave the church matrix, we discover that Jesus has been out there along. Jesus does not really need us to take him out into the world. Jesus is already there. God is there. The Spirit is there. The kingdom is there and taking root. You have to ask though, how much more fun is it if we, like Jeffrey, unbind and free our Jesus from the precious faithful church that has stolen him away? What would happen if we ran out to discover God in Christ Jesus that is out in the world, present in the lives of neighbors, in the wilderness, at the foot of people's crosses and in the midst of their illnesses and hearings? What a great adventure to join Jesus and God's gospel and run as fast as we can from the doors of the church. Out there, our conversion will happen. Out there is a world of people with many languages and cultures. Out there, awaiting us is our new family, Jesus's family. Out there together, with them, we might just find what we are made for. So, take the baby and run.

ACKNOWLEDGMENTS

I want to begin by thanking the Episcopal Diocese of Texas and its people who have continued to press me into conversations about the future mission of the church and why it matters. I am grateful for the support of my staff that has enabled me to have time to write. The Reverend Canon John Newton especially has been supportive of the work and an encourager along the way, as has the Reverend Canon Kai Ryan. My first reader and conversation partner for this book was The Reverend Patrick Hall, who has my gratitude for the work and time he put into the book, and the gratitude of my wife, JoAnne, who served as the first reader for the last five books. Of course, Richard Bass, my editor, and the team at Church Publishing who are always wonderful to work with and supportive of my projects. Finally, I am grateful to JoAnne, who knows I sneak off to the desk in the early morning hours and late at night to work on my writing and who is always caring, encouraging, and excited to hear what is next.

ENDNOTES

1. *Cloud of Unknowing* (New York: Penguin Classic, 1978), 54.

Foreword

1. *The Book of Common Prayer and Administration of the Sacraments and Other Rites and Ceremonies of the Church: Together with the Psalter or Psalms of David According to the Use of the Episcopal Church* (New York: Church Hymnal, 1979), 816.
2. Emil Brunner, *The Misunderstanding of the Church* (Philadelphia: Westminster Press, 1953), 14.
3. Ibid., 115. It seems important to simply state what Brunner and I shall mean by "religion." Religion is a human-oriented practice. This series of assumptions undergird one's apprehensions of reality. These assumptions are incarnated in liturgies—repetitive practices that bear our basic assumptions back to us. Liturgies abound, like shopping or watching the Super Bowl, and in our culture we have a peculiar habit of not acknowledging their religious origins. In this way, there is no such thing as a nonreligious person. Such a person would be incapable of interacting in society, because they could not make sense of anything in any way, or engage in any of our common liturgies that create the mutual bonds of connection. Religion should have this broader sense of worldview so that Christian religion might be about the assumptions, incarnated in church structures, liturgies, repetitive practices that symbolically bear our human-oriented practice and reflect our assumptions back to us. Unfortunately, we typically discuss religion as the rules. Therefore, like Capon, Brunner, and Stringfellow, I will be using religion in a more colloquial sense. By this I mean that religion is a kind of rule book for how I get right with God. We will unpack our immanent religious frame in chapter five.
4. These ideas are part of the work of Emil Brunner, William Stringfellow, Robert Ferrar Capon, and many more. We will of course explore them in detail in the pages below. Our goal is to juxtapose a pneumenal church of Christic imagination, the Ideal church, with all of the actual instantiations of church, hobbled by foibles and lacks. It will be important, as we unbind the gospel from the institutional church, to ensure that we don't sever the continuity between the actual, material church, and her ideal synonym. What we desire is that the institutional church be reformed such that it remains the analogical glue that binds the gospel to actual people in the world without it being an institutional millstone.

Chapter One

1. Lewis wrote that this was his thought about church shortly after becoming a believer. C. S. Lewis, *Surprised by Joy: The Shape of My Early Life* (New York: Harcourt & Brace, 1956), 233–34.
2. Richard Rohr, "Jesus as Paradox." Richard Rohr's Daily Meditation, Center for Action and Contemplation, July 29, 2014, http://myemail.constantcontact .com/Richard-Rohr-s-Meditation--Jesus-as-Paradox.html?soid=11030986686 16&aid=oce_J7-8kkI.
3. Lana Wachowski, and Lilly Wachowski, *The Matrix,* The Internet Movie Script Database (IMSDb), accessed March 25, 2016, http://www.imsdb.com/scripts /Matrix,-The.html.
4. *The Matrix Revisited*, directed by Josh Wreck, performed by Lana Wachowski and Lilly Wachowski (Warner Brothers, 2001).
5. Jean Baudrillard, *Simulacra and Simulation* (Ann Arbor: University of Michigan, 1994).
6. Ibid.
7. Mircea Eliade discusses this world of symbol in his phenomenology entitled *The Sacred and the Profane*. Mircea Eliade and Willard R. Trask, *The Sacred and the Profane: The Nature of Religion* (New York: Harcourt, Brace & World, 1959).
8. Baudrillard, *Simulacra,* 6.
9. Ibid.
10. Ibid.
11. Ibid, 1.
12. I am using here Paul Hegarty's outline of Baudrillard as the structure for discussing the sweep of church organization history. You may find a detailed argument of this history and illustration of community development in my book *CHURCH*. There you will find a more thorough treatment of the evolution of church community. Paul Hegarty, *Jean Baudrillard: Live Theory* (London: Continuum, 2004), 49.
13. Ibid.
14. Ibid, 94.
15. Ibid, 36.
16. Charles Taylor, *Sources of the Self: The Making of the Modern Identity* (Cambridge, MA: Harvard University Press, 1989), 186.
17. Thomas F. Tierney, "Punctual Selves, Punctual Death and the Health-Conscious Cogito: Descartes' Dead Bodies," *Economy and Society* 41, no. 2 (2012): 258–81, DOI: 10.1080/03085147.2011.635436.
18. This is a phrase often attributed to G. K. Chesterton and Archbishop William Temple, though there is no citation to be found.
19. Jay Pathak and Dave Runyon, *The Art of Neighboring: Building Genuine Relationships Right Outside Your Door* (Grand Rapids, MI: Baker Press, 2012), 101.
20. Ibid., 102.

Chapter Two

1. C. H. Spurgeon, *Flashes of Thought: 1000 Choice Extracts from the Works of C. H. Spurgeon* (London: Passmore and Alabaster, 1874), 66.
2. It seems important to pause here and consider this notion of morality a bit. Today we (all Westerners and the Western church) exist in a modern liberal society that is largely dominated by exclusive humanism. Both the liberal and conservative arms of the church are really two sides of a humanistic coin. This is largely due to the development of a Christian or theist notion that originally demanded a kind of social order that governed "rights bearing individuals." Today this order is disconnected in large part from the reformation movement that gave it strength and power. So much so that Christianity, while humanism's parent, is sometimes seen as its enemy. While the church and state are even now engaged in a battle over the setting of these norms (the culture wars), they are ostensibly arguing over completely immanent framework. They are debating about the upholding of rights. Moral code is now the name of the game and all vertical transformation completely removed from the picture. The "great weakness of modern moralism" is that it "sweeps dilemmas under the carpet, particularly the ones involving verticality," writes Charles Taylor (Charles Taylor, *Dilemmas and Connections: Selected Essays* [Cambridge, MA: Belknap of Harvard, 2011], 362-65). At its root, present-day religious and secular morality (though I think they are essentially and in large part the same form of moral teaching with different codes) all dictate "one or the other thing" within a horizontal framework of humanism. So for now we are going to set this aside, as there is not room in this text to undertake the complete work on this thought. Suffice it to say I believe there is a very good case that the last five hundred years of reformed morality has failed and that there is a new conversation underway. Moreover, we have turned this morality into a ghettoized base where religion dwells in the wider society. Religion has become the rule book by which we get right with God. We shall touch on this a bit in the chapter on engaging power. I would suggest for further reading Charles Taylor, Ivan Illich, James Gilligan, and René Girard.
3. William Stringfellow, *A Keeper of the Word: Selected Writings of William Stringfellow,* ed. Bill Wylie Kellermann (Grand Rapids, MI: W. B. Eerdmans, 1994), 31, 305.
4. William Stringfellow, *An Ethic for Christians and Other Aliens in a Strange Land* (Waco, TX: Word Press, 1973), 61.
5. Nathan Felmore, "The World Was Made for the Dead," *Dispatches to and from,* July 31, 2016, http://nathanfelmore.com/blog/2016/7/31/the-world-was-made-for-the-dead (accessed April 8, 2017).
6. James A. Fowler, "Christianity Is NOT Morality," Christ in You Ministries, accessed March 27, 2016, http://www.christinyou.net/pages/Xnotmor.html.
7. C. S. Lewis, *Mere Christianity: A Revised and Amplified Edition* (San Francisco: Harper, 2001), 244.
8. Ibid.

9. Ibid., 245.
10. Brunner, *Misunderstanding,*10.
11. Stringfellow, *Ethic,* 60.
12. Brunner, *Misunderstanding,*11.
13. Ibid., 13
14. Ibid., 15.
15. Ibid.
16. Ibid., 109.
17. Ibid.
18. Patrick Hall, conversations with the author.
19. Wachowski, *The Matrix,* Script Database.

Chapter Three

1. I am mindful here of the struggle that ethicist Timothy Sedgwick talks about in his book entitled *The Christian Moral Life: Practices of Piety.* In it Sedgwick talks about the ancient practice of worship that is an exchange in nature: worship exchanges a good for a good with God. Offerings made for a harvest, faithfulness for the winning of a battle, and sacrifices for the healthy birth of a child are examples of exchange practices in religion. Sedgwick argues that no matter with what fervor, the community seeks to practice true hospitality and relationship with God it inevitably returns to a practice of exchange. Personal conversations with author, March, 2017.
2. The Book of Common Prayer (BCP), 236.
3. Brooke Sherrard, "American Biblical Archaeologists and Zionism: How Differing Worldviews on the Interaction of Cultures Affected Scholarly Constructions of the Ancient Past," *Journal of the American Academy of Religion* 84, no. 1(2016): 235.
4. While the idea of a church lens redaction is of my own making, I am here referring tangentially to the book by Raymond E. Brown, *The Churches the Apostles Left behind* (New York: Paulist Press, 1984). I will refer back to his work later in this chapter.
5. Jon D. Levenson, *Sinai & Zion: An Entry Into The Jewish Bible* (San Francisco: Harper Press, 1985), 187.
6. The people freed from Egypt entered into the Promised Land and with them brought many stories of origin like the creation story and Noah, of important figures like Abraham and Job (commonly believed to be the oldest text in the Bible), stories of Moses who freed the people from Pharaoh, the judges who ruled, and prophets who kept the faith. These were held and told and repeated until the reign of David. The scribes of the era often called today the Yahwist, because they used the term Yahweh for God, wrote around 950 BCE. Other scribes writing at the same time, the Elohists, used the term Elohim for God. Many scholars believe that the first Scriptures were a merger of these traditions that make up the first five books of the Bible, called the Tanakh. The Tanakh includes the Torah (Law), the prophets, and other writings. Scholars believe that while we can trace different traditions throughout these texts, a final editor synthesized these sacred

books into one after Israel returned from exile in Babylon. We don't need to go into all the scholarship here. But it is important to understand that the postexilic redaction sought to explain the rise and fall of Israel almost two hundred years after the Elohists and Yahwists wrote. These final redactors are called the Deutoronomists, because they redacted the whole tradition.

7. We know that the books that form the Tanakh existed long before they were collected into one because part of the Scriptures references the discovery of other parts. During the time of Jeremiah, when Josiah was king, the temple of Solomon was going through some renovations. In the midst of this process, a scroll was discovered that included the book of Deuteronomy. After rediscovering the text, the priests read Deuteronomy to the people and they all repented. Josiah even sent it to a prophetess named Huldah who said that the book was "set apart" from all other writings (2 Kings 22:10–20; 2 Chron. 34:15–28). Following the return from Babylon, the Levitical priests continued to collate and edit the story of Israel, sharpening the narrative focus on Mount Zion and the temple.

Other books like Psalms, Proverbs, and the book of Daniel were not included in the Hebrew Scriptures at this time, or even upon the return of the people from Babylon. It wasn't until the sack of the temple in Jerusalem by the Romans, and the growth of the Christian movement and their own discussions about sacred books that a Hebrew council was convened to create a canon. In 90 of the common era (CE) rabbis and scholars gathered in Jamnia to adopt the Scriptures as sacred texts of Israel. We'll come to the New Testament in a moment.

8. Levenson, *Sinai & Zion,* 209.

9. Ibid., 212.

10. Ibid.

11. Ibid., 193.

12. Ziony Zevit, *The Religions of Ancient Israel: A Synthesis of Parallactic Approaches* (London: Continuum, 2001), 255. Tradition and archeology reveal that such shrines were common both in the north and south of Israel. They can be found at Arad, Beersheba Lachish, until 700 BCE. Some accounts believe Hezekiah had many of these closed during religious reforms and that by 500 BCE they were mostly gone according to known archeological sites. We know of course that there were shrines at Gilgal (1 Sam. 15:12–21, 33; Amos 4:4; 5:5), at Mizpah (Judg. 20:1–3, 8–10; 21:1, 5, 8; 1 Sam. 7:5–11; 10:17–24), at Mizpah in Gilead (Judg. 11:11, 30–31, 34, 39), at Hebron (2 Sam. 5:3; 15:7), at Bethlehem (Judg. 19:18), at Nob (1 Sam. 21:1–10; 22:16–19), at Gibeath Saul (2 Sam. 21:9).

13. Zevit, *Religions,* 238.

14. Levenson, *Sinai & Zion,* 192.

15. Ibid., 73.

16. Ibid.

17. Ibid., 192.

18. Ibid., 191. Deuteronomy 18:15–19 reads:

The LORD your God will raise up for you a prophet like me from among your own people; you shall heed such a prophet. This is what you requested of the LORD your God at Horeb on the day of the assembly when you said: "If I hear the voice of the LORD my God any more, or ever again see this great fire, I will die." Then the LORD replied to me: "They are right in what they have said. I will raise up for them a prophet like you from among their own people; I will put my words in the mouth of the prophet, who shall speak to them everything that I command. Anyone who does not heed the words that the prophet shall speak in my name, I myself will hold accountable."

19. Levenson, *Sinai & Zion*, 191.
20. Ibid.
21. Ibid., 195.
22. Ibid., 23.
23. Roy Heller, private email correspondence with author, March 30, 2016.
24. Ibid.
25. Stanley Hauerwas, "Naming God," ABC Religion & Ethics (Australian Broadcasting Corporation), September 24, 2010, http://www.abc.net.au/religion/articles/2010/09/24/3021305.htm.
26. John Milbank argues that Western thought cannot think itself out of an antagonistic dichotomy between the polis as the fundamental object of study, or the individual member of the polis as the object of study. One may argue that I am reproducing this aporia here, setting up an antagonism between the one-as-the-many (Zionism / institutional bad church) and the many-as-the-one (Sinai faith / small local church). We know and will talk about Paul's body of Christ analogy in coming chapters. For Milbank, it is this metaphor and a church founded upon it that can move past the dichotomy of Western thought—the one is the many, and the many are the one. I believe we will also cover this concern in chapter five and the work of Charles Taylor. (Conversations with Hall regarding August, 2016: John Milbank, *Theology and Social Theory* [London: Wiley, 1993], 340.)

Chapter Four

1. Stringfellow, *Ethic*, 59.
2. Brown, *Churches*, 15.
3. Baudrillard, *Simulacra*, 6.
4. Brown, *Churches*, 32.
5. Ibid., 40.
6. Ibid., 52.
7. Ibid., 55.
8. Ibid., 60.
9. Ibid.
10. Ibid., 62.
11. Ibid.
12. Ibid., 63.
13. Ibid., 74.
14. Ibid., 83.

15. Ibid., 84.
16. Ibid., 87.
17. Ibid., 97.
18. Ibid., 100.
19. Ibid., 112.
20. Ibid., 115.
21. Ibid., 114.
22. Ibid.
23. Ibid., 134.
24. Ibid.
25. Ibid., 138.
26. Ibid.
27. Ibid.
28. Wayne Meeks, *First Urban Christians: The Social World of the Apostle Paul* (New Haven, CT: Yale University Press, 1983),186.
29. Ibid., 80.
30. David Brakke, "Canon Formation and Social Conflict in Fourth-Century Egypt: Athanasius of Alexandria's Thirty-Ninth Festal Letter," *Harvard Theological Review* 87, no. 4 (1994): 395–419.
31. John Chrysostom, Hom. 50, 3–4, PG 58, 508–9.
32. Edward Foley, *From Age to Age: How Christians Have Celebrated the Eucharist* (Chicago: Liturgy Training Publications, 1991), 63.
33. Ibid., 87.
34. Bill Bryson, *At Home: A Short History of Private Life* (New York: Doubleday, 2010), 322-23.
35. Robert Farrar Capon, *Kingdom, Grace, Judgment: Paradox, Outrage, and Vindication in the Parables of Jesus* (Grand Rapids, MI: W. B. Eerdmans, 2002), 240. Max Weber offered in his writing on leadership and legitimacy that at first there was a charismatic movement that then became institutionalized. Applied to bishops, for instance, this moves from charismatic follower of Jesus to bishop within an adapted Roman structure. He did this in his "Three Types of Legitimate Rule" originally written in German called "Die drei reinen Typen der legitimen Herrschaft." A good friend and patristics scholar Christopher Bealey pointed out the theory to me when I was telling him about this book. He also reminded me of the work of Adolf Harnack, a contemporary of Weber, who then took up the charge to challenge Christianity for its development of doctrine. He did this in a piece written in 1885 and entitled *History of Dogma*. ("Adolf Harnack," Christian Classics Ethereal Library, accessed April 5, 2016, http://www.ccel.org /ccel/harnack.) He challenged the institution by calling into question the growth of its theology over against the inherited narrative of the followers of Jesus. His arguments about historical critical method and Scripture have been accepted to a great degree, but modern scholarship has shown that there was probably more structure there in the subapostolic age than he thought. Bealey recommends the work of Claudia Rapp, who in her book on the Episcopate, entitled *Holy Bishops In Late Antiquity*, shows that from the subapostolic era forward we have a mix

of leadership qualities, including institutional leadership. I don't deny this at all, but I am pointing out that within thirty years after the resurrection of Jesus an institutional skeleton is developing that was not present. Furthermore, the institutional presence disrupts the gospel over time by making the institution more central than the original. If we would but get back to a patristic era gospel or subapostolic gospel, we would indeed be far better off. But the symbol of ecclesia is so far removed it will take radical reform and even then we are only imagining the first symbol of the original.

36. Capon, *Kingdom*, 117.
37. David Foster Wallace, *This Is Water: Some Thoughts, Delivered on a Significant Occasion about Living a Compassionate Life* (New York: Brown, 2009).

Chapter Five

1. Robert Farrar Capon, *The Mystery of Christ—and Why We Don't Get It* (Grand Rapids, MI: W. B. Eerdmans, 1993), 24.
2. Charles Taylor, *A Secular Age* (Cambridge: Belknap of Harvard University Press, 2007), 775.
3. Ibid., 774.
4. Ibid., 542.
5. Ibid., 543.
6. Harvey Cox, *Religion in the Secular City: Toward a Postmodern Theology* (New York: Simon and Shuster, 1984), 159.
7. Taylor, *Secular,* 233.
8. Ibid., 230.
9. Nassim Nicholas Taleb, *The Black Swan: The Impact of the Highly Improbable* (New York: Radom House, 2007), 8.
10. Nassim Nicholas Taleb, *Antifragile: Things That Gain from Disorder* (New York: Random House, 2012), 179.
11. Daniel Kahneman, *Thinking, Fast and Slow* (New York: Farrar, Straus and Giroux, 2013), 87.
12. Ibid., 85.
13. Ibid., 86.
14. Ibid., 202.
15. Capon, *Mystery*, 25.
16. Robert Farrar Capon, *Between Noon and Three: Romance, Law, and the Outrage of Grace*, (Grand Rapids, MI: W.B. Eerdmans Pub., 1997), 287.
17. Roger Knight, *Edwin Muir: An Introduction to His Work* (London: Longman, 1980), 175.
    Malcolm Guite talks about this poem and Edwin Muir's work in his conversations with me in May 2016 and on his website https://malcolmguite.word press.com/, and in his interviews.
18. These thoughts came from an evening with poet the Reverend Malcolm Guite. During that time he offered the perspective of the passage from Luke about the healing of a man. After the reflection, the Reverend Elizabeth Parker reminded everyone of the John Donne poem "Batter My Heart, Three-Person'd God." I felt

all of this fit nicely into the conversation I was having in my head with you as I wrote this chapter.

19. Malcolm Guite, *Parable and Paradox* (London: Canterbury Press, 2017) 28.

20. Guite said in a short film on art, "Coleridge says that when we watch a play or read a poem we have a willing suspension of our disbelief. . . .What I am trying to do is get theologians to do is a willing suspension of belief." ("Art Made Flesh with Malcolm Guite," The Work of the People, directed by Travis Reed, 2014. http://www.theworkofthepeople.com/art-made-flesh.) I think this is a good way to think about our work as we seek to remove the church lens.

21. Ibid.

22. Shakespeare, William, and William Aldis, *A Midsummer Night's Dream.* (n.p.: Clarendon, 1894), 1.1.12–18. Malcolm Guite points out this text in his film "Art Made Flesh."

23. Guite, "Art Made Flesh."

24. Augustine of Hippo, *Confessions* (Grand Rapids, MI: Baker Book House, 2005), 216.

25. Martin Luther, *Works of Martin Luther: With Introductions and Notes,* trans. and ed. Henry Eyster Jacobs and Adolph Spaeth (Philadelphia: Muhlenberg, 1943), 368.

26. Malcolm Guite, "The Lectern with Malcolm Guite," The Work of the People, directed by Travis Reed, 2014, http://www.theworkofthepeople.com/the-lectern.

27. J. I. Packer, *"Fundamentalism" and the Word of God: Some Evangelical Principles* (Grand Rapids, MI: Eerdmans Publishers, 1958), 69.

28. Guite, "Lectern."

29. Ibid.

30. Malcolm Guite, "Flesh and Blood with Malcolm Guite," The Work of the People, directed by Travis Reed, 2014, http://www.theworkofthepeople.com /flesh-and-blood.

31. C. S. Lewis, *Beyond Personality: The Christian Idea of God* (New York: Macmillan, 1945), 43.

32. Ibid.

Chapter Six

1. Nadia Bolz Weber, "Pregnant Old Ladies and Other Signs That God's Story Is Better than the One We Tell Ourselves." Patheos, December 11, 2012. http:// www.patheos.com/blogs/nadiabolzweber/2012/12/pregnant-old-ladies-and -other-signs-that-gods-story-is-better-than-the-one-we-tell-ourselves/.

2. *Monty Python and the Holy Grail,* Scene 7, last modified November 1994, http:// www.sacred-texts.com/neu/mphg/mphg.htm.

3. Capon, *Kingdom,* 169.

4. Ibid., 173.

5. Ibid.

6. Ignatius, "The Epistle of Ignatius to the Magnesians," *CHURCH FATHERS: Epistle to the Magnesians (St. Ignatius).* chapter 9, accessed April 11, 2016, http:// www.newadvent.org/fathers/0105.htm.

7. Cynthia Bourgeault, *The Wisdom Jesus: Transforming Heart and Mind: A New Perspective on Christ and His Message* (Boston, MA: New Seeds, 2008), 29.

8. Ibid., 27.

9. Katherine Grieb, *The Story of Romans: A Narrative Defense of God's Righteousness* (Louisville, KY: Westminster John Knox Press, 2002), xxiv.

10. Ibid., 86.

11. These words are repeated in different forms in the Gospels, and in the Episcopal Book of Common Prayer on pages 362–63.

12. Ibid., 363.

13. Ibid., 362.

Chapter Seven

1. Jaime Clark-Soles, "ON Scripture: Jaime Clark-Soles on Matthew 22:34–46: On Loving God, Loving Neighbor and #OWS," *On Scripture* (blog), October 19, 2011, http://day1.org/3371on_scripture_jaime_clarksoles_on_matthew_223446_on_loving_god_loving_neighbor_and_ows_.

2. Taylor, *Secular*, 543.

3. Ibid., 317.

4. Ibid., 539.

5. Ibid.

6. Ibid., 540.

7. Ibid., 551.

8. Ibid., 589.

9. Wallace, *Water*, 36–41.

10. Marc J. Dunkelman, "Marc J. Dunkelman: Our Tolerance Has Led to the Balkanization of Society," *The Spokesman-Review*, September 14, 2014, http://www.spokesman.com/stories/2014/sep/14/marc-j-dunkelman-our-tolerance-has-led-to-balkaniz/

11. Ibid.

12. See Marc Dunkelman's work on these images and metaphors and vanishing melting pot opportunities. *The Vanishing Neighbor: The Transformation of American Community* (New York: W. W. Norton, 2014).

13. Capon, *Kingdom*, 204.

14. Ibid., 203.

15. Ibid., 203.

16. Ibid., 204.

17. Ibid., 205.

18. Ibid., 206.

19. Ibid., 201.

20. I was introduced to Ivan Illich's work through the reading of Charles Taylor's *Secular Age*. I am using Taylor's treatment of Illich. Ivan Illich's work entitled *The Rivers of the North of the Future* is worth a read. See Taylor, *Secular*, 714–15.

21. Ibid., 714.

22. Ibid. Taylor agrees with Illich here that what happens to the Samaritan story is that it is corrupted. A friend of mine, the Right Reverend Sean Rowe, remarked

to me recently, "Every movement must organize." When the movement falls into something more "normal" in worldly terms, says Taylor, it automatically begins to form rules and boundaries. It forms a new tribe and community. With this new normal there is a new set of tribal insiders and tribal outsiders. The church, Illich and Taylor argue, "develops into a need to shore up and institutionalize them, introduce rules, divide responsibilities" (715). We create a new modern bureaucracy. Illich argues that the Reformation really does something important to humanism by institutionalizing it. Taylor writes, "Rules then become modern bureaucracies based upon rationality and rules prescribe treatments for categories of people; so we fit into categories, our rights entitlements burdens depend on the shape of life these rules give us." Taylor, *Secular,* 716. Illich and Taylor clearly see this as "a corruption of the original" (716). What happens, Taylor explains, is that the organization of daily life is constantly creating a system of ins and outs and in so doing, undermines "a sense of mutual belonging" that is the intent of the parable. Jesus is not creating a system of morality, but a way of being in the world with one another. The randomness of our encounters invites us to continuously break the code and system in which we are formed (718).

23. Capon, *Kingdom,* 202.
24. Fleming Rutledge, "Who Is the Good Samaritan?" Generous Orthodoxy, May 1, 2005, http://generousorthodoxy.org/sermons/who-is-the-good-samaritan.aspx
25. Ibid.
26. Capon, *Mystery,* 25.

Chapter Eight

1. Rowan Williams, *A Ray of Darkness: Sermons and Reflections* (Cambridge, MA: Cowley, 1995), 82.
2. Taylor, *Secular,* 8.
3. Ibid., 310–12.
4. Ibid., 313.
5. Ibid., 312.
6. Ibid., 49.
7. Ibid., 50.
8. Ibid., 746
9. Ibid., 747.
10. Patrick Hall, conversations with author August, 2016.
11. Taylor, *Secular,* 529.
12. Ibid., 122.
13. Ibid., 528.
14. Robert Johansen, *Leaders Make the Future: Ten New Leadership Skills for an Uncertain World* (San Francisco: Berrett-Koehler, 2012), 50.
15. Ibid.
16. Joan E. Taylor, *The Immerser: John the Baptist within Second Temple Judaism* (Grand Rapids, MI: W.B. Eerdmans, 1997), 34, 43.
17. Ibid., 214–18.

18. Capon, *Kingdom,* 21.
19. Ibid., 344.
20. Ibid., 419.
21. Taylor, *Immerser,* 213.
22. Ibid., 214.
23. Ibid., 218.
24. Ched Myers, *Binding the Strong Man: A Political Reading of Mark's Story of Jesus* (Maryknoll, NY: Orbis, 1988) 128, 150–51.

Chapter Nine

1. Brian D. McLaren, *A Generous Orthodoxy: Why I Am a Missional, Evangelical, Post/Protestant, Liberal/conservative, Mystical/poetic, Biblical, Charismatic/contemplative, Fundamentalist/Calvinist, Anabaptist/Anglican, Methodist, Catholic, Green, Incarnational, Depressed-yet-hopeful, Emergent, Unfinished Christian* (El Cajon, CA: Emergent YS, 2004), 59.
2. Taylor, *Dilemmas,* 182.
3. Ibid., 183.
4. Ibid., 173.
5. Ibid., 183.
6. Ibid., 22.
7. Barbara Cawthorne Crafton, *The Also Life* (New York, Morehouse, 2016), 152.
8. Ibid.
9. Athenasius, "Discourse 1 Against the Arians," *CHURCH FATHERS: Discourse I Against the Arians (Athanasius),* New Advent Web Library, 1.39, 3.34, http://www.newadvent.org/fathers/28161.htm.
10. I borrow the "lost and least" from Capon's work and I am adding to it the word "other" from Miroslav Volf's reflections in *Exclusion and Embrace: A Theological Exploration of Identity, Otherness, and Reconciliation* (Soʾul: Ivp, 2013).
11. René Girard, *Job: The Victim of His People* (Stanford, CA: Stanford University Press, 1987), 154–68 (accessed online at: http://girardianlectionary.net/res /girard_job_ch21.htm).
12. Ibid.
13. Ibid.
14. Ibid.
15. Ibid.
16. Ibid., 156.
17. "Jesus being found guilty" is an important distinction. In most humanistic theologies the humans make a mistake or God finds us guilty and so Jesus may pay our price. In the Gospels what is true is that the powers of this world find that Jesus's ministry is destroying the order of things—which it is! So he is guilty by worldly just standards. He is only innocent in the reign of God, where he is doing what he is intended to do; and that is, to turn the tables on the powers of this world.
18. Girard, *Job.*
19. Ibid.

20. Ibid.
21. Ibid.
22. Taylor, *Dilemmas*, 17.
23. Malcolm Guite, *The Word in the Wilderness* (London: Hymns Ancient & Modern, 2014), 130.
24. Girard, *Job*.
25. Girard, *Job*. I wish to make clear that I am fully aware of the fact that I am skating close to the heresy of *apokatastasis*—universal reconciliation. I intend to take here, though, what I will call a "Barthian jog." All the great theologians agree Barth's doctrine of redemption rooted in the incarnation and creation logically implies universal reconciliation—though he never said it! (Roger Olson has a list: Donald Bloesch in *Jesus Is Victor!*, Hans Urs von Balthasar in *The Theology of Karl Barth*, G. C. Berkouwer in *The Triumph of Grace in the Theology of Karl Barth*, and Emil Brunner in *Dogmatics*, vol. 1 all agree.) What Barth cleverly does is to protect the freedom of God by stating that God does not have to, nor is required to by his nature, redeem anyone (*Dogmatics* II/2, 417). Barth then goes on to say on the very next page that neither can he limit God's freedom and grace to a limited salvation. Barth writes that God can and may upon the last day choose a "final opening up and enlargement of the circle of election and calling" to all people (ibid, 418). Olson reminds us of Barth's address to reformed ministers in 1956 entitled "The Humanity of God" (published in 1960) wherein he says he will not be pinned down to a "for" or "against" position on universal salvation. Barth writes: "One should at least be stimulated by the passage, Colossians 1:19, which admittedly states that God has determined through His Son as His image and as the first-born of the whole Creation to 'reconcile all things (τά πάντα) to himself,' to consider whether the concept could not perhaps have a good meaning." He then went on to say, "This much is certain, that we have no theological right to set any sort of limits to the loving-kindness of God which has appeared in Jesus Christ. Our theological duty is to see and understand it as being still greater than we had seen before." Barth believed that given the passages found in John 1:9, 1:29, 3:17, 8:12, 9:5, 11:9, and 12:46, "We cannot follow the classical [Reformed] doctrine and make the open number of those who are elect in Jesus Christ into a closed number to which all other men are opposed as if they were rejected. Such an assumption is shattered by the unity of the real and revealed will of God in Jesus Christ" (*Dogmatics*, 422). In the end, I must like Barth concede theologically not to box God in and at the same time that God in Christ Jesus intends to save all human beings—this is God's will according to Scripture. I am basing my work on my own reading of Barth's *Church Dogmatics* and am grateful for the theory proposed by Roger Olson on this subject in his essay that reminded me of the passages read so long ago in seminary! Roger Olson is Foy Valentine Professor of Christian Theology of Ethics at George W. Truett Theological Seminary of Baylor University. Karl Barth, *Church Dogmatics*, trans. G. W. Bromiley and Thomas F. Torrance (Edinburgh: T. & T. Clark, 1961); Roger Olson, "Was Karl Barth a Universalist?" *Roger E. Olson My Evangelical Armenian Theological Musings,*

Patheos, March 10, 2013, http://www.patheos.com/blogs/rogereolson/2013/03
/was-karl-barth-a-universalist-a-new-look-at-an-old-question/
26. Girard, *Job*.
27. Guite, *Word*, 233.
28. Ibid.

Chapter Ten

1. Greg Boyle, "The Jesus Strategy," The Work of the People, May 2016, http://
www.theworkofthepeople.com/the-jesus-strategy.
2. You can read more about Magee here: Martha Lund Smalley, ed, *American
Missionary Eyewitness to the Nanking Massacre, 1937–1938* (New Haven, CT:
Yale Divinity School Library, 1997). http://web.library.yale.edu/sites/default
/files/files/OccasionalPublication9.pdf. You can also see a brief description of Magee
on Wikipedia here: https://en.wikipedia.org/wiki/John_Magee_(missionary).
3. Smalley, *American*. You can watch the film on Youtube here: https://www.you
tube.com/watch?v=YeIxDezImGM)
4. Ibid. You can see the role that he played in the film entitled *Don't Cry, Nanking*,
1995.
5. Girard, *Job*.
6. Ibid.
7. Ibid.
8. Henri J. M. Nouwen, *Can You Drink the Cup?* (Notre Dame, IN: Ave Maria,
1996).
9. L'Arche communities are residences where people with and without intellectual
disabilities share life together. You can read more about their work here: http://
www.larche.org/
10. Pamela Cushing, "To Be Fully Human," Jean Vanier, accessed May 13, 2016, http://
www.jean-vanier.org/en/his_message/jean_vanier_on_becoming_human/to
_be_fully_human
11. Jean Vanier, *Becoming Human* (Paulist Press: New York, 1998), 10.
12. Jean Vanier, *Community and Growth* (Paulist Press: New York, 1989), 95.
13. Philip Yancey, *What's So Amazing about Grace?* (Grand Rapids, MI: Zondervan,
1997), 14.
14. Capon, *Kingdom*, 38.
15. Myers, *Binding*, 157.
16. Capon, *Kingdom*, 38.
17. Myers, *Binding*, 156.
18. Ibid.
19. Ibid., 206.
20. Ibid., 207.
21. Capon, *Kingdom*, 261.
22. Ibid., 118.
23. Ibid., 120.
24. Ibid., 263–66.
25. Ibid.

26. Eugene H. Peterson, *The Message: The Bible in Contemporary Language* (Colorado Springs: NavPress, 2002.

27. Capon, *Kingdom*, 402.

28. Ibid., 405.

29. I am struck by Raymond E. Brown's work on the prayer of Jesus that his followers be one as he and the Father are one found in John's Gospel, chapter 17. Raymond E. Brown, *The Gospel According to John. Vol. 2.* (Garden City, NY: Doubleday, 1966), 781.

Chapter Eleven

1. Elaine A. Heath, *The Mystic Way of Evangelism: A Contemplative Vision for Christian Outreach* (Grand Rapids, MI: Baker Academic, 2008), 13.

2. The Reverend Jim Liberatore said during a conversation with me, August 3, 2016, that he thought the missional church made people the subject of its mission and not the object as do so many programs in attraction churches. It stuck with me and I think it is a true statement about the life and work of Jesus.

3. Boyle, "Jesus Strategy."

4. Ibid.

5. Capon, *Kingdom*, 417.

6. Ibid.

7. Taylor, *Secular*, 769.

8. Ibid.

9. Ibid., 729.

10. Ibid.

11. Anselm, *Proslogion: With the Replies of Gaunilo and Anselm,* trans. Thomas Williams (Indianapolis, IN: Hackett, 2001), ix.

12. Taylor, *Secular*, 737.

13. Ibid., 739.

14. Ibid.

15. Ibid., 751.

16. Ibid.

17. Ibid., 765.

18. Ibid., 766.

19. Stringfellow, *Keeper*, 20.

20. Leonardo Boff, *Trinity and Society* (Maryknoll, NY: Orbis, 1988).

21. Rachel Held Evans, "On 'Going Episcopal,' " *Rachel Held Evans* (blog), March 25, 2015, http://rachelheldevans.com/blog/going-episcopal.

22. I believe that the nature of conversion itself parallels Hans-Georg Gadamer's work in truth and method. I read the text while in seminary. I am using articles from a review of the text here to digest the notions into a shorter paragraph. Richard Palmer, *Hermeneutics: Interpretation Theory in Schleiermacher, Dilthey, Heidegger, and Gadamer* (Evanston, IL: Northwestern University Press, 1969), 163.

23. Ibid., 209.

24. Ibid.

25. Francisco J. Gonzalez, "Dialectic and Dialogue in the Hermeneutics of Paul Ricouer and H.G. Gadamer" *Continental Philosophy Review* 39 (2006): 322–23.

Chapter Twelve

1. Barbara Brown Taylor, *Leaving Church: A Memoir of Faith* (San Francisco: Harper, 2006), 236.
2. The passage is taken from Matthew 4:1–11. The connections are taken from Daniel Harrington, *The Gospel of Matthew* (Collegeville, MN: Liturgical Press, 1991), 68.
3. Ibid., 70.
4. Walter Wink, *Walter Wink: Collected Readings,* ed. Henry F. French (Minneapolis: Fortress Press, 2013), 106.
5. Ibid.
6. Ibid.
7. Taken from an excerpt from René Girard's *Things Hidden Since the Foundation of the World.* (Stanford, CA: Stanford University Press, 1987), 220.
8. Girard, *Hidden*, 219.
9. Ibid, 220.
10. Ibid, 220.
11. Ibid, 221–22.
12. Ibid, 221.
13. Girard writes, "The complete absence of any sexual element has nothing to do with repression—an explanation thought up at the end of the nineteenth century and worthy of the degraded puritanism that produced it. The fact that sexuality is not part of the picture corresponds to the absence of the violent mimesis with which myth acquaints us in the form of rape by the gods. This idol—what we have called the model-obstacle—is completely absent" (All such images of sexual extasy arrive much later in art and are placed as a lens on top of the story.) (Girard, *Hidden*, 222.).
14. See arguments from the midcentury on. We might think of John Spong's rejection or any other. But Tillich too saw no point in it. Girard writes, "Paul Tillich dismisses in the most peremptory way the theme of the virgin birth because of what he calls 'the inadequacy of its internal symbolism'" (Girard, *Hidden*, 222).
15. Ibid, 223.
16. Ibid, 222.
17. Ibid.
18. I am going to follow Wink's biblical analysis of Jesus's confrontation of the powers and domination system in the paragraphs to follow. See Walter Wink, *The Powers That Be: Theology for a New Millennium* (New York: Doubleday, 1998), 78.
19. Ibid., 80.
20. Ibid., 78.
21. Ibid., 81.
22. Ibid., 88–89.
23. Ibid., 92.

24. Taylor, *Dilemmas*, 195.
25. Wink, *Powers*, 82.
26. Taylor, *Dilemmas*, 195.
27. Ibid.
28. Ibid., 196.
29. Taylor, *Dilemmas*, 196.
30. Ibid., 203.
31. Ibid., 207.
32. Ibid., 209.
33. Stringfellow, *Ethic*, 111.
34. Wink, *Powers*, 82.
35. Ibid.
36. Stringfellow, *Ethic*, 59.
37. Robert Bellah, *Beyond Belief: Essays on Religion in a Post-traditional World* (New York: Harper & Row, 1970), 169.
38. Ibid., 186.
39. Dwight D. Eisenhower, quoted in Will Herberg, *Protestant-Catholic-Jew* (Garden City, NY: Doubleday & Co, 1955), 97.
40. I am taking here Taylor's side and I am using Robert Bellah's definition of Taylor's point for clarity. Robert Bellah, "The Immanent Frame," The Immanent Frame RSS. May 25, 2016, http://blogs.ssrc.org/tif/author/bellah/.
41. Taylor, *Dilemmas*, 138.
42. Ibid., 139.
43. Willis Jenkins, *The Future of Ethics: Sustainability, Social Justice, and Religious Creativity* (Washington, DC: Georgetown Press, 2013), 100.
44. Ibid., 91–92.
45. I believe two questions come up at this point of equal interest and importance. The first is this: If Jesus intends a "different system than dominating hierarchies," is hierarchy inherently violent? The second question is: Given the ubiquity of systems of domination, and the fact that every rejection of them is also a tacit embrace of them, might this undermine your premise that a genuine movement IS possible from a more compromised way of life to a less compromised way of life? In other words: If it is the lot of humankind to be enmeshed and admired in these systems of domination, then what is the benefit of trying to throw off a present compromised system in favor of a future compromised system? I believe both these questions tap into the essential nature of our discussion: that is, if the Jesus movement must always organize itself, how does it do so without engaging in violence? (Something it has been unable to avoid most of these two thousand years.) I am placing this conversation here in the footnotes because I believe this is a question of organization and not hermeneutical and belongs outside the text for consideration.

First, I believe that I have made the case that any system that abstracts the "other" and creates levels of powers and authorities is inherently going to be violent. There is a universal human nature that leans toward domination. This tendency for violence, oppression, and domination is called sin in the church.

Our desire to create codes will always bring us into both a rejection of sin and a participation in a ever new system of domination. It is the work of the church, though, to continually throw off this domination and seek the ecclesia and community for which Jesus speaks. Simply because we live in a sinful world and can name our sin does not mean we are given permission to live in it and throw up our hands. Rather, we are continually invited to be reformed and changed. The thought here is the work of *ecclesia reformata, semper reformanda* (the church reformed, always reforming)—courtesy of Karl Barth and other theologians post World War II. Here, then, is the idea that when Scripture clearly speaks to us, we should reform our institutional/structural church practices.

Regarding the organizational question before us, I rely here on the work of Arthur Koestler, author and journalist; Kenneth Earl "Ken" Wilber II, an American writer whose work on "integral theory" is known; and Rolf Sattler, professor, plant biologist specializing in plant morphology, and student of Wilber's. Here the new science offers organizational thinking around the gospel thinking.

The first thing to understand is the nature of hierarchies as an observed reality and not necessarily a domination system. I have been talking in this chapter about dominating hierarchies. I am here rejecting this idea but holding onto the nature of hierarchy as a system or organizing principle. Wilber adopts the word "holarchy" in order to differentiate between observable ordering of organisms and dominating and violent hierarchies. Holarchy was a term first used by Arthur Koestler in his work where "holon" (the basis for a holarchy) is a piece and part of the levels around it. In this way, a divided top-down power structure is divided. Koestler offers this as an example of holarchic relationship: subatomic particles ↔ atoms ↔ molecules ↔ macromolecules ↔ organelles ↔ cells ↔ tissues ↔ organs ↔ organisms ↔ communities ↔ societies. See Arthur Koestler, *The Ghost in the Machine* (New York: Macmillan, 1968); Ken Wilber, *The Collected Works of Ken Wilber* (Boston: Shambhala, 2000), 29. Sattler helps to understand this, "A holarchy or hierarchy is a system of holons at different levels. In this system lower level holons compose a higher level holon, and a higher level holon comprises lower level holons. Any holon is a part with regard to the higher level holon it composes, and at the same time a whole with regard to the lower level holon(s) it comprises. Therefore, a holon is a part/whole. For example, an organ is a part of an organism, but a whole with regard to the cells of which it is comprised" (Rolf Sattler. "Wilber's AQAL Map and Beyond," *Beyond Wilber*, accessed July 21, 2016, http://www.beyondwilber.ca/AQALmap/bookdwl /files/WAQALMB_1.pdf).

Wilber uses the ideas of Chinese boxes and baskets. Barbara Cawthorne Crafton uses this metaphor in her book *The Also Life*. What Wilber helps us to understand is that while we may categorize through holarchy, the reality is that holons are "interpenetrating" (Ken Wilber *The Collected Works of Ken Wilber* [Boston, MA: Shambhala, 1998], 61). Stattler takes this then and expands it based upon Wilber's work to say that if interpenetrating, then what we see "is a whole, a continuum, a unity, because processes by their very nature are interconnecting, and a network of processes is an undivided whole" (Stattler). While reality is homogenous, there is differentiation and because of this differentiation there can be some sense of the holons. We see this in the way we talk about the color of light or the organs of plants. While we can see the other, to make the other a separate entity from ourselves is to reintroduce hierarchy. There is no "radically separate and isolated and bounded entity" (Ken Wilber, *The Collected Works of Ken Wilber* [Boston: Shambhala, 1999], 469).

So while we may organize ourselves, the regulator is always to have in mind this interconnectedness that we have been talking about in the whole book. There is not a classification of lost and then a classification of found people where the found people are to look for the lost. Instead, what Jesus is teaching us is that we are all lost and all found by God. We may choose to live in some kind of abstracted hierarchy of abusive power that denies God's collective finding, but that is a false system, organization, and church community. Stattler is quick to point out, "I am not against hierarchies. I recognize their value as an ordering principle and a means to hierarchical holism that reveals emergence, an important phenomenon that often is not recognized in modern reductionist science and flatland views. However, hierarchical thinking is not the only way. We can also think in a nonhierarchical way and this kind of thinking reveals another important aspect of manifest reality that cannot be grasped through hierarchical thinking" (Stattler). The point is that understanding this interconnectedness that Jesus and science reveal helps us always be aware of the oppression inherent in hierarchies and to seek to reform us toward the image of holarchy that Jesus is speaking about.

This is what theologian and Christian philosopher Catherine Pickstock calls "abstract universal" a power that shows itself within hierarchy. You can read more of Pickstock's work in Catherine Pickstock, *After Writing: On the Liturgical Consummation of Philosophy* (Oxford, UK: Blackwell, 2015). A holarchy as described above is much more like Paul's shared vocations. The truth is that as a church with hierarchy we will be forced to deal with this over and over again in some kind of eternal return.

Systems like church must always grasp with Paul's vision vs. the hierarchy of human organization. It is our continual work, then, to understand this different way of hierarchical thinking. In my own denomination this is how we are organized, though we struggle with powers of domination. The orders of the church are not hierarchical but rather in relationship with one another. The hierarchy of the Episcopal Church is organized through the conventions themselves. As America cast off the hierarchy of monarchy in the revolution, the church did the same. Of course, the organizational body politic can and does become a dominating hierarchy. This it seems is the task, though in every organization of church to grasp the wholeness of being that is intended by the gospel. Shared relationship within the wider body is not an abstraction but the crux of the matter if the organism, organization, is to keep from replicating the domination system of the world. I think that this will become clearer as we explore, in future chapters of this book, how God sends his followers out to do their ministry and

how the first generation understood this call and how they sought to undertake the mission.
46. Capon, *Kingdom*, 185.
47. Ibid., 354.
48. Ibid., 185.
49. Kenneth E. Bailey, *Finding the Lost: Cultural Keys to Luke 15* (St. Louis, MO: Concordia Pub. House, 1992), 65.
50. Ibid., 107.
51. Capon, *Kingdom*, 187.
52. Ibid., 187–88.

Chapter Thirteen

1. Williams, Rowan. "The Life of Dietrich Bonhoeffer: His Views on Culture, Piety and Ecumenism." Lecture at the International Bonhoeffer Congress, Wrocław, Poland, February 3, 2006.
2. If you wish to read more on the subject of God's scattering of people, see both Robert Alter's and Carol Kaminski's texts on the subject. Their books are: Robert Alter, *The Five Books of Moses: A Translation with Commentaries* (New York: Norton, 2004), 58; Robert Altar, *Genesis* (New York: W.W. Norton, 1996), 26; Carol M. Kaminski, *From Noah to Israel: Realization of the Primaeval Blessing after the Flood* (London: T & T Clark, 2004).
3. Taylor, *Secular*, 729.
4. Capon, *Kingdom*, 383.
5. Ibid.
6. Ibid.

Epilogue

1. Edwin H. Friedman, Edward W. Beal, and Margaret W. Treadwell, *A Failure of Nerve: Leadership in the Age of the Quick Fix: An Edited Manuscript* (Bethesda, MD: Edwin Friedman Estate/Trust, 1999), 26.
2. Ibid. I am using Friedman's apologetic here for his work. It has a wonderful way of flowing and explaining the reason for needed change.
3. Ibid., 2.
4. Ibid., 3. I am using Friedman's idea here to capture what I have offered.
5. Ibid.
6. Capon, *Kingdom*, 135.

WORKS CITED

"Adolf Harnack." Christian Classics Ethereal Library. Accessed April 5, 2016. http://
www.ccel.org/ccel/harnack.

Alter, Robert. *The Five Books of Moses: A Translation with Commentaries.* New York:
Norton, 2004.

———. *Genesis.* New York: W. W. Norton, 1996.

Anselm. *Proslogion: With the Replies of Gaunilo and Anselm.* Translated by Thomas
Williams. Indianapolis, IN: Hackett, 2001.

Athenasius. "Discourse 1 Against the Arians." *CHURCH FATHERS: Discourse I
Against the Arians (Athanasius),* New Advent Web Library. 1.39, 3.34 http://
www.newadvent.org/fathers/28161. Accessed April 7, 2016.

Augustine of Hippo. *Confessions.* Grand Rapids, MI: Baker Book House, 2005.

Bailey, Kenneth E. *Finding the Lost: Cultural Keys to Luke 15.* St. Louis, MO:
Concordia Pub. House, 1992.

Barna, George, and Mark Hatch. *Boiling Point: It Only Takes One Degree: Monitoring
Cultural Shifts in the 21st Century.* Ventura, CA: Regal, 2001.

Barth, Karl, G. W. Bromiley, and Thomas F. Torrance. *Church Dogmatics.* Edinburgh:
T. & T. Clark, 1961.

Baudrillard, Jean. *Simulacra and Simulation.* Ann Arbor: University of Michigan,
1994.

Baudrillard, Jean, and Mark Poster. *Selected Writings.* Stanford, CA: Stanford
University Press, 1988.

Bellah, Robert N. "The Immanent Frame." *The Immanent Frame RSS.* May 25, 2016.
http://blogs.ssrc.org/tif/author/bellah/

Bellah, Robert N. *Beyond Belief; Essays on Religion in a Post-traditional World.* New
York: Harper & Row, 1970.

Boff, Leonardo. *Trinity and Society.* Maryknoll, NY: Orbis, 1988.

*The Book of Common Prayer and Administration of the Sacraments and Other Rites and
Ceremonies of the Church: Together with the Psalter or Psalms of David According to
the Use of the Episcopal Church.* New York: Church Hymnal, 1979.

Bourgeault, Cynthia. *The Wisdom Jesus: Transforming Heart and Mind: A New
Perspective on Christ and His Message.* Boston, MA: New Seeds, 2008.

Boyle, Greg. "The Jesus Strategy." The Work of the People. May 2016. http://www.the
workofthepeople.com/the-jesus-strategy.

Brakke, David. "Canon Formation and Social Conflict in Fourth-Century Egypt:
Athanasius of Alexandria's Thirty-Ninth Festal Letter." *Harvard Theological
Review* 87, no. 4 (1994): 395–419.

Brown, Raymond E. *The Churches the Apostles Left behind*. New York: Paulist, 1984.

———. *The Gospel According to John*. Vol. 2. Garden City, NY: Doubleday, 1966.

Brunner, Emil. *The Misunderstanding of the Church*. Philadelphia: Westminster, 1953.

Bryson, Bill. *At Home: A Short History of Private Life*. New York: Doubleday, 2010.

Capon, Robert Farrar. *Between Noon and Three: Romance, Law, and the Outrage of Grace*. Grand Rapids, MI: W. B. Eerdmans, 1997.

———. *Kingdom, Grace, Judgment: Paradox, Outrage, and Vindication in the Parables of Jesus*. Grand Rapids, MI: W. B. Eerdmans, 2002

———. *The Mystery of Christ—and Why We Don't Get It*. Grand Rapids, MI: W. B. Eerdmans, 1993.

Clark-Soles, Jaime. "ON Scripture: Jaime Clark-Soles on Matthew 22:34–46: On Loving God, Loving Neighbor and #OWS." *On Scripture* (blog). October 19, 2011. http://day1.org/3371on_scripture_jaime_clarksoles_on_matthew_223446_on_loving_god_loving_neighbor_and_ows_.

Cox, Harvey. *Religion in the Secular City: Toward a Postmodern Theology*. New York: Simon and Shuster, 1984.

Crafton, Barbara Cawthorne. *Also Life*. New York: Morehouse, 2016.

Chrysostom, John. "Don't Adorn the Church but Ignore the Poor—Chrysostom." Crossroads Initiative. August 28, 2016. https://www.crossroadsinitiative.com/media/articles/dont-adorn-the-church-but-ignore-the-poor-john-chrysostom.

Cushing, Pamela. "To Be Fully Human." Jean Vanier. Accessed May 13, 2016. http://www.jean-vanier.org/en/his_message/jean_vanier_on_becoming_human/to_be_fully_human.

Dunkelman, Marc J. "Marc J. Dunkelman: Our Tolerance Has Led to the Balkanization of Society." *The Spokesman-Review*. September 14, 2014. http://www.spokesman.com/stories/2014/sep/14/marc-j-dunkelman-our-tolerance-has-led-to-balkaniz/

———. *The Vanishing Neighbor: The Transformation of American Community*. New York: W. W. Norton, 2014.

Eisenhower, Dwight D. *Protestant-Catholic-Jew*. Edited by Will Herberg. Garden City, NY: Doubleday & Co, 1955.

Eliade, Mircea, and Willard R. Trask. *The Sacred and the Profane: The Nature of Religion*. New York: Harcourt, Brace & World, 1959.

Evans, Rachel Held. "On 'Going Episcopal.'" *Rachel Held Evans* (blog). March 25, 2015. http://rachelheldevans.com/blog/going-episcopal.

Felmore, Nathan. "The World Was Made for the Dead." Dispatches to and from. Nathan Felmore, 31 July 2016. http://nathanfelmore.com/blog/2016/7/31/the-world-was-made-for-the-dead.

Finkelstein, Israel, Amihay Mazar, and Brian B. Schmidt. *The Quest for the Historical Israel: Debating Archaeology and the History of Early Israel: Invited Lectures Delivered at the Sixth Biennial Colloquium of the International Institute for Secular Humanistic Judaism, Detroit, October 2005*. Atlanta, GA: Society of Biblical Literature, 2007.

Foley, Edward. *From Age to Age: How Christians Have Celebrated the Eucharist*. Chicago: Liturgy Training Publications, 1991.

Fowler, James A. "Christianity Is NOT Morality." Christ in You Ministries. Accessed March 27, 2016. http://www.christinyou.net/pages/Xnotmor.html.

Friedman, Edwin H., Edward W. Beal, and Margaret W. Treadwell. *A Failure of Nerve: Leadership in the Age of the Quick Fix: An Edited Manuscript.* Bethesda, MD: Edwin Friedman Estate/Trust, 1999.

Girard, René. *Job: The Victim of His People.* Stanford, CA: Stanford University Press, 1987,

———. *Things Hidden Since the Foundation of the World.* Stanford, CA: Stanford University Press, 1987.

Gonzalez, Francisco J. "Dialectic and Dialogue in the Hermeneutics of Paul Ricouer and H.G. Gadamer." *Continental Philosophy Review* 39 (2006): 322–23.

Grieb, A. Katherine. *The Story of Romans: A Narrative Defense of God's Righteousness.* Louisville, KY: Westminster John Knox, 2002.

Guite, Malcom. "Art Made Flesh with Malcolm Guite." The Work of the People. Directed by Travis Reed. 2014. http://www.theworkofthepeople.com/art-made-flesh.

———. "Flesh and Blood with Malcolm Guite." The Work of the People. Directed by Travis Reed. 2014. http://www.theworkofthepeople.com/flesh-and-blood.

———. "The Lectern with Malcolm Guite." The Work of the People. Directed by Travis Reed. 2014. http://www.theworkofthepeople.com/the-lectern.

———. *Parable and Paradox.* London: Canterbury Press, 2016.

———. *Word in the Wilderness: A Poem a Day for Lent and Easter.* London: Hymns Ancient & Modern, 2014.

Harrington, Daniel J. *The Gospel of Matthew.* Collegeville, MN: Liturgical, 1991.

Hauerwas, Stanley, "Naming God." ABC Religion & Ethics (Australian Broadcasting Corporation). September 24, 2010. http://www.abc.net.au/religion/articles/2010/09/24/3021305.htm.

Heath, Elaine A. *The Mystic Way of Evangelism: A Contemplative Vision for Christian Outreach.* Grand Rapids, MI: Baker Academic, 2008.

Hegarty, Paul. *Jean Baudrillard: Live Theory.* London: Continuum, 2004.

Ignatius. "The Epistle of Ignatius to the Magnesians." *CHURCH FATHERS: Epistle to the Magnesians (St. Ignatius).* Accessed April 11, 2016. http://www.newadvent.org/fathers/0105.htm.

Jenkins, Willis. *The Future of Ethics: Sustainability, Social Justice, and Religious Creativity.* Washington, DC: Georgetown University Press, 2013.

Johansen, Robert. *Leaders Make the Future: Ten New Leadership Skills for an Uncertain World.* San Francisco: Berrett-Koehler, 2012.

Kahneman, Daniel. *Thinking, Fast and Slow.* New York: Farrar, Straus and Giroux, 2013.

Kaminski, Carol M. *From Noah to Israel: Realization of the Primaeval Blessing after the Flood.* London: T & T Clark, 2004.

Knight, Roger. *Edwin Muir: An Introduction to His Work.* London: Longman, 1980.

Koestler, Arthur. *The Ghost in the Machine.* New York: Macmillan, 1968.

Levenson, Jon D. *Sinai & Zion: An Entry Into The Jewish Bible.* 1st ed. San Francisco: Harper, 1985.

Lewis, C. S. *Beyond Personality: The Christian Idea of God.* New York: Macmillan, 1945.

————. *Mere Christianity: A Revised and Amplified Edition, with a New Introduction, of the Three Books, Broadcast Talks, Christian Behaviour, and Beyond Personality.* San Francisco: HarperSanFrancisco, 2001.

————. *Surprised by Joy: The Shape of My Early Life.* New York: Harcourt, Brace, 1956.

Luther, Martin. *Works of Martin Luther: With Introductions and Notes.* Translated and edited by Henry Eyster Jacobs and Adolph Spaeth. Philadelphia: Muhlenberg, 1943.

The Matrix Revisited. Directed by Josh Wreck. Performed by Larry Wachowski and Andy Wachowski. Warner Brothers, 2001.

Mauser, Ulrich. "Front Matter." *Philosophical Transactions: Biological Sciences* 356.1415, Complex Clocks (2001): 1681-1682. *Theology Matters.* Presbyterians of Faith, Family, Ministry, Dec. 2000. Web. 24 June 2015.

McLaren, Brian D. *A Generous Orthodoxy: Why I Am a Missional, Evangelical, Post/ Protestant, Liberal/conservative, Mystical/poetic, Biblical, Charismatic/contemplative, Fundamentalist/Calvinist, Anabaptist/Anglican, Methodist, Catholic, Green, Incarnational, Depressed-yet-hopeful, Emergent, Unfinished Christian.* El Cajon, CA: Emergent YS, 2004.

Meeks, Wayne A. *The First Urban Christians: The Social World of the Apostle Paul.* New Haven, CT: Yale University Press, 1983.

Metzger, Bruce M., and Roland E. Murphy. *The New Oxford Annotated Bible with the Apocrypha: New Revised Standard Version.* New York: Oxford University Press, 1994.

Monty Python and the Holy Grail. Last modified November 1994. http://www.sacred -texts.com/neu/mphg/mphg.htm.

Myers, Ched. *Binding the Strong Man: A Political Reading of Mark's Story of Jesus.* Maryknoll, NY: Orbis, 1988.

Nouwen, Henri J. M. *Can You Drink the Cup?* Notre Dame, IN: Ave Maria, 1996.

Olson, Roger. "Was Karl Barth a Universalist?" *Roger E. Olson My Evangelical Armenian Theological Musings.* Patheos. March 10, 2013. http://www.patheos .com/blogs/rogereolson/2013/03/was-karl-barth-a-universalist-a-new-look-at-an -old-question/

Packer, J. I. *"Fundamentalism" and the Word of God: Some Evangelical Principles.* Grand Rapids, MI: Eerdmans, 1958.

Palmer, Richard. *Hermeneutics: Interpretation Theory in Schleiermacher, Dilthey, Heidegger, and Gadamer.* Evanston, IL: Northwestern University Press, 1969.

Pathak, Jay, and Dave Runyon. *The Art of Neighboring: Building Genuine Relationships Right Outside Your Door.* Grand Rapids, MI: Baker, 2012.

Peterson, Eugene H. *The Message: The Bible in Contemporary Language.* Colorado Springs: Nav Press, 2002.

Pickstock, Catherine. *After Writing: On the Liturgical Consummation of Philosophy.* Oxford, UK: Blackwell, 2015.

Rapp, Claudia. *Holy Bishops in Late Antiquity: The Nature of Christian Leadership in an Age of Transition.* Berkeley: University of California, 2005.

Rohr, Richard. "Jesus as Paradox." Richard Rohr's Daily Meditation. Center for Action and Contemplation. July 29, 2014. http://myemail.constantcontact.com /Richard-Rohr-s-Meditation--Jesus-as-Paradox.html?soid=110309866861 6&aid=oce_J7-8kkI.

Rutledge, Fleming. "Who Is the Good Samaritan?" Generous Orthodoxy. May 1, 2005. http://generousorthodoxy.org/sermons/who-is-the-good-samaritan.aspx

Sattler, Rolf. "Wilber's AQAL Map and Beyond." Beyond Wilber. Accessed July 21, 2016. http://www.beyondwilber.ca/AQALmap/bookdwl/files/WAQALMB_1.pdf.

Shakespeare, William, and William Aldis. A Midsummer Night's Dream. n.p.: Clarendon, 1894.

Sherrard, Brooke. "American Biblical Archaeologists and Zionism: How Differing Worldviews on the Interaction of Cultures Affected Scholarly Constructions of the Ancient Past." Journal of the American Academy of Religion 84, no. 1(2016): 234–59. https://doi.org/10.1093/jaarel/lfv063.

Shmoop Editorial Team. "The Brothers Karamazov." Shmoop.com. November 11, 2008. http://www.shmoop.com/brothers-karamazov/.

Smalley, Martha Lund, ed. American Missionary Eyewitness to the Nanking Massacre, 1937–1938. New Haven, CT: Yale Divinity School Library, 1997. http://web .library.yale.edu/sites/default/files/files/OccasionalPublication9.pdf.

Spurgeon, C. H. Flashes of Thought: 1000 Choice Extracts from the Works of C. H. Spurgeon. London: Passmore and Alabaster, 1874. Accessed March 23, 2016. https://books.google.com/books?id=2AEDAAAAQAAJ&printsec=frontcover& source=gbs_ge_summary_r&cad=0#v=onepage&q&f=false.

Stringfellow, William. An Ethic for Christians and Other Aliens in a Strange Land. Waco, TX: Word, 1973.

———. A Keeper of the Word: Selected Writings of William Stringfellow. Edited by and Bill Wylie Kellermann. Grand Rapids, MI: W. B. Eerdmans, 1994.

Taleb, Nassim Nicholas. Antifragile: Things That Gain from Disorder. New York: Random House, 2012.

———. The Black Swan: The Impact of the Highly Improbable. New York: Random House, 2007.

Taylor, Barbara Brown. Leaving Church: A Memoir of Faith. San Francisco: Harper San Francisco, 2006.

Taylor, Charles. Dilemmas and Connections: Selected Essays. Cambridge, MA: Belknap of Harvard University Press, 2011.

———. A Secular Age. Cambridge, MA: Belknap of Harvard University Press, 2007.

———. Sources of the Self: The Making of the Modern Identity. Cambridge, MA: Harvard University Press, 1989.

Taylor, Joan E. The Immerser: John the Baptist within Second Temple Judaism. Grand Rapids, MI: W.B. Eerdmans, 1997.

Tierney, Thomas T. "Punctual Selves, Punctual Death and the Health-Conscious Cogito: Descartes' Dead Bodies." Economy and Society 41, no. 2 (2012): 258–81, DOI: 10.1080/03085147.2011.635436.

Vanier, Jean. Becoming Human. New York: Paulist, 1998.

———. Community and Growth. New York: Paulist, 1989.

Wachowski, Lana, and Lilly Wachowski. *The Matrix*. The Internet Movie Script Database (IMSDb)."Accessed March 25, 2016. http://www.imsdb.com/scripts /Matrix,-The.html.

Wallace, David Foster. *This Is Water: Some Thoughts, Delivered on a Significant Occasion about Living a Compassionate Life*. New York: Little, Brown, 2009.

Weber, Nadia Bolz. "Pregnant Old Ladies and Other Signs That God's Story Is Better than the One We Tell Ourselves." Patheos, December 11, 2012. http://www .patheos.com/blogs/nadiabolzweber/2012/12/pregnant-old-ladies-and-other -signs-that-gods-story-is-better-than-the-one-we-tell-ourselves/.

"Whose Hands? Another Possible Case of Cumulative Authorship." Mockingbird's Imitations (Blogger Edition). November 7, 2011. http://mimuspolyglottos.blog spot.com/2011/11/whose-hands-another-possible-case-of.html.

Wilber, Ken. *The Collected Works of Ken Wilber*. Boston, MA: Shambhala, 1998.

Williams, Rowan. "The Life of Dietrich Bonhoeffer: His Views on Culture, Piety and Ecumenism." Lecture at the International Bonhoeffer Congress, Wrocław, Poland, February 3, 2006.

———. *A Ray of Darkness: Sermons and Reflections*. Cambridge, MA: Cowley, 1995.

Wink, Walter. *The Powers*. Philadelphia: Fortress, 1984.

———. *The Powers That Be: Theology for a New Millennium*. New York: Doubleday, 1998.

———. *Walter Wink: Collected Readings*. Edited by Henry French. Minneapolis: Fortress Press, 2013.

Yancey, Philip. *What's So Amazing about Grace?* Grand Rapids, MI: Zondervan, 1997.

Zevit, Ziony. *The Religions of Ancient Israel: A Synthesis of Parallactic Approaches*. London: Continuum, 2001.

ABOUT THE AUTHOR

The Right Reverend C. Andrew Doyle, the ninth bishop of the Episcopal Diocese of Texas, summarizes his autobiography in six words: "Met Jesus on pilgrimage; still walking." He is author of *Small Batch, Generous Community, CHURCH, Unabashedly Episcopalian, Orgullosamente Episcopal,* and *Unity in Mission.* He and his wife, JoAnne, live in Houston and have two daughters.